THE
LAST HERO

Bill Tilman: A biography of the explorer

Tim Madge

THE
MOUNTAINEERS

ISBN 0–89886–452–6

Copyright © 1995 by Tim Madge

First published in Great Britain in 1995 by
Hodder and Stoughton,
a division of Hodder Headline PLC
338 Euston Road, London NW1 3BH

Published in 1995 in the United States of America by
The Mountaineers, 1011 SW. Klickitat Way, Seattle WA 98134
Published simultaneously in Canada by Douglas & McIntyre Ltd.,
1615 Venables St., Vancouver B.C. V5L 2H1

Typeset by Hewer Text Composition Services, Edinburgh
Printed and bound in Great Britain by
Mackays of Chatham plc, Chatham, Kent

To my father

and to Rufie
Nil mortabilus ardui est

Reckless O soul, exploring, I with thee, and thou with me,
For we are bound where mariner has not yet dared to go,
And we will risk the ship, ourselves and all.

O my brave soul!
O farther farther sail!
O daring joy, but safe! are they not all the seas of God?
O farther, farther, farther sail!

Walt Whitman, 'Passage to India'

CONTENTS

MAPS

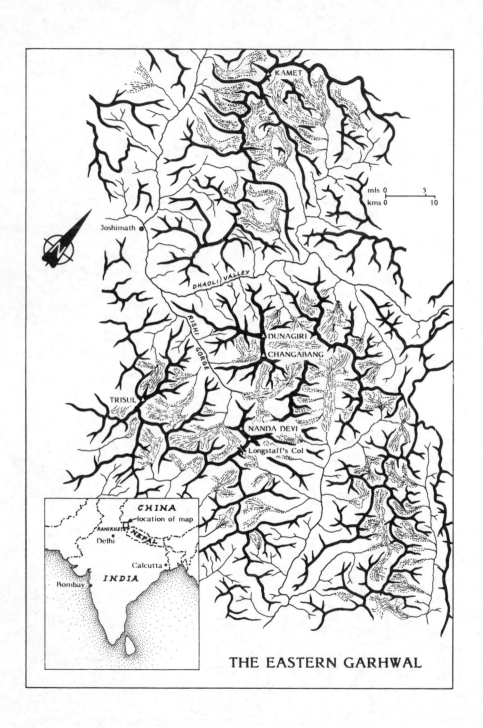

KAMET

mls 0   5
kms 0   10

Joshimath

DHAOLI VALLEY

DUNAGIRI
CHANGABANG

RISHI GORGE

TRISUL

NANDA DEVI

Longstaff's Col

CHINA
location of map
RANIKHET
Delhi   NEPAL

Calcutta

Bombay   INDIA

THE EASTERN GARHWAL

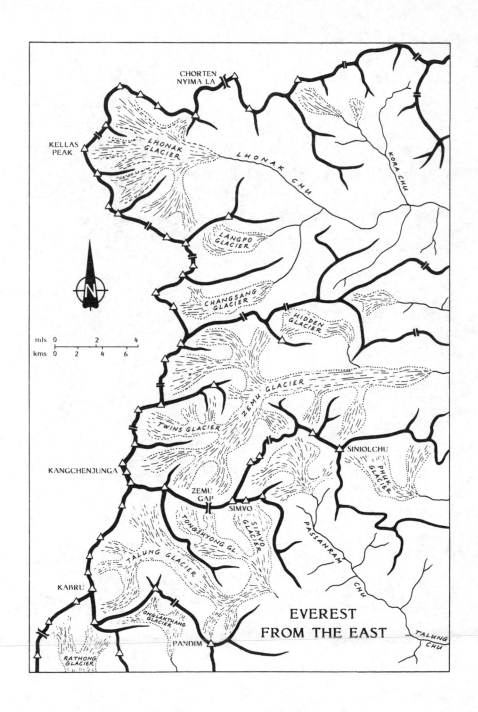

CHORTEN
NYIMA LA

KELLAS
PEAK

LHONAK
GLACIER

LHONAK CHU

KORA CHU

LANGPO
GLACIER

N

CHANGSANG
GLACIER

HIDDEN
GLACIER

mls 0   2   4
kms 0   2   4   6

ZEMU GLACIER

TWINS GLACIER

SINIOLCHU

PHUKR
GLACIER

KANGCHENJUNGA

ZEMU
GAP

SIMVO

SIMVO
GLACIER

TONGSHYONG GL.

PASSANRAM CHU

TALUNG GLACIER

KABRU

ONGLAKTHANG
GLACIER

PANDIM

EVEREST
FROM THE EAST

RATHONG
GLACIER

TALUNG
CHU

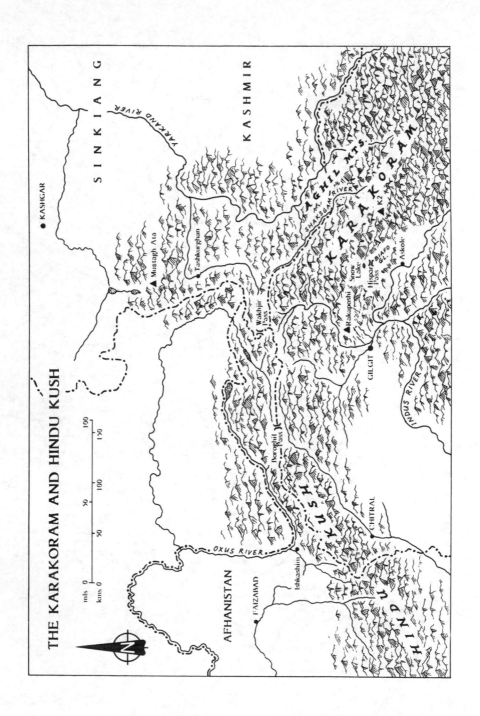

THE KARAKORAM AND HINDU KUSH

SINKIANG

KASHMIR

KASHGAR

YARKAND RIVER

Mustagh Ata

Tashkurghan

AGHIL MTS.

SHAKSGAM RIVER

KARAKORAM

K2

Askole

Snow Lake

BIAFO GLR.

Hispar Pass

Rakaposhi

Wakhjir Pass

GILGIT

INDUS RIVER

Baroghil Pass

HINDU KUSH

CHITRAL

OXUS RIVER

Ishkashim

AFGHANISTAN

FAIZABAD

mls 0   50   100

kms 0   50   100   150

N

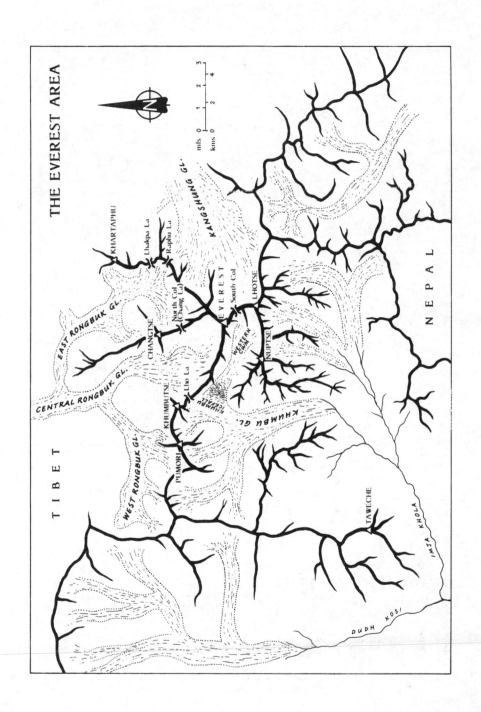

THE EVEREST AREA

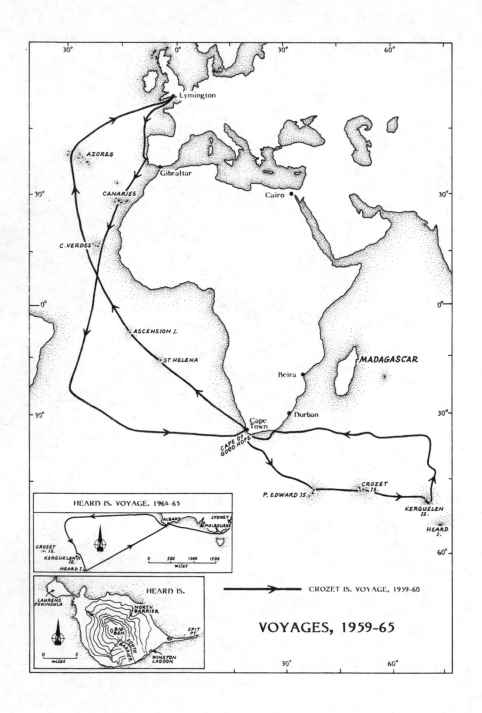

VOYAGES, 1959-65

CROZET IS. VOYAGE, 1959-60

HEARD IS. VOYAGE. 1964-65

HEARD IS.

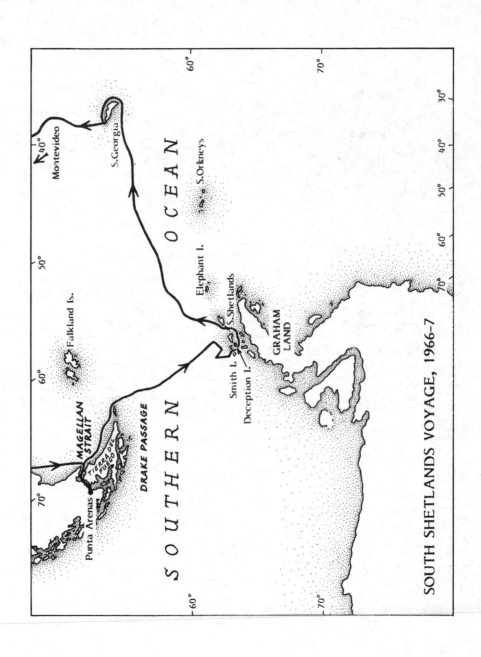

SOUTH SHETLANDS VOYAGE, 1966-7

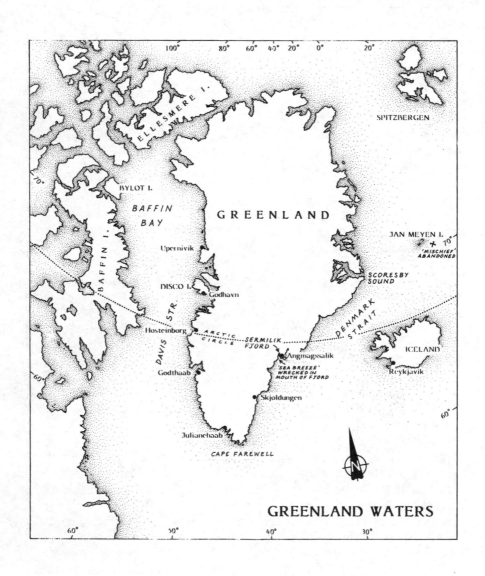

GREENLAND WATERS

ACKNOWLEDGEMENTS

My principal thanks go to Mrs Pam Davis, Bill's niece, whose interest
in this book has been intense, anxious as she has been to ensure that
her uncle had a fair hearing, and that, in particular, his wicked sense of
humour was finally unmasked. She has given freely of her time in the
several years it has taken to assemble all the material; she has allowed
me access to Bill's papers; and generously allowed his obituary for
Mischief to appear more or less in full for the first time in any book.

I would also like to thank Dr John Ross, Bill's Italian campaign
comrade, Professor Victor Gozzer, his Italian translator, and all the
surviving partisans of Belluno and its environs, who have helped put
together details of that epic struggle in the mountains.

Among the climbers, I owe a debt of gratitude to the many with whom
I have corresponded and especially to Charles Houston, who gave me
valuable background information about the 1950 Nepal expedition and
Bill's relationship with Betsy Cowles. On the sailing side, Sandy and
Mary Lee of Lymington were immensely fruitful sources, as was
Michael Rhodes, Bruce Reid, Brian Hill and Roger Robinson. Jim
Gaitens provided an insight into Bill's last voyage north. There are
many others, from both the climbing and the sailing days. Dorothy
Richardson was most useful on the questions surrounding the voyage
of *En Avant*, and Diana Shipton gave me information about Bill and
Eric's last adventures in China. John Mead of Harlech television lent
unbroadcast videotapes of the many people interviewed for the ITV
documentary on Bill; John Anderson's widow was kind enough to allow
me to shuffle through her late husband's papers and files on Bill, and in
particular to allow me to borrow photostats of the always valuable and
informative diaries.

In the course of my researches, I interviewed many people who had
known Bill, in his various careers as soldier, sailor and climber; to them
all, if they are not mentioned by name above, may I express my lasting
thanks for their time and efforts. Bill Tilman's life spanned many eras,
many continents and many activities which brought him into contact with
a huge range of people, few of whom ever forgot the encounter. One
testament to this remains the huge correspondence Bill had with people
he knew all over the world. He was a diligent letter writer, as well as a

diarist, at least of those parts of his life which he deemed interesting; for that we should be most grateful.

The H. W. Tilman archive, formerly with the Gwynedd County Council Archives, is now housed in the Royal Geographical Society, London. This consists of thousands of letters mostly from Bill Tilman to his sister, Adeline; many more are to him from colleagues and acquaintances across the years. As well, it consists of thousands of other papers, some published, some not, and includes bank statements and other private material not normally available to even the most assiduous biographer.

It also contains the original diaries of many of the expeditions and voyages, and photostats of the remaining sea voyage, logs and diaries brought back by the author from Wyoming in 1992.

The University of Wyoming has a valuable collection of Bill's diaries and logs because they wrote and asked him for them in the 1960s and he, typically, was tickled by the idea that anyone, anywhere, should actually want what he considered to be a lot of redundant paper once he had written his books. The University also contains, by a happy coincidence, Betsy Cowles' original diaries and papers, including those of the 1951 Nepal trip. I am grateful to Dr Gene Gressley for giving me access to these archives which may be seen, on request, in the smart new surrounding of the Laramie campus. Bill would smile could he but see where his papers have ended up.

T.M.

PART ONE

Youth – Heart of Darkness

CHAPTER 1

Childhood, School and Adolescence

Harold William Tilman (known as Bill) was the third child of John and Adeline Tilman. He entered the world of a prosperous and forceful Liverpool sugar merchant and his wife on St Valentine's Day: February 14th, 1898. His sister Gertrude Adeline was seven, his elder brother Kenneth was two. Even for the late Victorian era, theirs was a modest-sized family.

It was a wealthy family though, a product of those same Victorian values which Mrs Thatcher, while Prime Minister in the 1980s, was so anxious to reinforce in the British. In many respects the Tilmans epitomise, if not quite rags to riches, then certainly middling well-off to extremely comfortable; a tale that could be told for many of the Victorian success stories.

His grandfather, William, had started work as a cobbler's assistant in Liverpool, then one of the powerhouses of the great industrial revolution which had helped to propel Britain to world status. William married Caroline Hinkes and John, Bill's father, was born in 1861. By now William was prospering – a boot and shoe manufacturer.

John Hinkes Tilman left school at fourteen and became an office boy with a firm of Liverpool sugar merchants. By 1895, twenty years later, he had set up business with George Rome as sugar brokers, a trade from which he was to derive his fortune. His wife, Adeline Rees, came from a line of Cumberland hill-farmers; she considered, it is said, that she had married a little beneath her. After all, John Tilman was, albeit successful, still 'trade'.

Mr and Mrs Tilman lived for a while in Birkenhead and then moved to Wallasey, first to Radnor Drive, then to a big house – Seacroft – in Grove Road where they lived for the rest of their lives and to which Bill must have addressed thousands of letters. There is a photograph of Seacroft taken some time in the 1920s, showing a garden party. It was a large rambling detached pile, liberally served with cooks, maids, and all the domestic baggage of the well-off. This was Bill's world as a child and well into middle age.

The late Victorians were riding the crest of a wave. There had been peace across western Europe since 1815, nearly a hundred years before. The great *Pax Britannica* enforced by the Royal Navy was still a recognisable part of foreign policy, ensuring that the British writ ran worldwide. In 1898 the British could look back to a year earlier and the Spithead Review celebrating sixty years of Victoria's rule.

On that summer day in 1897 the Queen had sailed down the lines of 165 warships from many nations, all of them dominated by the Royal Navy. Of all the British warships present, her admirals no doubt pointed out, not one had been withdrawn from the Empire. What she saw was the home fleet alone.

What she was seeing on that day, too, was the tip of a huge economic system. The British merchant fleet was enjoying the pinnacle of its greatest successes. Never again would so many British ships carry so much of the world's trade. The Empire was not the basis of most of this trade, merely serving as part of the seamless web of British power and influence. The Empire was – as it always had been – a net burden on the home state.

The Empire, though, was the expression of a growing jingoism – that form of nationalism calculated to infuriate other nations. At the end of Victoria's reign the onset of Edwardian decadence would signal the first public signs of real decline in British fortunes. The Boer War would be another such sign.

In fact Britain, in 1898, was already in sharp economic decline, the outward trappings of pomp and circumstance a dangerous diversion from the truth. The Tilmans might prosper in the sugar trade but overall economic growth was plunging (down to only 1.5 per cent annual industrial production in this period). British exports, expanding at five per cent between 1840 and 1870, were down to one per cent between 1890 and 1900. The decline of course was relative: Britain was the world's wealthiest nation in this period and its slowly growing economy was still huge. Second, invisible earnings – such as shipping and foreign investment – were bringing in massive annual receipts.

The lack of a major conflict over the previous eighty years had also ensured prosperity. But the British attitude bordered on hubris by the time Bill came into the world. No doubt Bill's father, an arrogant and self-assured businessman of repute, would have espoused all this in his public utterances, at his workplace and in his club. The late Victorian businessman, large and small, was exactly the model Mrs Thatcher had in mind. They believed completely in what they did, and they believed, too, that it was the only way forward for success – in business and in life. To doubters they would have simply swung their arms and pointed at – in John Tilman's case – the bustling docks and their hinterland. This was success manifest.

To these major and minor economic grandees, the traders and brokers in particular, who had a better grasp of world economics, Britain was unassailably the best. Its achievements would everywhere have been celebrated, its power applauded and its opinion – on every subject – marched out on every occasion. This was the greatest success story ever known; in invention and industry the world had never seen anything like it.

Young Bill would have absorbed all this with his mother's milk. The world was settled, set and certain. At the age of two, when the new century was proclaimed, he would have believed his father when he said that the next hundred years would lead to greater and greater glories for the nation, and better and better living for the Tilmans.

Had 1914 never happened, Bill would have gone to university; after, who knows. He might have gone on to teach, to become an academic perhaps, for it is clear that Bill was, from early on, a thoughtful and quiet child, much given to reading. It is possible he might have been persuaded into his father's firm to become, eventually, a partner. Can we read any significance into the fact that Kenneth, the elder brother, chose to go to sea to get away from the dominating influence that John Tilman clearly was? And how important was that dominance? John Tilman could be a very forceful character but in the many letters Bill wrote home from the front in the First World War he tends to take a bantering line with his father, calling him the 'Guv' or 'Guvo'. This suggests the dominance was not of brutal authority but more born of the time and culture of the period.

Yet John Tilman was forceful. Bill's previous biographer, John Anderson, quotes a Mr T. Eland, who was once John Tilman's office boy, for a description of what he was like. *Inter alia* he said:

> Occasionally he would storm into our office and in stentorian tones shout, 'Eland! Get me to the Dock Board!' On arrival he would ask, 'Why is the pilot boat at the stage in weather like this?' It meant little that gale-force winds were forecast – in fact they had only come in to change crews . . . He favoured good discipline, and if we met in the street would not even acknowledge my presence with a nod.

John Tilman, at the time of this anecdote, was a member of the Mersey Docks and Harbour Board, a position he clearly relished. Another account of him suggests that he lived, ate and slept business, thinking anything else, apart from some charity work, a waste of time. Might that have included Bill's adventuring or was he, as Pam Davis remembers, overtly proud of his younger son?

The attitudes Bill's father espoused came from the hard times that were the other and constant face of the Victorian world. The welfare state, that great twentieth-century invention, was more or less non-existent; if you sank you drowned in poverty and the line between success and failure could be a very narrow one. Trade – including that of sugar – fluctuated. We may judge John Tilman harshly – in some respects too harshly – but he must constantly have had the fear of failure in his mind.

There would also have been the issue of status. Having come up from humble origins John Tilman would have been acutely aware of his social status and its relative fragility, dependent on his continued success. Self-made businessmen were much in evidence in ports like Liverpool around the turn of the century but even the most successful of them would have doffed his top hat to a real 'nob', like the landed gentry.

It is important to understand that John Tilman's own insecurity was based on reality. His own humble origins would have haunted him – he was known for saying from time to time when the stock market fell that they were all ruined. Just because the children were brought up in a middle-class environment did not mean they were not prey to older, darker fears: insecurity being perhaps the principal one.

As I shall argue later, Bill became prone to the two great neuroses of our times: insecurity and guilt, the former learned from, if not imparted by, his father, the latter from his own experiences – and survival – in the First World War. Whatever John Tilman was like as a father – and he could be kind and generous – he also probably had impossible expectations of his male offspring. Kenneth went to sea and eventually was killed in an air accident. Did Bill spend much of his life thereafter (if not before) trying to fulfil the impossible hopes of his father? Was the quest for endless adventure in the end a quest for his father's approbation – or even his final approval?

If there are only question-marks here, it is because there are so many unknowns. Bill kept so much to himself throughout his long life. We can never know the definitive answers to most of these questions, even if we scour all Bill ever wrote, published and unpublished. On the surface everything seems to be fine. Very occasionally, there are hints that Bill is not entirely secure in himself, or that he blames himself more than reason would dictate, for all manner of things. What is apparent is his cosmic restlessness and his fear of inaction. This suggests a man who is not at peace – in any way – with himself. The truly big question is, however, whether this came more from his experiences in the First World War than from his father, or any aspect of his home life.

At the turn of the century, in the seminally important years of early childhood, the settled social hierarchy of Victorian and Edwardian Britain was complete; indeed it was part of a larger economic problem because the parvenus were trying to marry their children into the aristocracy and thereby get their missing status at one remove, rather than encourage them to continue in commerce or industry.

There is no question that John Tilman would have despised this attitude; equally, though, he would have been a prisoner of the snobbery which insisted that land meant more than trade. It is in the clash of what John Tilman knew in his head, with what social niceties told him in his heart, that he brought up his family. Bill never lost a sense of deference – to members of the royal family, for instance. There is nothing odd in this; it was part and parcel of his upbringing and it reached back to those early days when the world was Britain's to toy with.

John Tilman's first passport is illustrative of this. A large piece of parchment, written out by hand and dating from 1895, its copperplate writing ends with the signature of Lord Salisbury, the Secretary of State for Foreign Affairs. It is, in effect, a personal letter from the Foreign Secretary to anyone who needs to know, stating that the bearer is under his personal protection. The personal authority such a passport confers was another part of both the intimacy of British society and its remoteness. Likewise, we may surmise that the Tilman family would have been ruled by John Tilman as a patriarch.

There is a photograph of Adeline and John Tilman which reveals a great deal; she, a broad-faced rather plain woman, resigned in her expression, her boots poking out from a long Edwardian dress, her hands awkwardly placed on her lap. She looks out of place, a hill-farmer's daughter thrust into a commercial world. Her husband, John, by contrast, sits by her side, legs crossed, spats showing on polished boots, a buttonhole in his coat. His hands are carefully placed, his smile an arrogant witness to his belief in himself. He is the very model of a self-made man and he looks at the camera with a completeness, a knowledge which is hard to penetrate

Appearances can be deceptive, though. Pam Davis, Bill's surviving niece, remembers her grandmother as rather a regal lady, reinforcing the idea that she may well have thought she had sacrificed status for love. We may assume, rightly, that it was love that brought her out of the hills to the bustling world of Liverpool. Bill, then, with his brother and sister, was brought up in a comfortable middle-class home, where laughter and affection, albeit trammelled by the conventions of the time, were commonplace.

Following a middle-class tradition, both sons were sent to prep school in New Brighton; from there they went on to the fee-paying Wallasey Grammar School. In 1909 Bill, then eleven, followed his elder brother to Berkhamstead School in Hertfordshire. The school's headmaster was the Reverend T. C. Fry, one of the outstanding men of his day, whose reputation would have been studied closely by John Tilman in choosing the school for his boys.

Fry was succeeded as headmaster, a year after Bill arrived at the school, by Charles Greene, the father of both Graham Greene, the novelist, and Hugh Greene, who later became a controversial Director-General of the BBC. A third son, Raymond, became a distinguished mountaineer. Bill and Kenneth were both in School House; in 1913 Bill was awarded a Foundation Scholarship which meant that his school fees were now paid for. In the same year he became a prefect.

From the surviving school report it seems that he was a middling all-rounder. He played football for the First Eleven, became a captain at 'fives' (an invention of the public schools rather like squash without the rackets), and he excelled at gym. But already he was a very shy boy of whom a contemporary wrote that one never really knew him. 'Likeable but remote', a description which John Anderson says fitted him all his life.

Like all schoolboys at boarding school, he wrote regularly to his parents. The tone of these letters is almost a parody of what we have come to associate with a *Boys' Own Paper* world of the early part of the century. They are completely unselfconsciously written, though, and should be read as such.

My Dearest Own Mater and Pater,

Awfully glad to hear you arrived back safely after your ripping holiday,

Poor old Rex [the dog] I expect he was awfully bucked. No excuse for mater not going to the Island if she can cross the Channel, nor Adds either. I don't think I will be able to manage the Dee party, the earliest I will be able to get is the 1–15 which does not get in till 6–35, rather a farce isn't it?

I hope your pal from Surrey has a decent time, how long is she going to stay?

Charles [Greene] invited about fifteen chaps to tennis and croquet last Monday. We had an American journalist like we had at St Bees. My partner and I won (imagine what the rest were like) and we got a box of chocolates each. We gorged cherries and cakes and topping ginger beer in a revolving summer house. Then we played 'crazy croquet', a weird game. I got into the final but Charles knocked me out. We had a glorious time, awfully decent of Charles.

On Tuesday I took the 2nd class swimming test, you have to do a decent dive and 15 lengths in 7$1/2$ minutes, 5 with breast stroke, 5 side stroke and 5 on the back.

I got through in 6 min 21 secs. It was an awful sweat, 2nd class people are allowed to wear flax swimming bags.

Uppers lost the final of the 2nd XI House Match against Bees yesterday, they left us 90 to make and three quarters of an hour to do it in and we only made 30 in about twenty five minutes, and so we lost.

Sorry I cannot enclose the promised photo but it is too big, I will show it you when I come home.

Love to Adds, ever your loving son, Harold

Truly, a world lost.

One of the last letters he wrote from Berkhamstead, in the autumn of 1914, and just after war was declared, brings exciting news; already Bill is exhibiting his talent as a writer, combining a good story with humour and wit in what is a definable style.

My Dearest Own Mater and Pater,

I am writing this from within the precincts of the Pres' Room, so you can guess that something funny has happened. I now have to do all sorts of rum things, such as seeing the dormitory to bed, waking 'em up and sending 'em down, taking prep from a glorified arm chair, saying prayers, and in the near future I shall have to read the lesson in chapel! O Lord! I have just taken prayers this morning. I felt like a Salvation Army Holy John. You bet I didn't keep them attending long. Besides all this, through the decease of comrade Boil, I find I have to run uppers. This entails all sorts of rot such as jawing to House collectively, selecting the footer teams, etc., etc.

You know I was talking about Dr Buckholdt in the hols, one of our language masters, well the little squit was arrested. Charles, like an idiot, baled him out for 100£ and he is now put under the five mile limit, we have got a new man in his place. He will probably be arrested again and sent to a concentration camp, as he told a whole pack of lies at his trial. I will let you know when this happy event takes place.

Charles [Greene] is a special constable. Surely if this is all we can raise in the way of special constables, the British race is decadent. By the way, before I forget, the victory of the Allies is assured, Capt Hopkins, with marvellous discernment has given me command of a section in No 1 Platoon. Vive Hoppy! Vive Corporal Tilman!

This term the corps are having two parades a week, Monday and Friday, and also field work every other Wednesday afternoon. We also have to provide a guard for the armoury every night from seven pm to seven am. The guard consists of six men with loaded rifles and fixed bayonets, each man has two hours on and four off. There are about 2,000 recruits from Sunderland in the town. Nearly every house has to take four or more.

Please don't expect another letter as long as this again, it can't be done. It's not my fault there's such a lot of news. I hear there are already over 300 OBs serving in different things. How is Ken getting on, have you heard again from him? I hope Adds' box is filling up.

Love to all of you, ever yours, Harold

The five-mile limit Bill refers to with regard to the German schoolmaster 'spy' was a requirement under the emergency Defence Regulations that an alien must not travel further than five miles from his or her place of residence without permission from the police.

Bill had taken his School Certificate (forerunner of GCSEs) in 1913. With a reasonable academic bent he could confidently have expected to pass through the sixth form and on, in due course, to a university. This last is pure speculation, for with the declaration of war Bill was about to be plunged into the harshest school of all.

The First World War was not the first 'modern' war in the history of mankind. The American Civil War and the Franco-Prussian Wars both exhibited a large measure of what we have come to know as 'total' war. This is a war in which certain characteristics are manifest: mass slaughter, 'industrial' weapon systems, involvement of civilians, limitless geographical extent among them.

The First World War was to exhibit all of these, adding one more weapon of horror – gas – to that other dreadful killer, the machine-gun. But even the trenches, which have become the abiding symbol of the war, were not a new idea; it was their eventual extent across northern France that was.

The war was a war between empires, and to that degree it was unique. It was the first truly global conflict, involving European powers as well as Asiatic (largely Japan) ones. It was a war not particularly sought but probably inevitable, given the militaristic attitudes of the times, attitudes much displayed by schools in their Officer Training Corps, for instance.

The start of the war was welcomed across Europe as a 'cleansing', an idea so alien to us it is impossible fully either to describe it or explain it. Suffice it to say that, taking just Britain, many people in positions of political and cultural authority believed that without a war the nation's youth were set on a path of decadence and decline. They believed that a war would purify the nation and its goals, and keep the future bright. In this the British were certainly at one with the Germans and the French. Ideas of national purity were to carry the Germans along the road to Nazism and the world to the Second World War. In Britain these ideas were, literally, killed off by the carnage which was to come between 1914 and 1918; but then the British, if not exactly winning, did not, like the Germans, lose.

What happened to Bill Tilman between 1914 and 1918 was to change his life utterly, as it did for millions of other young men – and a large number of women – who went through this holocaust and, in large measure, survived. The key influence in Bill's life, apart from his father, to whom we will return later, was his wartime experience between 1916 and 1918. The war began when he was in his seventeenth year; it ended when he was just twenty.

CHAPTER 2

The First World War: 1914–18

The First World War began on August 4th, 1914. It was a war for which, uniquely in the modern world, we are in full possession of all the documents (the Russian communists briefly opened all the files on the Tsarist government's action in August 1914, just after they had seized power). It was a futile war, in the sense that it solved none of the outstanding international problems and led, inexorably, to the Second World War.

Its bizarre beginnings, in the assassination of Archduke Ferdinand, the heir to the Austro-Hungarian throne, by an obscure Serb nationalist in Sarajevo, led to war through a series of stumbling steps each side failed to prevent. The Austro-Hungarians used the assassination to attack Serbia, whereupon Russia declared war on them. This led Austro-Hungary's ally, Germany, to declare war on Russia.

The twist came with the systems of alliances on each side. Germany was tied to Austria-Hungary and Italy in the Triple Alliance; Britain was tied to France and Russia in the Triple Entente. When Germany declared war on Russia it did not attack the Russians but the French in the west, where its military master plan was located. This had to be through neutral Belgium, according to the Schlieffen Plan. This plan had been devised in the event of a two-front war against Russia and France, and was posited on the assumption that the more dangerous of the two was France. A holding operation in the east would ensue, until France was crushed.

It was the attack through Belgium which brought Britain into the war. Italy, as a footnote to history, finally joined the Franco-British-Russian side, after much dithering, and then fought a bitter mountain war in the Dolomites with Austria.

In the west the Germans were successful early on but the arrival of the British Expeditionary Force in late August, 100,000 strong and all regular troops, coupled with a stout French defence, finally held the German attack. The Battle of Mons on August 23rd, and the Battle of the Marne, in early September, were both critical. If the Allies had lost the latter the history of the twentieth century would have been completely different. But by December these early battles of manoeuvre had stopped, their place being taken, for the next three and a half years, largely by fixed trench warfare.

Bill Tilman had by December 1914 already decided his future: it would be with the Royal Artillery. Like so many of his generation, and like the vast majority of the British, Bill had been intoxicated by the war. Many people believed it was for the best and that, in any case, it would soon be over. If this seems today like some kind of collective insanity, especially given the hindsight of the casualty lists, at the time few would have had any doubts.

The British were no longer at the apogee of their imperial power but they felt as if they were. Since Waterloo the British had been masters of the universe. They had the Royal Navy – in which there was total confidence – and they had a highly trained professional army. Unfortunately that army had only had foreign tribesmen as a foe – excepting the Boers whose bloody conflict with the British might have sounded a warning note but did not. In 1914 the chief fear among those who rushed to volunteer was that they would be too late to take part in giving the Germans a fiercely bloodied nose.

The greatest illusion was that war was romantic; it was the stuff of poets such as Rupert Brooke, and it was welcomed. Bearing that in mind, Bill's own eagerness to get into this fight should not be a surprise. He left Berkhamstead School in December 1914, at the end of his first term as a sixth-former and, after Christmas at home, joined the Royal Military Academy at Woolwich, home of the Royal Artillery, in January 1915. He had already been accepted, passing 55th out of 111 candidates in the November exams. A faded press cutting, kept by the family, records his unremarkable result.

He wrote home:

I arrived here about 4.30 last night. The station you go to is Woolwich Arsenal and you have to get an old cab to go up to the Academy. I am of course amongst the 'Snookers' and the Senior and Second Term men keep us in our places. We are not allowed to put our hands in our pockets, or leave our coats unbuttoned, or turn any coat collar up. You have to be awfully smart on parade. There is a parade before each meal close to the gun park, and at the luncheon parade the blighter literally crawls round you inspecting you, and the least speck of dust on your clothes, or an unshorn face, and you parade the next morning as a defaulter . . .

As far as I can make out the training consists of the following: squad drill and signalling, FA (field artillery) training, riding, sword drill, French, workshops (forge etc.), tactics and administration, gym, map-reading and various lectures . . .

The grub is excellent. For breakfast this morning we had bacon and kidneys, tea or coffee, brown or white toast, marmalade and jam. For lunch roast beef, Yorkshire pudding, roast potatoes, cauliflower, plum pudding, sauce, cheese. Drinks were beer or ginger beer. For dinner we have several courses – the number you get depends on what servant you have, sometimes you can get five.

Bill was training to be a regular army officer and he was scathing about the volunteers who came through the 'Shop' (the regular army name for the Woolwich Academy). The artillery officer of 1915, had he but known it, was about to see a transition in his operations from essentially nineteenth-century ideas and equipment to twentieth-century. The biggest change would come later in the First World War: the increasing use of trucks to pull the guns. Bill had to deal with horses.

He rode every day except Sundays, although he found it hard going. He also had trouble being smart, at least once at Woolwich being defaulted for untidiness. His kit had to be bought partly out of his own funds – another throwback to the past. It included a sword, as well as spurs, field glasses, puttees and a revolver. His upbringing had already lent him caution when spending money – even the army's – and he told his parents that in the matter of field glasses he had bought the cheaper of the two on offer but with graticules (a grid-iron pattern of squares inside the lens to help pinpoint a bearing), 'absolutely necessary for RA officers', which brought the final price close to that of the dearer pair.

On July 28th, 1915, Bill was commissioned as a second lieutenant in the Royal Field Artillery. He was then just short of seventeen and a half and he was posted to 2A Reserve Brigade, Preston. Soldiers were prevented from going to France before they were eighteen, although this rule was to be breached for Bill, as for many thousands of other young men.

The war had been going badly for the Allies in the west. Turkey's entry into the war on the side of Germany, in late 1914, had cut off the Russians, and led to the disastrous landing on the Dardanelles in 1915. In the east the Russians were in retreat. In France and Belgium the Germans had nearly broken through at Ypres, using poison gas (chlorine) for the first time and terrorising the French. There had been Zeppelin raids on London (mentioned by Bill in his letters home). At the end of the year the British commander-in-chief, Sir John French, had been replaced by Douglas Haig and Lloyd George, a member of the coalition government, was in charge of the Ministry of Munitions.

There had been an appalling casualty rate. Around 612,000 Germans, 1,292,000 French and 279,000 British had been killed or wounded.

There had been no appreciable shift in the battle lines between the North Sea and the Swiss Alps. The Germans had worked out, sooner than the Allies, that the increase of lethal firepower – field artillery and the machine-gun in particular – had completely changed warfare. The advantage, for however long it lasted, had passed to the defence, which was able to bring up reserves to limit an enemy breakthrough before any penetration could be exploited.

As a result the Germans adopted a flexible trench line in two or more separated groups, with a high concentration of machine-guns and supported by artillery in depth. Any breakthrough by the Allies into the first German trenches could be immediately met by accurate fire from the succeeding lines, pounded by artillery well beyond the range of the attacking guns. The machine-gun – memorably described by one historian as the industrialisation of killing – was the most feared weapon of all. A good gunner, by tapping his gun as he fired, could put a bullet into every inch of his traverse; no one could escape this wall of death.

Yet these simple facts, evidenced by the casualty lists, escaped the notice or the concern of high commands of all the armies. Faced with a static line they elected, time and again, to throw hundreds of thousands of lives away in futile attempts to walk across the no-man's land between the trenches in order to assault them. In essence, until the arrival of the British-invented tank, unprotected men, carrying rifles, made this short journey to injury or death. Officers on the British side frequently only carried a swagger stick, or a revolver. They led their men into this holocaust of lead and barbed-wire in battle after battle. Few failed in their 'duty' in this regard; a very few who did were shot as cowards or deserters.

On the other side of the Channel in Britain, even though it was possible to hear the guns firing in France by standing on the cliffs at Dover, life went on very much as it had before the war, certainly up to the end of 1916, when conscription finally came. There was a lack of direction, most apparent in the shell shortage. Income tax was still 3s 6d in the pound (17.5p); trade unions resisted replacing men off to fight with unskilled labour. The question of using women as replacement workers was not on the agenda at all. Statesmen still wore top hats, although unstarched collars among lesser mortals were appearing at weekends, where maids might hand out sandwiches for afternoon tea, rather than footmen.

In Preston, Bill was fretting over not being sent to France. In November his name was sent in for a course of instruction in France but his age was prominently mentioned on the form and he did not go. He wrote home: 'we are frightfully sick with life.' Later the same month he took a draft of forty horses to a remount camp at Ayr and after a Christmas break at home he was put in charge of 250 men on their way to a reserve brigade in Glasgow. He had to march them three miles through the city to the barracks.

On January 9th, 1916 he wrote to Adeline:

I intended ringing up on Saturday to see if you were alone, when we could have had a dinner and theatre but I felt pretty sure you would be booked up with someone or other . . . I've just returned from Glasgow; been taking a draft of 250 men up there for 6A Res Bde. We got in at 10 o'clock Saturday night, the population of Glasgow lined the streets, 'twas a grim sight . . .

He talked of coming home the next weekend for leave, which he duly did. While there, on January 15th, and a month short of his eighteenth birthday, a telegram was delivered ordering him immediately to Preston and thence to France. He arrived on January 18th at the port of Le Havre. He moved up to the line on January 22nd, posted to B Battery, 161st Brigade, Royal Field Artillery. This brigade was a part of 'Kitchener's Army'. John Keegan, in the *Face of Battle*, calls the British Expeditionary Force of 1916 'one of the most remarkable and admirable military formations ever to have taken the field'.

Kitchener, Secretary of State for War, had originally called for 100,000 men to supplement the regular army, supported by the still famous 'Your Country Needs You' poster campaign. He got, by the spring of 1915, 600,000, from which he formed five 'new' armies of six divisions. The greatest number of these volunteers came from the northern and Midland cities and the men chose their own titles for their units, in some cases even their own officers. In almost every case they chose their comrades: these were the 'Pals' battalions.

Of them Keegan writes:

Perhaps no story of the First World War is as poignant as that of the Pals. It is a story of a spontaneous and genuinely popular mass movement which has no counterpart in the modern, English-speaking world and perhaps could have none outside its own time and place: a time of intense, almost mystical patriotism, and of the inarticulate elitism of an imperial power's working class; a place of vigorous and buoyant urban life, rich in differences and sense of belonging – to work-places, to factories, to unions, to churches, chapels, charitable organisations, benefit clubs, Boy Scout, Boys' Brigades, Sunday Schools, cricket, football, rugby, skittle clubs, old boys' societies, city offices, municipal departments, craft guilds – to any one of those hundreds of bodies from which the Edwardian Briton drew his security and sense of identity . . .

In physique, in subordination, in motivation, in readiness for

self-sacrifice, the soldiers of the Kitchener armies, 'citizen soldiers'
as the propaganda of the period, for once getting its categories
right, called them, were unsurpassed . . .

The influence of men like these, who had given up everything, and
were in many cases to give up their lives, must have been profound on
Bill Tilman, an eighteen-year-old regular army officer, still in many ways
a schoolboy in military dress. The 161st Brigade was from Yorkshire,
two of its four batteries raised at York, one at Scarborough, the other at
Wakefield; Bill fought with the Scarborough Pals. It was new in France,
like Bill, first sent to Bresle, north of Amiens, then to the neighbourhood
of Albert. The battery occupied a position near the River Ancre on a
quiet part of the front.

Bill wrote many letters home, most of them preserved. They are
usually in pencil and, to begin with, they express a schoolboy's sense of
the great adventure he clearly thought he was embarked upon. The early
ones (to the end of 1916) are also quite long. Later they become short,
terse, and often very harsh. But, to begin with, there is little sense of
the nightmare quality of what he was seeing every day. Hence, perhaps,
an early letter which, *inter alia* says: 'All the dugouts are in a shallow
ravine about 50 yards to the left [of the guns]. We're jolly comfortable
and live more or less like lords. Bullets which just miss our first-line
parapet come over the crest and down the ravine, otherwise it's very
jolly.' He talks about 'bits of rifle fire and machine-guns' and watching a
British spotter plane being brought down. 'I believe either the pilot or
observer were hit,' he remarks.

On February 4th, he wrote:

Things have livened up considerably since I arrived!! Yes, I think
so. The wily Hun has located the gallant 161 (poetry). The other
day a battery came up on our left, not only did they come up, but
they came up in broad daylight, we think their flashes are also
visible. Any rate since their arrival, our life has become almost a
burden, we got their hate as well as our own.

Last week I was laid low for two days by a fell disease, and as
I lay abed and thought – down the valley came a packet, Selah! I
wonder if one will hit my dugout, I say to myself. At once came
the reply 'I hope not, I hope not sincerely!' Since then this has
been a daily, or nightly performance and . . . the battery fights
on its stomach.

We've had nothing but gas alarms the last few days, only one
was genuine, it was very slight, but having a helmet on for half
an hour quite made up for the weakness of the gas.

Only a short time later, also in February, he talks of more gas alarms and how things have livened up some more but he also adds that he would like some magazines to be sent over; a week later he writes: 'We lost our best sergeant the other day, up at the OP [observation post]. A Whizz-bang came through the window as he was looking out. It's always the way – the best fellows get done in, the rotters escape.'

Already, though, Bill was volunteering for this kind of observation post work – it was liaison duty with the infantry in order to co-ordinate the requirements of the front line troops with that of the artillery. Often it meant crawling out into no-man's land to a forward position, using a telephone to communicate to his battery. A loner by inclination, Bill must also have been thinking he was fulfilling his duty to the best of his ability by taking on these tasks.

On his eighteenth birthday, on February 14th, he reported that he had had 'a bottle of fizz' in a very long letter home. By February 28th he was on a course: 'It's rather a relief to get away from the battery a bit, you get fed up with these locally raised units after a bit.' Early in March he was telling Adeline that she smoked too much.

Life for officers in the trenches in 1916 was often very short, their casualty rate being frequently much higher than that of their command. In March 1916 Bill was wounded by a rifle grenade while passing along a section of trench which, he said, 'has been bashed in, no proper trench left. They evidently saw or heard us . . .' His wound, to a thigh, although not very serious, meant he was evacuated to the base hospital where, he reported, 'there are some awfully decent Sisters down here, and that makes a lot of difference.' Still he regretted not being at the front.

He returned to the front on April 8th and later in the month took part in a raid on the enemy lines. These were being conducted at this time to gather intelligence on the strengths and weaknesses of the German army in time for the great set-piece Allied offensive of the summer, the Somme. Bill wrote home: 'We had a tremendously successful raid last week, both raiding party and artillery did splendidly. The prisoners, driven across with kicks, clubs and curses, were in an awful funk. They fully expected to be shot offhand and when Tommies went up with clasp knives to cut buttons off them as souvenirs they thought they were going to be knived.'

The Battle of the Somme, which lasted from June 24th to November 13th, began with the greatest day of slaughter in the history of the British army: 60,000 casualties on the first day of the infantry assault, 19,000 dead. The question has often been asked since the First World War: what possible motive could the average British soldier have for walking into the gale of machine-gun bullets battles like the Somme produced?

Keegan says their motives were many, including compulsion: stragglers were rounded up in the trenches and sent forward by 'battle police'; compulsion was also in the German defence. After the artillery bombardment lifted the soldiers who reached the German trench parapet first would win (the Germans having hidden deep in their dugouts while being bombarded). But he is emphatic that the underlying and consistent reason for fighting – at least up to 1916 – was the calibre of the leadership in the front line. As this is entirely pertinent to the story of Bill Tilman I shall quote him at length. Although Bill was an artillery officer, what Keegan says is as true of Bill as it was of any other subaltern.

We have seen that on the Somme, on 1 July, there were special factors at work which were implicit in the composition and experience – or inexperience – of the Fourth Army. But over and above its cohesion, sense of mission, mood of self-sacrifice, local as well as national patriotism, there were other elements in play. Self-confidence and credulity were certainly present, and powerfully effective at persuading the Pals to jump the parapet. But to emphasise the popular character of the Kitchener armies is to minimise the importance which leadership played in taking it into battle. And arguments can be found to suggest that leadership – conscious, principled, exemplary – was of higher quality and greater military significance in the First World War, at least in the British army, than before or since.

'The Lost Generation' and the 'Public School Officer' are clichés which seem too well worn to be worth repeating or re-examining in this context. Certainly by the end of the war, the officers of the British Expeditionary Force had ceased to be a socially exclusive group, indeed perhaps more broadly recruited than their equivalents in the Second World War . . . critics of the pre-1914 public schools commonly condemned them as militaristic. But unlike the German military schools, which segregated the future officer from childhood and brought him up in a strictly military regime, the public schools educated the whole English upper-middle class and exposed it to a variety of influences, athletic, scholastic, ethical and religious as well as military. The eighteen-year-old who went on to the Royal Military College was treated when he arrived there as someone already formed in character and attitude and only needing tactical training to take his place in his regiment.

This is exactly how Bill writes of the 'Shop' and his place in it; to that extent, it was merely an extension of Berkhamstead. But Keegan cogently argues that the formation of leadership qualities, already largely in place by the culture of the public schools, was reinforced by the men's understanding of their place in this society: that is, they were completely accepting and trusting of the officers who were in charge of them.

Simply by being themselves, therefore, the first amateur officers provided their untrained soldiers both with an environment and a type of leadership almost identical to those found in a regular, peacetime regiment. They organised games for the men, and took part themselves, because that was the public school recipe for usefully occupying young males in their spare time. They organised competitions between platoons and companies – in cross-country running, rifle shooting, trench digging – because competition was the dynamic of public school life. They saw to the men's food, health, cleanliness, because as seniors they had been taught to do the same for junior boys. They administered automatically the military code of rewards and punishments, because it mirrored the system in which they had been brought up. And they took their men to church because it was there on Sundays that the school went *en masse*.

It went further in some minds, writing at the time: there was a conscious comparison between many of these young officers and Christ: many subalterns attended to their men's feet – lancing blisters, watching for 'trench' foot, ensuring the men could keep on marching – the crucial means of movement in the First World War. These same officers then led their men, with a stick, cane, or maybe a revolver, from the front; huge numbers died, precisely the sacrifice that Christ made – a conscious decision to die that men could live. Keegan says: 'The equation of courage with morality, a sort of heroic Puritanism, is distinctive of the public school approach to the First World War at least in the early stages.'

How far did Bill Tilman fit this image? I think to a considerable extent, although he would have been horrified to be compared with Christ – and he of course lived to the end. Certainly the public-school attitude was manifest in him throughout the war – the bantering tone of his letters, even when they grow more serious as the war lengthens, tells us that. With hindsight we may wish to believe that the comparison of the horror of the war with an extended game is deliberate psychological distancing, to keep sane amidst madness, horror and death. In the context of the times, though, this tone was not uncommon.

The Somme was a turning point of the war and, as such, even from the worm's-eye view Bill would have had of the battle, would have had a profound influence on him. It was preceded by a huge artillery bombardment, meant to destroy the German front trench line and to cut the barbed-wire. The bombardment lasted for a week, and expended around 1.5 million shells. This, however, meant in reality that only 900 tons of high explosive fell on the German lines, or, put another way, that each ten square yards under attack had received only a pound each, each square mile thirty tons. In Normandy, thirty years later, the Allies would lay down 800 tons to the square mile – and in minutes, not days.

The give-away to the failure of the artillery to do anything useful was the enormous fountains of earth thrown up by the impact of the shells, dissipating the explosive force upwards, not down to the deep bunkers where the Germans waited.

The second illusion about artillery was the concept of the barrage. The idea was that, once the infantry came out of their trenches, a huge barrage of artillery shells would precede their walk across no-man's land, protecting them from the Germans in front. At each critical phase this barrage would 'lift', the enemy trenches would be taken and the barrage would begin again, further forward. In theory this barrage could take the entire British army through the German lines without casualties. In both these artillery tactics Bill would have been intimately involved.

Bill's battery actually fired 16,000 shells between June 24th and July 16th. Bill wrote: 'From the 24th to the 1st was a pretty strenuous week for the gunners, and from the 1st onwards for everybody.' He mentions wire cutting, which was a more or less total failure:

Wire cutting, the 18-pounders job during the preliminary, is absolutely our *bête noire*. If you are at the OP you observe till your eyes nearly drop out of your head, if you're at the battery you fire all day till your head sings, and at the end there's nothing to show for it – no Boche killed, no trenches blown in, only, if you're lucky, a few strands cut, and a few stakes bowled over.

This comment is telling and, seventy-five years on, gives pause to wonder why, if the artillery officers on the ground were reporting the wire was not being cut according to the plan, the troops were sent over the top regardless.

Bill was in no-man's land on July 1st, the day of the assault. He remarked, laconically, that 'the front line is popularly supposed to present no difficulty; such was not the case on this particular front.' On July 3rd Bill's battery was attacked by phosgene shells, a very nasty form of poison gas; they were repeatedly attacked in this way. Although they were sent out of the line later in July they had returned by September.

At the end the British had made a few gains. The simple truth was that despite their gallantry and leadership the army could not stand up to machine-gun fire poured down on to them by a German defensive system of interlaced trenches and strongpoints going back miles from the front line. Although the British first used tanks in this battle they were too few and, where they broke through, no follow-up of reinforcements was made. Communication, once the soldiers had left the trenches, was more or less non-existent.

What the battle did was to bleed the German army of its experienced non-commissioned and junior officers. Whilst the British sustained

420,000 casualties, and the French 195,000, the Germans lost 650,000 to wounds and death.

Bill fought more or less all through the Battle of the Somme, and its effect on him is hard to judge. It seems inconceivable, given what he would have witnessed, that he did not harden his heart in order to stay in any way sane. His letters retain a curiously childish tone but that can hardly be surprising – he was still only eighteen and in a world in which cynicism and doubt were still largely absent. He was almost certainly still a virgin, opportunity hardly presenting itself, other than in local prostitutes of whom, we may be sure, Bill would have had uncharitable views.

Part of his sustenance would have come from his comrades but Bill was always a loner by inclination and he would have mixed, if not badly, then indifferently. Much of his moral courage came from his links with home – the fact that he kept up a huge correspondence all his life suggests this. Letters have one great advantage: they give the writer (and receiver) time to think about what to say, and they provide contact and distance at the same time. Bill was always awkward on the telephone in later years, and not just because he was going deaf.

Partly because of the static front the postal system in the First World War remains legendary, letters frequently only taking a few days to arrive at or from the front. Parcels were plentiful, too, and soldiers from Britain also knew that home was only a hundred miles or so away, just across the Channel. Bill received – and sent – hundreds of letters in the First World War. He also had home leave, just before Christmas 1916; Christmas Day he spent with his men. 'We gave them a huge blow out, more power to them,' he wrote home.

Then, in January 1917, he was severely wounded. There is little indication as to why the British-named 'Munich Trench' had to be captured on January 11th. It was known to be strongly defended, part of the German line at Auchonvillers. Bill was detailed, with two telephonists and two runners, to select observation posts in the trench after it had been taken by the 91st Infantry Brigade and he was wounded as he was moving to the captured trench. Even so he continued to work until the telephone line was established. For this he was awarded the Military Cross.

This had been awarded immediately but he did not learn of it until February (a nice birthday present!) when he wrote home: 'Isn't it great about the jolly old MC . . . I suppose it's for the FOO stunt on the 11th, though I don't quite see why. What pleases me is that it is an immediate award by the Corps Commander, and not given out as a divisional allotment like a good many are.'

The wound was serious and despite his letters home suggesting he would soon be up and about, he was in hospital first in France and then in England for nearly three months. He appeared before a medical board which pronounced him fit for duty in April. The letters he sent home from his Somerville College Hospital bed are among the most telling he wrote. Now, the doubts have begun.

On January 27th, he wrote to his parents:

I'll just explain why I'm not up, a sort of history of the case, you know, not too technical you know, although I'm getting a bit of a high flyer at medical terms. Soon after I got here they took the stitches out of the wound (pronounced properly please [it was said as 'wind' as in long and winding road]) which had healed. But unfortunately there was a whacking great blood clot inside dying to get out, so of course, the wound burst open again. Since when they've been busy getting the blood out, which is now nearly finished when I hope it will begin to heal. Only for this I would be up by now.

Apparently the Le Touquet people, not too cleverly, sewed it up so close tight that absolutely nothing could get out. I thought I would just tell you this by way of explanation.

Apart from his parents, he was writing regularly to Adeline and to Alec Reid Moir, the man who would one day marry her. Alec was a staff officer, somewhat senior in rank to Bill but this did not prevent them communicating in a light-hearted way. To Alec, on the same day, he wrote: 'May I hasten to remove the impression that seems to exist (Ken thinks the same) that I'm a confirmed and highly successful wangler. To a man with a highly developed sense of duty like myself to have to leave France was a wrench that time alone can heal.' This was a masterly piece of irony, and Bill knew it. Humour, in all its forms, kept men sane in the charnel house of this war. If Bill had a sense of humour as a youth, it was honed into an often black and wicked purpose by his time in the trenches.

To Adeline, on his birthday, he wrote: 'Dear Old Thing, Ever so many thanks for your jolly letter and for share in that top hole cigarette case,' but he ends the letter with 'P.S., We've got a concert next Sat. I'm going to try and get to it. "Bath chairs and coffins 9 pm."'

Occasionally, his humour turns sourer, to the point of despair, in fact, most especially when he knows he will, soon, be going back to France. On February 17th he wrote to his parents a long letter which included the following:

But a shadow is spreading itself over hospital life, the convalescent home scare spreads consternation everywhere (poetry). Hotels are to be taken over for convalescents, these are only allowed out between 1 pm and 6 pm with blue-bands so that theatres are inaccessible and drinks unobtainable. What a war! old boy, what a war! After, say, six weeks in the rollicking home of innocent jollity and mirth, the unfortunate sufferer is released for a space of ten days, when he is again gathered to the fold for light duty. After perhaps a day or two of this restful and exhilarating life, the unhappy man is boarded and passed fit for General Service.

Events now move rapidly, two hours see him in France, three and he is in the forefront of the battle. Two alternatives now present themselves to the 'arrassed 'ero – a Blighty [a wound bad enough to get him back to England, as Bill's had been] and the prospect of a repetition of what he has just gone through, or a bloody end sur le champs d'honneur! Choosing the lesser of two evils the afore-mentioned 'H H' stops a five.nine [a large artillery shell] with his heaving breast, thus passing into a land where convalescent homes are not and light duty is unknown.

This little picture (in no way overdrawn) of what is impending, is more than sufficient to make the blind walk, the lame see, the incurables die without waiting, and people like meself get better on time.

He continues with a description of various chaplains fighting over his bed and how, to get rid of them, he agreed with them all. 'The vicar of Bray is as the unchanging sea compared with me,' he said.

He got better slowly. The medical board in Preston declared him fit for general service in April but stayed on in Britain for his investiture with an MC. He was in France once more by mid-May.

The year 1917 is now best known for the events in Russia, which were to take it entirely out of the war and precipitate a crisis on the western front in early 1918. It was also the year the United States finally came into the conflict on the Allied side – on April 6th while Bill was still recuperating. The Germans, meanwhile, had declared unrestricted submarine warfare (part of the reason the USA declared war) and Britain faced a serious risk of being starved out of the war. At the same time Ludendorff, the German Chief of the General Staff, had ordered that the western front be turned into a defensive line. This involved a withdrawal to the Hindenburg Line, twenty miles behind the over-extended line from Arras to Soissons. Undertaken in great secrecy, the withdrawal began in February and was completed by April. It meant the German front could be held with fewer divisions, affording them a much greater reserve to be used where needed.

For the British army in France, 1917 was a grim year, in which distrust of the high command – after the Somme – was growing and where the overall attitude was one of determination just to hold on. Many were beginning to believe the war would last for ever or at least until all the young men of the Allies – and of Germany – had been killed or maimed. The year was dominated by a squabble between Haig and the French commander-in-chief, Nivelle, and it saw futile battles in the Aisne by the French – followed by a French mutiny – and at Passchendaele, where the British lost 300,000 men for a gain of five miles in the Ypres salient.

Bill's life was affected by all these events in small ways. He mentioned the Russian collapse, for example. He had settled back to life at the front and his letters now tended to be shorter and to concentrate on food, leave and items of clothing or equipment he needed. He discussed, too, investments with his father. On September 13th he wrote: 'I told you about receiving the boots OK. The Guvo and I seem fated to differ with regard to tailors, bootmakers, etc. Comrade Laxton can talk as much as he likes so long as he delivers the goods.'

He told his family on October 1st: 'The other day I was offered a job as creeper, orderly officer to the CRA of our division (Brig Gen) though of course only pro tem as the other officer was away on leave; however I resisted the temptation or rather escaped being sent by a narrow margin.'

On October 12th he wrote: 'The other day Cotton [his commanding officer] put my name in for Horse Gunner [the coveted Royal Horse Artillery]. Lizzie!!! But whether I'll get it or not or whether it's for pendant or après la guerre I don't know so will you please keep it a family secret till something, if anything, happens.' [The reference to 'Lizzie' is to a wartime bugle call announcing the mail had arrived.]

In November the British made a major change in tactics at Cambrai, using tanks in large numbers (200) in a surprise attack on the German lines; significantly, there was no long warning artillery bombardment. The initial breakthrough took the Germans entirely by surprise but once again there was no sustained follow-up.

Earlier in the summer there had been a number of crucial actions in all of which Bill took part, back with his old battery. He rejoined his unit for the Battle of Messines Ridge on June 7th. The British had tunnelled into the ridge – held by the Germans – and planted a million pounds of high explosive which they detonated on the 7th. Within three hours they had taken the ridge and it was a significant gain for the Passchendaele offensive which was to follow.

Bill's unit had by then been moved to the far west of the line close to Nieuwpoort on the Belgian coast which was held by the Germans. He wrote home that he had marched his men twenty miles to the North Sea for a bathe. Unfortunately for Bill he was stung by a jellyfish; he thought it might be a new German secret weapon. The move by his battery had been part of a plan to take Nieuwpoort in a combined army and navy operation but the Germans attacked first, on July 10th. Bill was in charge of the battery as his seniors were all on leave. He was, by now, a full lieutenant.

The attack was a severe one; 700 of the Northampton Regiment, for instance, were captured, along with 400 of the Kings K[enya] Rifle

Corps. The artillery was also coming under tremendous pressure. Among the few letters Bill wrote at this time was the following:

On the 10th I fear we met our Waterloo. What a party! It beat everything in the way of Boche bomboes we have struck, it brightened our ideas considerably. I was OC battery at the time. The Boche could not have known it (perhaps he did, though!), I was also unfortunately at the OP which was blown in as a preliminary. As you see, I did not follow the O Pippers example, although an officer of the heavies who was also there, did.

Bill was referring, somewhat elliptically, to the high casualty rate among observation post men. There were other injuries to deal with, though. On August 10th he wrote: 'Unfortunately we've had rather a lot of casualties. My batman, a priceless possession, one of the best, lost his hand. I was round to see him today in hospital, he was in wonderfully good cheer. He was a valet at the British Embassy in Washington avant la guerre, so you can guess what sort of servant he made. I feel quite lost without him.'

The same letter contained another piece of news: Bill had been given a bar to his Military Cross. He never knew why, precisely, but it seems most likely to have been awarded for his stalwart efforts as temporary OC in July under the terrible bombardment by the Germans. In all, during the time they were in the Nieuwpoort area, Bill's battery suffered sixty casualties. It is during this time that his letters home become less frequent, more laconic; often pages are missing and although this might be attributed to the years intervening, it suggests that he may well have posted them without checking their contents.

From Nieuwpoort the battery moved to Ypres, to the Plickheim Ridge where conditions were far worse. Apart from the mud, which all veterans of Passchendaele remembered with loathing, their position was very exposed. Added to this the Germans were using aircraft to bomb artillery positions. As the British painfully advanced into the mud, so Bill's battery followed them. They were now in a scene out of hell. At a point only 500 yards from the German lines, Bill's unit had to move shells up by night through a landscape of shell-holes full of dead and decaying men and horses.

The Scarborough Pals post-war account of this time says:

Leading our horses three miles we made our way through St Julien, past torn up railway lines, derelict tanks, dead animals and men, smashed wagons, along the remains of a road, splashed from head to foot by equally mud-smothered horses, and sometimes dragged backward or forward by their frantic struggles at gun flashes, near bursts, and the dreadful sights and smells they encountered.

Horses, as well as men, drowned in this mud, unseen, unheard, sometimes even unmissed. The same account mentions that, at the end of this terrible journey 'the imperturbable Lieut Tilman superintended operations, often under enemy fire.'

Bill did get his transfer to the very grand and snobbish RHA and in November 1917 left the battery to join I Battery, Royal Horse Artillery, attached to the 1st Cavalry Division.

On January 3rd, 1918, he wrote: 'I hope you saw the New Year in usual way; we did in great style though personally had it been five minutes late in coming I should not have seen it in at all.' By 1918 Adeline and Alec had decided to get married that spring and a month later Bill wrote: 'I fear my chances of getting home for the wedding are pretty slim. I've been detailed for a course at the RHA school. I don't know how long it lasts.'

The year before had ended with little change on the western front, the Ypres attack having petered out. It was known that the Germans were planning an attack, now that they had been able to withdraw so many troops from the former Russian front. Leave was becoming hard to get. On February 22nd Bill wrote: 'I wouldn't mind having an even fiver that some rotten offensive starts and all leave stopped just before [this is Bill getting round the censor by telling them what he thinks will be happening soon]. Nothing like being a blooming optimist what! Pity there are not a few more weddings if they induce Ken to get a new uniform. The swob hasn't written me for years.'

Bill went on his course for RHA officers, one which he evidently passed. Then, in March, the Germans attacked. They had been moving divisions from the Russian front for many months and, in desperate economic trouble back home and near starvation, of fuel as well as food, this was to be their last and decisive attack.

Ludendorff was desperate to make his move before the United States had a chance to shift its huge manpower reserves to Europe. He had also worked out that whilst the French were most anxious to protect Paris, the British were equally anxious to retain communications with the Channel ports. His battle plan envisaged driving a wedge between the two armies and then to destroy the British before turning on the weaker French. There were two prongs to the attack: one against the British at Ypres; the other against the French on the Somme.

Bill's battery, as part of the mobile reserve the cavalry and the RHA constituted, entered a period of rapid deployment from one arena to another. On March 23rd they were ordered to cross the Somme, Bill and one gun being the last to withdraw when the Germans' attack was successful. On March 25th Bill again used his guns to cover a withdrawal. Firing over open sights in a fast-moving battle of tactics, Bill was enjoying himself in a way he would not again – in wartime – until he was in northern Italy in 1944–45.

He had some narrow escapes but the thrill of what was taking place is clear from a letter he sent home: 'At the present moment I have not eaten for 24hrs and have neither washed nor shaved nor taken off my boots for days. Wouldn't have missed it for a lot. Today has been great fun, we have had the Boche in view most of the time. The weather is priceless. This is *war.*'

Inevitably, he missed the wedding, writing on April 7th, 'So glad to hear the wedding was a success. I had a letter from Adds down at Ludlow. She appeared to be full of beans and having a splendid time. I hope Alec was not recalled.' A few days later he was writing: 'Looks like no more leave, everyone seems determined to finish it one way or the other this summer. What ho for some more open warfare.'

The Allies held, although the Germans kept up their attacks up to mid-July. Then the Allies counter-attacked. By July the Germans had lost half a million men, the Allies rather more. But American reinforcements were now arriving at a rate of 300,000 a month and the Germans were exhausted – at the front and at home.

Bill wrote home on August 10th:

We're having a priceless time, worth ten years of one's life, though, as a matter of fact. The Hun went so fast that we didn't have much time for a shoot but had our work cut out to keep up. Our Brigade alone took 1,000 prisoners. The joke of it is that we're going over the same ground as we came back last spring. Last night we bivouacked on one of our old positions. No good loot so far but excellent prospects.

The letter was written on German *feldpostbrief* paper.

In late August Bill went on another course. On September 9th he wrote to his parents:

The course goes well it lasts until the 28th. It is proving expensive as well as instructive, visits to Dieppe tell heavily on the exchequer but what's money for except to be blued (loud 'hear hear' from two sides of the breakfast table).

Our mess gave a dance last Friday night. It was a great show, we raised a band and about fifty ladies, French mostly, some American and some English. I had quite a lot of dances, but it was grim silent work as my French is not. It also required considerable skill as there was a bit of a crush. We got to bed about 3 am. The only blot on the proceedings was that most of the servants got tight. We hope to have another before the end of the course if we're not all broke.

Bill was enjoying these last few weeks of the war no end. On September 19th he told his parents: 'I ran into Renie Edwards in

47

Dieppe the other day and last evening I had tea with her. She hopes to go on leave soon and then talks about coming out with a Lena Ashwell concert party as a sort of secretary. I asked her to our dance next Friday.'

In October Bill's parents had news that he had been wounded. He wrote hastily to reassure them. Then, on November 11th, it was all over. He wrote home on November 14th: 'Hope you've all recovered from celebrating, did the Guv get blotto? We're all getting ready for the march [into Germany], posh clothes, standards pennons, bands etc. etc.'

The front line in France and Belgium, which had held for more than four years, had collapsed as the weight of Allied troops, armour and aircraft began to bear. By September it was clear the Germans were in retreat and it was only a matter of time. An early request for an Armistice was rejected by the US President, Woodrow Wilson, who said he would not deal with a military dictatorship. Finally, on November 11th, at 11.00 a.m., the Armistice came into effect. The First World War was over.

Bill's battery made a forced march through the Ardennes, hoping to be the first into Germany; they crossed the frontier on December 1st, 1918. On December 3rd he wrote home: 'We are now in Prussia at a little place called Bonn. We crossed the frontier at 8.40am on the first. We shall finish up somewhere east of Bonn about the middle of the month. The people here seem more or less apathetic, the majority seem quite pleased and are out to help, one or two don't care about it.'

Then, on December 8th he wrote: 'Our dreams have been realised, a castle on the Rhine. We are now a mile or two northwest of Bonn and living in Baron —'s Schloss, well hardly a Schloss, sort of a villa they call it. Anyhow it's very nice indeed, priceless bedrooms and a topping big dining room all done in oak and lit by about fifty electric lights all cunningly placed.' He added there was no hope of getting Christmas leave, though.

He was very uncertain as to what he was going to do. In a letter sent on December 28th he looked at the various options.

With things as they are and nothing in particular to go on leave for I'm rather inclined to let things slide a bit and see what happens. On the other hand if there is any particular date you fancy (Ken and Alec being home or something like that) I could most probably fix it up. What do you think about it all? I mean it isn't as if there was a war on when it would be tempting providence not to get home on every possible occasion.

A month's leave of course would rather alter things, I don't see any hope of getting it unless I hang on to May and by that time with the Grace of God and a bit of luck we may know what's going to

48

happen to us. This state of uncertainty and not knowing what to do is assuredly devilish depressing.

As it happened Bill found he could resign his commission much more quickly than he had anticipated and, because of that, a new phase of his life was about to begin, the other most formative part of his young manhood: Africa.

The men who survived the First World War without serious, or lasting, injury, including the loss of a limb, saw themselves as a privileged group in a way few now can understand. Living on borrowed time is a phrase which can be applied to all of us, but to come through the bombardments and the bullets of four years (in Bill's case, three) of war in the trenches must have seemed like a pure miracle.

For the rest of his life Bill put himself into considerable hazard – and discomfort. Nothing of what he was about to experience would have compared with what he had been through, what he had seen. The philosophical side of Bill had been formed in these years, alongside the influences of his parents, especially his father. To the insecurity the dominant side of his father engendered in him, can we add that other great enemy of internal peace: guilt? The guilt of the survivor when most are dead or injured, maimed physically or mentally.

How far is it possible to assert that Bill was made insecure by his father? And how far did he feel guilt, rather than a humble remorse at surviving the war? On both questions we must wait until we have had a chance to examine the final elements of Bill's youth and early manhood: his hearth and home after the First World War in that most mysterious of continents: Africa.

CHAPTER 3

Africa – Where a Man Can Thrive

'To those who went to the war straight from school and survived it, the problem of what to do afterwards was peculiarly difficult.' Those words could have been written by a social historian at any time since 1918. In fact they were the opening lines of Bill's first book, *Snow on the Equator*, published in 1937, and the only coherent account of what he did in the fourteen years he spent in Kenya as a colonial planter. These were years of great struggle, the years that formed the backcloth to all his young adulthood, and they were years in which his solitary character was finally solidified.

He had wasted no time in deciding to go abroad. He came home from the occupied Rhineland in April 1919. By August he was on a ship to East Africa. No correspondence exists from this period but, from his own account, he returned from Germany with no fixed plans. His father wanted Bill to follow him into the sugar trade; for every possible reason, Bill resisted. As a result, relations between them cooled considerably for a time.

Instead he took up one of the government post-war schemes for resettling demobbed soldiers and was granted a square mile of land, on the basis of what Bill called a lottery, more accurately decided by who applied first. In this he was lucky for the land he got was well watered and wooded, on the south-west edge of the Mau Forest, fifteen miles from Kericho in the newly formed colony of Kenya, formerly the protectorate of British East Africa. The site was at 6500 feet which meant that, close to the equator though it was, the climate was generally very pleasant, up to 30°C in the day, 10°C at night.

Bill paid £35 for his one-way passage from Liverpool; one wonders how his mother and father and sister must have felt as they saw him off, after three years of not knowing whether he would survive the next day. It was an uncomfortable voyage. 'Five of us were quartered in a steel deck-house on the poop, flanked on either side by a pen of live sheep, and immediately below was the lascar crew's galley, whence the fumes of cooking never ceased rising,' he later wrote.

As they passed through the Red Sea, the temperature – and their tempers – rose. The voyage lasted six weeks – desperately slow – but by October Bill had arrived at the site of his new home. There, he inspected his land. 'I was viewing from the top of a tree the square mile of land which was to be my home for the next ten years. This unusual method of inspection was adopted because heavy bush, through which there were no paths, for there were no inhabitants, prevented access to it.'

What he saw, he liked, although he realised his was to be a back-breaking task in bush clearance before his chosen crops, first flax, then coffee, could be planted. It is an irony of the situation in which Bill and his fellow settlers found themselves that they missed tea, which grew wild, as the crop which would have made them rich.

It was a solitary life altogether. There were other settlers but for much of the time all were engaged in a struggle against nature. In many respects Bill and his companions had chosen a peacetime extension of their army life: an implacable enemy – heat, disease, despair – which only constant battle could defeat, and with the growth of strong male bonds, a common purpose. There were very few women. Among the male friends Bill kept in close touch with, Ron Buchanan, Robin Sneyd and Richard Royston constituted an inner circle.

Early on Bill faced tremendous logistical problems, against which later expedition supply crises must have paled into nothing. There was a dirt track to Kericho, four miles away from Bill's plot, but the Itare River was between him and it. Getting from the railhead at Lumbwa, forty miles away, could take four days – and by ox-cart as the car and the lorry had hardly begun to penetrate this region. One of the first tasks undertaken by Bill and Ron Buchanan was to build a bridge – of timber and barbed-wire – across the Itare River. It lasted a year. Eventually they built a steel and concrete bridge over the River Kiptiget, on the other side of their land, which gave them a better route to the main road.

Bill first lived in a tent and then built a mud and wattle hut. He begrudged the time spent on building this structure, and the ones that followed. The floors were of earth which had its own drawbacks, one being dust when it was swept, another being the vegetation which regularly grew through it. As well, there were delights like jigger fleas, ants, termites, the occasional snake, and the hens (carriers of the fleas) who liked to come in and lay their eggs in the dark corners. For the bats which swept in, he had an answer: 'I found it impossible to sleep so long as one remained fluttering about. I used to light the lamp and lie in bed holding a .22 rifle to pot them off one by one whenever they settled and hung down from a beam . . . A quicker and more sporting method was to bag them with a tennis racquet.' Bill rather relished telling the stories of these unwelcome visitors to his houses in the bush.

The only letter from this early period was written at the beginning, to his sister, by then in the United States with her husband. Dated October 26th, 1919, and written in pencil, it says:

Dearest Adds,

I am writing this from the site of my future farm, at present a square mile of African bush of the most prodigious thickness. We are 50 miles from the railway, by a most precarious road, 15 miles from the township of Kericho which as you see [he sent photographs] consists of a Post Office. I have no doubt whatever that with the expenditure of a few thousands and in the course of a decade or so the farm will be in a position to keep its owner!!!!

However, it's an upping country. We are half a degree south of the equator and 6500 feet up. The mornings are all English summer days. Every afternoon it rains merrily.

Am at present staying with Buchanan, one of the eleven who has already started work on his land. As a matter of fact he's been making three miles of road and a 60 foot bridge to take us on to the 'main' road. I'm giving him a hand and trying to pick up the language and a few hints before starting on my own. We live in tents, rise at crack of dawn, breakfast and then having a gang of 30 wa-Lumbawa 'boys' till it begins to rain about 1 o'clock. Lunch and then odd jobs between storms till 4.30.

After tea the rain generally stops and we push off for a walk in the bush. At sundown we get into pyjamas cardigans and coats and light a huge fire, bath, dinner, smoke, turn in.

Of course on my own place I shall have work and worry ad lib. There are only pigeons and partridge to shoot round here but a few days safari south is a great game country, including elephants. I think you and Alec ought to chuck New York and come out here. Alec's hard-earned would come in useful (I shall touch him for some anyway one of these days). He'd make an excellent horny-handed son of the soil, you would lend the softening influence to see that we didn't become too horny-handed, ride a horse, see that we got some decent grub and invite people to stay with us.

If the altitude and rainfall didn't appeal to you, we sell out at enormous profit and buy a farm at lower altitude. You could roast to your heart's content. Drop me a line when you intend coming. Love to Alec, hope he's not becoming indecently wealthy,
    Yours, Billy

There is a clear touch of loneliness in this letter. The sheer effort of clearing the land, the difficulties of language and supply, must all have worried at Bill's resolve, perhaps most of all in the early days. But he cleared the land and began to grow crops. He socialised but not by all accounts very much. Most of all he read, it being a family legend that in his time in Africa he got through all Dent's Everyman Library. While he was reading, he could look out at the view. 'The most attractive part of the view, at any rate to me, was, in course of time, the neat parallel rows of alternating coffee-bushes and shade trees stretching away from below the house for half a mile.'

Then, in 1924, Kenneth died in an aircraft accident off Majorca at the age of thirty-two. In a letter to his wife, Group Captain Kilner, his old instructor, wrote:

I am writing to express to you on behalf of myself and all the officers our very sincere and deep sympathy in the great loss you have sustained on the death of your husband. I have known him for some years, in fact he was a pupil of mine in training, when I commanded Redcar in 1917, and I well knew and appreciated his sterling character and loveable disposition. Perhaps I may tell you what happened.

He went up as an observer on the morning of the 11th March during fleet exercises off Palma, the aeroplane swung to the right just as it was leaving the deck and went into the sea, turning upside down practically at once. The destroyer attending us went immediately to the rescue, and got both your husband and the pilot out and rendered all aid possible.

Unfortunately, your husband had been stunned by the fall and was beyond human aid. Artificial respiration was continued for four hours and he was immediately rushed off to the attending hospital ship. If it is any consolation to you I am assured by the Medical Officers that he could not have had a moment's suffering, and his end was quite peaceful. He only had a large bruise on his temple, but otherwise was quite normal to look upon.

We buried him this afternoon just off Polensa Bay in Majorca, alongside a Lieutenant Commander, Royal Navy. It was a most impressive service conducted by the Chaplain of his ship and attended by over 300 officers and men, including the Admirals' representatives commanding the Atlantic and Mediterranean fleets. I am having a cross made from a propellor, and placing it on his grave.

John Tilman was so upset by Ken's death he wrote a letter to the Air Ministry in London demanding an explanation; a long letter in reply came saying that at that time they had no idea why the aircraft – flying off the Royal Navy's first purpose-built aircraft carrier, HMS *Argus* – should have swung off the deck and fallen into the sea. 'The engine had been tested and found correct,' the letter said, and it went on to say that perhaps the court of inquiry would throw more light on the matter. It would have been cold comfort to the Tilmans to know that the pilot had survived.

A few years later Adeline went on a Mediterranean cruise with her father and they visited the grave, bringing back a white geranium. A cutting from that plant lives on at Bodowen to this day; the other physical memory of Ken is in a clock, set in the centre section of the propellor of the aircraft in which he was killed, now with Ken's great-nephew, Pam's son, Simon. The Tilmans may, as Pam admits, be undemonstrative in their public grief or memories of their dead but they have their own, equally moving, private memories in this way.

Bill came home from Africa for the funeral and took Adeline, also back for the funeral, off to the Lake District for a short holiday. He and she were then discussing the problems she was having with her marriage to Alec. She by now had two daughters: Joan, born in 1920 and Pam, born in 1922. Bill had liked Alec a lot and, in the wilds of Africa one can surmise his own grief at the turn of events. So strongly did he feel about Alec that he journeyed to the States to try to patch things up between Adeline and Alec; to no avail. Adeline packed her bags and she and her daughters made their final voyage back home to Liverpool together, late in 1924.

The visit home may also have healed some of the rift between Bill and his father created by his sudden decision to emigrate. Two years later, in 1926, John Tilman travelled to Kenya to visit Bill. Although Bill had expressed great anxiety over this visit to friends, it seems to have gone well. What his father might have thought about Bill's idea of accommodation was mitigated by his recognition that farming in East Africa had a bright future. One result of the visit was that John Tilman invested in his son's enterprise. Bill now bought nearly 2000 acres of land at Sotik, for coffee-growing.

Shortly before this visit, he had gone into partnership with a compatriot, Richard Royston, whose family lived near Wallasey. Royston became manager of the Kericho farm and Bill moved to Sotik. The Sotik land was actually two good strips divided by a swamp. Back home John Tilman advised them on the means by which they should market their coffee. In all, it was the best time Bill had in Africa, and the most settled. It was also the last part of his African sojourn, for he did not move to Sotik until 1929.

The truth was that Bill was getting restless. He freely admitted, in *Snow on the Equator*, that

> the daily routine of attending to planted coffee was much less congenial to me than the earlier struggle to carve a home out of the forest and to tame the wilderness; to watch the landscape – a

waste of bush and jungle, but a familiar one – change daily under one's eyes; to see a new clearing here, a shed there, paths and roads pushing out in all directions, while seeds, which one had oneself planted, grew into trees big enough to make timber.

He was afraid of gathering moss and, apart from his visits to England and an annual shooting excursion, had simply worked. With an able business partner capable of taking much of the burden of daily farming off his shoulders, Bill was clearly looking for an outlet for his energies. Into his new life at Sotik was to come climbing and fulfilment, a more satisfying pursuit than his shooting trips with Ron Buchanan, which previously had been his only true relaxation.

Bill gives an account of one of these hunts in *Snow on the Equator*. 'Possibly the most urgent desire of the newcomer to a country of big game is to go out and kill something. Fortunately for most, this unsporting blood-lust is soon satiated,' he wrote. On his own land there were few opportunities for this, and in all the time he was at Kericho he only managed to shoot a serval (a medium-sized wild cat). A local leopard was killed by the natives and a wild pig by his dog. Bill was not a particularly good shot; in the Mau Forest, nearby, he managed only three bush buck in ten years.

'For more fun and less work', as he put it, they went to the Plains, the vast area of what is now the Serengeti along the Kenya–Tanzania border. Bill's first proper safari to this region was in pursuit of elephant. Licences to shoot elephant were expensive but this cost could be offset against the value of the ivory in the tusks; how times have changed – as well as attitudes.

They found a small herd but were inept at tracking it.

What with fear of the elephants and fear of the Game Laws, we suffered a deal of nervous wear and tear while we barged about submerged in the grass sea or watched expectantly from the branch of some thorn tree, bitten the while by ferocious tree ants. How we avoided blundering into or being charged by some peevish cow, or through sheer nervousness, shooting some undersized beast, remains to me a mystery.

On their way back to camp, however, they came across some herd stragglers, including a bull, which offered them a perfect target.

'We do it wrong, being so majestical; to offer it the show of violence', was certainly how we felt about it, but he seemed warrantable, and I had with me a new heavy rifle which I was itching to try on something worthy of its weight. One shot between the eye and ear dropped him stone dead, leaving us aghast at the suddenness of it and feeling like murderers with an outsize corpse on our hands.

The native porters saw to most of that, however, and Bill discovered the next day that he had shot an elephant carrying 100 pounds of tusk ivory which, while by no means a record, was good going. Fired with this success, they decided to try for a buffalo. In this they failed, and for an embarrassing reason. Bill's own style cannot be matched so here is the tale as he tells it:

Cautious and hurried whispering elicited the information that the buffalo herd were grazing almost in camp. Apparently a boot thrown out of the tent could not fail to hit one, and, luckily, the porters were too petrified to stir.

My first thoughtless impulse was to strike a match, but B[uchanan], hearing me fumbling, hastily stopped me. Then I remembered that my heavy rifle had been taken down to be packed away in its case, and that the only ammunition handy was soft-nosed. (A buffalo has a very tough hide, so that to make sure of sufficient penetration it is advisable to use a solid bullet . . .) The same thought had evidently struck B for he was on the floor, routing about in the haversack which contained the ammunition, cursing softly but vehemently. Afterwards I learned what the trouble was. B had false teeth, which in the dark and confusion he had mislaid, and he was now trying to distinguish between solid and soft-nosed bullets in the dark, without being able to bite them.

By the time they got outside, the buffalo had all gone.

Their final attempt to bag big game was with rhino. This was adrenalin-raising stuff for the bush where the rhinos were was extremely dense. 'The only warning of the close proximity of a rhino would be an appalling, explosive splutter, like the sound of some gigantic soda syphon in action.'

By Bill's own admission, towards the end of their safari they had camped across a well-used rhino path. The snortings started at midnight and, despite banking up the fire, continued. 'B and I took the precaution of loading our rifles, but it was raining, we could see nothing, so we remained in bed – unwisely, I thought, because if the rhino did decide to charge through the camp to reach the water-hole, he would very likely vent his fury on the tent in passing.' The porters, in a rather larger tent, obviously believed theirs would be the target and they all piled into Bill and Ron Buchanan's tent. 'We just sat still, and at each explosion of the perambulating syphon smiled a wan and sickly smile.'

57

Eventually they heard no more; it had apparently finally dawned on the rhino, wrote Bill, that a small deviation in its normal path would take it to the water-hole around their camp.

Returning home from these excursions, it was exciting to see how the flax had grown, or how the last planting of young coffee seedlings had 'taken', but we had, invariably, to steel our minds against the recital of a chapter of accidents by the head boy whom we had left in charge; the oxen that had strayed or died, the boys that had deserted; how the plough had broken the day we left, and had done no work since. So ran the tale, while other less obvious items, such as disease in the cattle or the coffee, we had the fun of finding out later for ourselves.

Bill substituted an ice-axe for a rifle in 1930 on Mount Kenya and Mount Kilimanjaro but he was to take part in one more safari, this time with his friend, Horace Dawson. Dawson had been made a temporary Vermin Control Officer, in which capacity he was ordered to control (not, Bill explained, exterminate) a herd of 2000 elephants which had been playing havoc with local farming. In one of his patrols, he invited Bill to go along. His activities as a great white hunter might appear as evidence of a callous indifference to wildlife to modern eyes. But he relates himself how he never relished killing things much; what does stand out is his enthusiasm for hazard, or even actual danger.

The cull with Dawson revealed another side to Bill's character – his love of the absurd. Among the elephants they killed were cows carrying young; Dawson, whose activities were known of in England, had been asked to obtain, if at all possible, the foetus of one of these elephants for study.

Neither of us knew the first thing about an elephant's interior arrangements, nor had we gone closely into the means of preservation and dispatch beyond providing ourselves with a five-gallon drum of methylated spirits. This drum we had solemnly carted about with us from camp to camp, much to the chagrin of the porter who had to carry it. Our men were curious as to the contents, and from the way we cherished it thought it must be some potent spirit, as indeed it was: but had we explained the base uses to which it was to be put they would have been more than ever convinced of our madness.

Bill and Dawson had the notion that all they had to do with the foetus, when they extracted it, was to tip it into the drum and solder it up. First, they had to get their foetus. 'When at last it was laid at our feet for inspection, we found it measured about four feet by two and weighed every bit of two hundred pounds. Our five-gallon drum, which was standing open-mouthed in readiness, looked rather foolish – our own mouths must have stood open in sympathy.'

Dawson, though, was not to be defeated; he remembered that he had a forty-gallon drum on his farm, a mere seventy miles away. Despite Bill's objections, he decided to take the foetus in the car. 'By now it was nine o'clock, and getting warm. Already the air bore to the sensitive nostril something more than a hint that speed was essential if our gift was to be at all acceptable to science.' Dawson, taken ill a little later, gave the car over to Bill who confessed to never liking to be the driver while its owner was sitting alongside.

'Neither of us was feeling very amiable. It was a disgustingly hot day, our kit kept dropping off, and the luckless passenger at the back was beginning to make its presence felt.' They stopped at an administrative post where there was a hospital to get advice but the size of their specimen defeated the doctors. Eventually they arrived at Dawson's farm.

It was ticklish work getting it into the drum, with D hopping about and cursing everyone in his anxiety lest at the last moment his flawless specimen should receive some irreparable injury. To say it was poured in would be an exaggeration – insinuated, perhaps, describes it better; but, anyhow, in it went and now all depended upon our precious five gallons of methylated spirits.

This, fortunately, covered the foetus and they all retired, happy with their work.

It was not quite the end of the story.

I left the next day, and that was then last I saw of D and the oil-drum for some time. I often wondered how it had fared on the long journey of 70 miles to the station, five hundred miles in the fierce heat of a steel truck to the coast, and the yet fiercer heat of the Red Sea; and even more did I wonder what the biological consignee thought of it. The true story is shrouded in mystery, and I fear it will never be revealed. Perhaps the drum was never delivered, because, shortly after, I read in a paper of a truck on the Uganda Railway being derailed by the explosion of an oil-drum. I had an uneasy feeling that there might have been some connection.

Bill ends his account by a typically elliptical remark about Dawson delivering his own child: 'I believe he even found a solution to another problem in practical biology, but it was probably one of less formidable dimensions than ours.'

On holiday in the Alps, in August 1932, he got a letter that had him hurrying back to England, to pack once more for Kenya. Gold had been discovered to the north-east of Lake Victoria. The letter was from Horace Dawson and, once back in Africa, they set up a partnership and set about the business of gold prospecting.

Bill delighted in telling the stories surrounding this episode all through his life, and it fits entirely with a man who loves living rough, chancing his arm against a sudden – and in this case, very lucrative – discovery. Dawson had already staked ten claims by the time Bill caught up with him. Their prospecting was of the old-fashioned, crudest kind. Crushing tons of quartz, and then 'panning' it, looking for the heavier gold sediments, or 'tailings'. If found in any quantity, the idea was then to follow the vein of quartz back to the main 'reef'.

They lived in a mud and grass hut and undertook this back-breaking work for, in Dawson's case, four, in Bill's case, six months. They had no luck and at the end of it they sold up – getting £25 for one of their claims. It had been an exciting if fruitless time. By then he had begun to wonder if he could make a living at writing – with no clear idea of what kind of books he might write. The great literary love of his life was Jorrocks, that classic of nineteenth-century hunting, but there is no evidence that Bill ever seriously thought of fiction.

What he may well have thought out is that a good book requires a good story; what better way to introduce himself to his readers than by making an unusual (at the time he did it, more accurately a wildly eccentric) exit from Africa, by cycling across it, from east to west?

In *Snow on the Equator*, after discussing the failure of the gold prospecting, Bill says that he had not decided his next move. He cheerfully confessed that he and Horace Dawson had illegally entered an area yet to be declared open for prospectors: 'On our return journey a large number of quartz samples had, by some strange chance, found their way into the car. But the wicked do not always flourish, and so it was with us, for every sample we tested proved to be barren.'

Thus, having had a last fling at the gold, he came to the conclusion he would go home for a while. 'Being in no particular hurry, this seemed the opportune moment for carrying out a scheme with which I had been toying for some time, namely, the finding of an alternative to the usual east-coast route to Europe.' By a process of elimination, he says, he arrived at the bicycle. In truth, this seems to be too good to be true: one strongly suspects his reasoning in the book was the post-hoc justification his readers would need. Modern exploring cyclists – Hallam Murray, Nick Crane, for example – instantly recognise Bill's true purpose. The bicycle is in many respects the best way to travel; not too slow but fast enough. It is an extension of walking, moreover, Bill's own preferred method of locomotion, in giving its rider the same kind of access to the landscape through which he is travelling, and to the people who live there.

He began his journey on September 14th, 1933, travelling by train from Nairobi to Kampala. He had bought a British bicycle for £6. He took no tent, planning to sleep rough on the ground under a mosquito net in a sleeping bag (he had a good quality eiderdown one). He took a rucksack with a few spare clothes and washing things. He had, to begin with, about twenty pounds of food but, in the main, he intended to live off the land, on a staple of plantain. He had good maps of Uganda but he could get no maps at all of the Congo.

The journey, in all, was about 3000 miles; he covered sixty on the first day, camping by Lake Victoria. 'The natives were always horrified at my sleeping out, and it was not easy to make them understand my reasons for it. On two occasions in Uganda, I heard lions grunting at night, but there was little to fear from them, while there was a good deal to fear from the tick-infested huts.' Often the local headman would provide a couple of spear-carrying guards, who sat by a large fire they built for themselves and Bill. As much as anything, they were all amazed at the spectacle of a white man cycling alone and many headmen clearly worried lest any harm come to him while he was in their vicinity.

It is sad to reflect that the passage of sixty years has led to a situation where only a madman would even dream of making much of this journey now, unless by armoured car. The ending of colonialism may have brought many benefits to native Africa; a settled peaceful order it has not.

It took Bill a week from Kampala to cross into the Belgian Congo (now Zaire). The frontier he found deserted, only a wooden post marking the change from British to Belgian rule. Just over the border he had one of the worst patches of riding on the entire journey as he had to cross a stretch of broken lava; it was here that he accepted his only lift – from an Indian lorry driver.

From Lake Kivu he headed towards Stanleyville (modern Kisangani). It was 650 miles as the road went north before turning west. There was a long stretch upwards and then twenty-five miles of downhill. Finally he came across the great Congo rainforest.

I beheld, far below me, a smooth expanse of dark olive green stretching away into the distance, flat and unbroken, like the sea. It was the Congo forest, reaching westwards to the sea and extending to four degrees north and south of the equatorial line. That afternoon I entered what was to be my environment for the next fortnight. Within this tract of low-lying virgin forest, terrifying for its silent immensity, the atmosphere is that of a hothouse, sapping the energy of both mind and body. The only road crossing this sea of vegetation in which I was now submerged stretches endlessly before one like a thin red band at the bottom of a canyon of living greenery. The dark wall of foliage towers up on either hand for nearly two hundred feet, to arch and almost meet overhead, as if to reclaim for the forest this pitiful strip that man has wrested from it.

Some 200 miles short of Stanleyville he had his first puncture. During the repair his pump connector gave out so he pushed the bike for five miles to a big Muslim village. There, to his astonishment, was a man with a bicycle – and a pump, but with no connector. However, the owner showed Bill how to pump his tyres using just the pump and a piece of wet rag – hard work but effective.

Bill spent one night in a hotel in Stanleyville before moving on. He crossed the border from the Belgian Congo into French Equatorial Africa where he was detained for a weekend by French officials while they obtained clearance for his bicycle to be imported. From here he had a long haul to the French Cameroons. Fifty-six days out of Kampala he saw the Atlantic. He ended his epic journey by loading himself and his bicycle on to a train for the last stretch from Edea to Duala. Bill had to wait a few days for a ship, contemplating his achievement.

In some ways, he admitted, he was disappointed at the sameness (he thought tameness, too) of the landscape through which he had passed; the people were not so diverse as he had anticipated, either. Finally, he was surprised at the ease with which he had managed it all; he blamed, in part, the coming of the internal combustion engine – for improvements in the roads.

My ship came up the river and I prepared to embark by buying myself a coat and a pair of trousers. I was glad that ships tie up alongside a quay at Duala, thus allowing my faithful 'grid' to be wheeled on board instead of suffering the indignity of being hoisted through the air like so much inanimate freight. Sailing day arrived, bringing with it for me the mingled feelings of more 'last days'. Countries, if lived and worked in long enough, have a queer way of making a man feel an affection for them, whether they have treated him well or ill. For fourteen years – a fifth of our allotted span – Africa had been my task-mistress, and now I was leaving her. If she had not given me the fortune I expected, she had given me something better – memories, mountains, friends.

We dropped down the river whose muddy waters were soon to be lost in the clean blue immensity of the sea, while the Cameroon mountains, showing faintly astern, waved to me Africa's last farewell.

As a footnote to this journey, the bicycle survives still (1995) in the bicycle museum in Coventry. On his return Bill wrote to the makers telling them of his journey, rather hoping they would send him a new bicycle as a reward. He got only a letter back, thanking him for his interest.

What did Africa, that larger manufacturer, give Bill? Much of what he gained is contained in *Snow on the Equator*, the most accessible of his books, apart from *Mischief in Patagonia*. His words at the end are clearly heartfelt: it gave him mountains and friends. He had not found a settled relationship, even if we make the assumption that he was looking for one. What he had discovered was himself, and that he could live with what he was.

CHAPTER 4

The Tilmans Back Home

Bill spent a lifetime writing, keeping his family firmly in the distance; little of his home life, or that of any of his family may be gleaned from the fifteen books he wrote over a period of forty years. Yet he relied on a stable household, much of it provided by his sister. Adeline had returned with her two small daughters to the family home in Wallasey late in 1924, there to look after her parents. Joan was six, Pam four. Pam says she had crossed the Atlantic three times by the age of three.

Adeline's marriage might have been over but she never came to terms with her divorce. This, as much as anything else, determined the course of her life, for although she had at least one possible suitor – about whom she confided to Bill, still in Africa – her innate sense of morality would not allow her to break her vows to Alec. She remained a separated wife for the next fifty years.

Pam believes that, as far as her grandparents were concerned, they might have been secretly pleased by the turn of events.

> My grandfather did not help the marriage. They got what they wanted, their only daughter back with their grandchildren, whom they adored. They got their daughter to run the house for them, which she then did. She saw to the maids and she saw to the food, and my grandmother handed it all over to her. She drove my grandmother about, they played bridge together, they played golf, what could have been nicer?

Adeline had become part of their retirement plan, as she could – and did – act as housekeeper to them both. A new family was in the process of forming: the grandparents, a divorced daughter and her two children. Into this scene Bill would occasionally drop, the exotic uncle from far away.

This is how Pam recalls him, then:

My first recollection of my uncle was meeting him at Seacombe Ferry, Wallasey, when he was returning on holiday from Africa. I was very young, I suppose about six, and my mother took my sister and me in the car which was a tourer with mica detachable windows. These windows were a source of anxiety to us. They must not be leant against or scratched. They would shatter at a touch, and all sorts of dire threats hung over our heads at the mere thought of damaging them in any way.

We waited at the ferry and up the slipway came this smallish, tanned man wearing khaki-coloured bush clothes with a large bush hat with a snakeskin band around it. I was entranced. The bright blue eyes twinkled as he sat in the front of the car chatting and laughing with my mother. Suddenly he turned round to say something to us in the back and crack! – his elbow had gone clean through the mica window.

I waited, appalled – what would happen now? My uncle said, 'Damn silly car, this,' and my mother replied, laughing, 'The trouble with you is that you're too used to wide-open spaces.' Not another word was even mentioned about windows to my knowledge and I think it was from that incident that I realised that this uncle of mine must be quite special.

To a small girl he was the most glamorous figure, appearing from faraway places, always with a present – a string of turquoise beads, a small tribal stool, an elephant tail fly whisk, an amber bracelet. He would stay for a while and then be off again. Always, there was the same celebration for his first homecoming dinner, a Christmas pudding which my grandmother had made and, put on one side the night he left, a sherry trifle.

He was a very kindly, laughing figure in my childhood. Once, my sister and I were incarcerated with measles or chickenpox, and we decided to open a museum. Collecting all our treasures, bird's feathers, pretty shells, the usual bric-à-brac which children collect, we labelled it all and charged 1d or 2d to view. I can visualise Bill now in his dinner jacket (he and my mother were going out to a dance), solemnly paying his money and expressing great interest in all our treasure.

He took me climbing at Helsby and in the Lake District and patiently hauled me up difficult pitches where I could not reach the next rock hold. I remember standing on a ledge with a large oxygen cylinder strapped to my back – he was testing it out for Everest – and as I reached up a gush of water went down my arm from a stream. It was very cold and it soaked me to the skin. But I got hauled up and the 'well done' at the top warmed me through.

Back at the hotel when the wretched heavy cylinder was taken off and I breathed fresh air, someone said, 'You'll give her pneumonia wearing that at low altitudes.' 'It didn't do her any good for climbing either,' was my uncle's reply. Perhaps from that dated his antipathy to the use of oxygen in climbing.

He was a romantic, exciting, kindly uncle and lucky indeed is the child who never has reason to change those opinions in later life.

Her grandfather, was nothing like Bill, Pam recalls. He was very small, a little podgy with red cheeks and very blue eyes. Bill's mother was afraid of him, in a very Victorian way, and catered for his every desire.

Pam thought of him as great fun:

I was the favourite and I knew it. I used to call him pop. They were awfully good to us. I remember them always bringing us back presents when they went away. One time I remember crawling into the drawing room as a Red Indian; of course they knew we were there but they entered into the spirit of it all.

I always got the knuckle off the lamb; my grandfather would be carving and he would make a point of giving it to my grandmother and make a terrific play of it and I would think, Oh, I haven't got it, and then it would reach my grandmother and she would slip it off into the vegetable dish so that when it reached me I could take it. Everybody knew it was happening – every single time we had lamb. There was a lot of humour and kindness.

He took such care over us going to school, coming round with us and checking, seeing which was the most suitable for his grandchildren to go to – Malvern won out. He was a twinkly little man but an awful lot of people were terrified of him – I wasn't, I thought he was wonderful.

Bill was more silent; my grandfather would chat and hold forth. He was head of the household and very much so – a real Victorian head. Bill was away so much and when he came home there was always this great excitement. It is hard to say how much in awe – if at all – of his father he was.

Bill's parents, Pam's grandparents, died within six months of each other in 1936. The last letter Bill received from his father was written on April 28th, 1936. He wrote: 'I am making steady progress – for four days in succession I have been out in the car.' On the back of this letter, Adeline had written, 'Dearest Bill, I'm afraid you must read the other side with kindly eyes, Father is very weak, and literally crawls into the car on hands and knees. Mentally he is rather muddled but his spirit is splendid.'

John Tilman died on September 5th, four days before the news of Bill's triumph on Nanda Devi reached home. Typically, Adeline had written to Bill not to hurry home. Six months later, in March 1937 his mother died in the car returning from a visit to Pam and Joan at their school, with Adeline driving her. Bill now only had his sister and his nieces as close family.

John Tilman had died a wealthy man – by the standards of today, a millionaire. His final comment on his younger son, though, was in the will: he left the bulk of his money in trust to his nieces, preventing Bill from realising the capital, should he so wish, although both Bill and Adeline had use of the interest for the rest of their lives. To the last, John Tilman was leaving a clear sign that he did not perceive Bill as capable of running his own affairs without the assistance, from beyond the grave, of his father.

'Then came the war,' Pam remembers (the Second World War):

and Bill soon went off to France telling my sister and me, casually, 'By the way, if I'm taken prisoner don't expect me back, I'll be shot escaping. I'll never stay in a prison camp.' We never told our mother, but I expect she knew. Then came Dunkirk and the agonising wait for news. The phone call came and blueing some precious petrol I drove to Lime Street station to meet him. The troop train arrived and tired soldiers flooded off, unshaven, dirty and in incomplete uniforms. Not Bill: his fore and aft cap jaunty on his head, shaved and buttons all done up, still carrying a rifle. When I asked him what that was for he replied, 'I picked it up off the beach, wasn't leaving that to those damned Boche.'

Bill survived the second world war, arriving in time – just – to give Pam away on her wedding day. She remembers it well.

In July 1945, I was to be married. We knew Bill was about to be demobbed but we didn't know where he was. The day of my wedding dawned and the usual hubbub reigned at the house. The bride, in her dressing-gown, and having just washed her hair, was imbibing a late breakfast when she looked up to see Bill coming up the garden path.

I greeted him with, 'Oh, you're just in time to give me away.' A startled look crossed his face but, good chap that he was, he appeared in uniform at 2.20 in time to accompany me to the church. As we paused at the start of the long walk down the aisle he muttered, 'This is the worst bit of the war.' When the vicar said his bit, 'Who giveth this woman' etc., Bill took a firm step forward and, in true parade-ground voice, replied, 'I DO.' There followed a complete collapse of the bride, groom, and most of the congregation.

Pam's abiding and overriding memory of Bill is that he was immense fun and she freely acknowledges that he was self-centred as far as his life at home was concerned. The fun side to Bill, she believes, has been largely missed by even those who were quite close to him; as he got older, this aspect faded as his back hurt more and his other travails increased, not the least of which was deafness.

None of this defines his character though; it does not yet illuminate the man inside the man. Who was Bill Tilman?

To discover that we have to look in the greatest detail at the man as he wished to be seen: first as a climber and mountaineer, later as a sailor. These two distinct adventuring careers were split for although Bill ostensibly took up sailing to climb remote peaks, in practice his great climbing days ended in 1939. The Second World War represents an inevitable transition for him and although he climbed after it, his triumphs were few.

Bill Tilman took up climbing first in Africa, during the later part of those long years as a colonial planter. It changed his life completely, bringing him before the general public as a heroic adventurer. With climbing he may be said to have discovered, at last, his life's work as an explorer.

PART TWO

Lift Up Thine Eyes Unto the Hills and Rejoice!

CHAPTER 5

African Adventures

Bill Tilman lived in East Africa, in Kenya, from October 1919 until September 1933, a period of fourteen years, broken by holidays, some back home in England. Bill's African experiences were to be the final tempering of the steel in his soul, forged by the First World War. In Africa, alone, Bill grew up. He was never to change, only to mature further inside his rock-hard fortitude, his desire to be alone with himself.

The most important legacy of his years in Africa was his love of mountains. Eric Shipton remembers their beginning thus:

> Early in 1930 I had a letter from H. W. Tilman, who had been given my address by Melhuish [an older fellow climber]. This turned out to be a most fortunate contact and we were destined to share many mountain ventures together. At that time Tilman had not done much climbing, having only started during his last home leave in the Lake District. But I have met few people so admirably adapted to it both physically and temperamentally. He was very strong and tough, he had a natural aptitude for moving about difficult country, I have never known him rattled, and he had a remarkable ability to put up with – even a liking for – unpleasant conditions. As a companion the qualities I liked best were his tremendous sense of humour and his constant readiness to embark upon any project.

Thus began the most famous climbing partnership of the twentieth century, and one, moreover, that revolutionised climbing in the Himalaya to this day. Although, ironically, they achieved few summits together in that mighty range, their inspiration, their techniques and above all their attitude, to both climbing and the lands through which they travelled and the people they met there, live on.

Bill's account, as you might expect, is quite different: 'On the last day of February 1930, S and I foregathered at Nairobi, whence we left

73

by car for the mountain [Kilimanjaro]. S, who like myself, was a coffee planter, had a farm north of the railway about 160 miles from mine.'

Bill was nine years older than Eric Shipton; the latter had not been through the First World War as a soldier. But Eric was the better climber and Bill had no difficulty in allowing himself to be guided. As individuals they were startlingly different. Bill was taciturn, even surly at times; Eric was talkative, sociable. As an example, here is Bill describing their difference in attitude to a lady whose car had broken down when they were on their way to climb in the Ruwenzori in 1932. 'It was a case of assisting a damsel in distress,' Bill wrote, 'so the delay was suffered gladly by one of us, and by the other without impatience.'

For Eric, the difference in temperament was summed up like this:

How I hated Tilman in the early morning. He never slept like an ordinary person. Whatever time we agreed to awake, long before that time (how long I never knew) he would slide from his sleeping bag and start stirring his silly porridge over the Primus stove. I used gradually to become aware of this irritating noise and would bury my head in silent rage against the preposterous injustice of being woken half an hour too soon. When his filthy brew was ready he would say 'Show a leg', or some such imbecile remark.

Thus they complemented each other in temperament and, over the years, became firm friends. After their climbing years together they stayed in touch (Shipton died in the same year as Bill, from cancer). Shipton's son came on one of Bill's later sailing trips and Eric followed in Bill's footsteps, making a number of expeditions to the southern Andes and the Patagonian ice-cap. It took them years to call each other Bill and Eric, though.

As with many stories told about this pair, the cautious researcher has to check and re-check the facts. In this case, they do seem to be as legend has it. This is that one day, years after they started climbing together, sitting on a mountainside high in the Himalaya, Eric taxes Bill with the issue of why Bill has never called him by his first name. Isn't it time, Eric asks, that you called me Eric. Bill is emphatic that he will not but Eric continues to press him as to why he refuses. Eventually, Bill is forced to say that he can't because Eric is such a silly name. He did, however, end by calling him by it.

Their first climb together was of Mount Kilimanjaro, the highest peak in Africa (which they recorded at 19,710 feet) and in fact an extinct volcano. It lies 180 miles south of Nairobi, just inside what is now Tanzania, and it had first been climbed in 1848 by two Germans. (East Africa had been largely settled by Germans; the British acquired these colonies after the First World War. As a mountain, Kilimanjaro is not a difficult climb although the height above sea level means its would-be conquerors might well suffer from altitude sickness, as Bill did.

The pair had decided they would attempt both Kibo, the higher part of the volcanic rim, and Mawenzi, which although lower presented a tough rock climb. 'We must have gone there at the wrong season,' wrote Eric Shipton, 'for we struck continuously bad weather and reached the top of Kibo only after a hard struggle through masses of soft snow. To see better in the bad visibility we removed our snow glasses and suffered for it a few hours later with a mild dose of snow blindness.'

Bill describes the summit:

On top of Kilimanjaro is a great flat-bottomed crater, possibly a mile across at its longest diameter, filled with ice and snow. The rim is gained by a notch at its lowest point, which is close on 19,000 feet, and then the climber turns left-handed to follow the crater wall round to the south and west. I was not feeling very well myself; in fact I was being sick at frequent intervals; but we ploughed slowly on through waist-deep snow.

They did not quite make the summit and turned back, debating when they got down as to whether they should even attempt Mawenzi.

They did and were successful, although again the weather was bad. Fortified by this beginning, six months later they determined to try for another, much bigger target: Mount Kenya.

Mount Kenya, about 130 miles north of Nairobi, has two main peaks, Batian (17,040 feet) and Nelion (17,000 feet). Eric Shipton had climbed both peaks with Wyn Harris and Gustav Sommerfelt in 1929; now Shipton suggested to Bill that they try to traverse both peaks, a formidable undertaking for Shipton let alone Bill with his very limited climbing experience. Shipton, though, had decided that Bill was up to such a climb. The whole trip was planned to take a fortnight.

'We camped the first night in a grassy glade on the outskirts of the forest. I always enjoyed the first camp. One felt so deliciously free, stretched out luxuriously on the soft grass in front of a blazing fire that flickered on the dark clumps of jungle, listening to the strange night noises,' wrote Eric, while Bill condensed this first night to 'a happy evening under the cedars sitting round a noble fire'.

The next day they marched through the forest, the trees slowly giving way to bamboo which in turn yielded to moorland, studded with giant groundsel. They finally reached a cave, at about 14,000 feet, having by then shed many of their porters and the accompanying ponies. Their first task was to recce the west ridge of the mountain.

To do this they made two first ascents of rock pillars, known as Dutton and Peter, which showed that the ridge could be reached from a col at its foot. This col lay at the head of the Joseph Glacier. Their first objective after this was Batian. To reach it they had to get over a series of large rock 'steps', the largest of which Shipton had already named the Grand Gendarme, a name which has stuck; it was preceded by a smaller step, the Petit Gendarme.

Shipton wrote of this climb: 'I know no mountain in the Alps, with the possible exception of Mount Blanc, that presents such a superb complexity of ridges and faces as the twin peaks of Mount Kenya.' Partly because of this, they had to get a closer look at the ridge and, accordingly, they left the day after climbing the two pillars to work themselves as high as possible.

They left camp at 7.00 a.m. and reached the snout of the Joseph Glacier at 8.30 a.m. They spent a long time cutting steps up this glacier, eventually reaching a steep ice and snow gully that led on to the saddle. At this point they had to get across a bergschrund. 'By the time we had reached the saddle we were dismally conscious that we had undertaken a very tough proposition,' wrote Shipton.

The col was narrow [said Bill], and sitting astride it, *à cheval*, we gazed with fascination at the terrific view of the west face of the mountain. The little we could see of the lower part of our proposed route up the ridge was not encouraging.

Sitting on the col, while the mists boiled up and shrouded the ridge from our straining eyes, we debated whether to attack it the next day. We had seen as much of the route as ever we would, steps were cut up to the col and would not last much more than a day or two, and the weather seemed settled.

The next day, Shipton's birthday, they were up at 3.00 a.m., the occasion for his later outburst at Bill's ability to be up and alert at such an ungodly hour. They set out, reaching the glacier at 4.30 a.m., where they found their steps intact. They were on the ridge by 8.00 a.m. and from there they roped up. Climbing in the 1930s was a generally crude affair, ropes being of hemp, boots being heavy and nailed by the simple expedient of banging them in by hand. Crampons were sometimes used – as they were here – but all the paraphernalia of modern climbing aids and the science which has now been devoted to their manufacture were missing. Even the ice-axes Shipton and Tilman carried were cumbersome and rudimentary.

The traverse they made to the Petit Gendarme was slow: the rocks were exposed, steep, and plastered with snow and ice. They moved, one at a time, crossing a series of rock ribs which effectively cut off the route ahead. 'We liked the thing so little,' wrote Bill, 'that there was some talk of retreat, but we agreed that we should at least gain the notch before admitting that we had bitten off more than we could chew.'

Having got on to the Petit Gendarme they now took a close look at the Grand Gendarme where they found, to their relief, that the rocks were clear of ice and snow. They had taken a tremendous risk in traversing the Petit Gendarme, as Shipton acknowledged. In their exposed position, if one had slipped he would have taken the other with him. Now, considering their position – and the time – they concluded it would be easier, and safer, to go on.

'Here the climbing was more straightforward, and except in a few places we could both move up together. We could never see very far ahead, and had little idea where we were getting to. Suddenly after about an hour and a half we reached the crest of the main ridge again, and were delighted to find that we were standing on top of the Grand Gendarme,' wrote Shipton.

Their efforts were by no means over. On the ridge above the Grand Gendarme they were confronted by a series of pinnacles; the ridge was so narrow and so sheer that each had to be tackled head on, up and down. The first of these was undercut at its base, and was in general a very hard climb, especially for Bill, inexperienced as he was. Even Shipton admitted that this one pitch gave him the frights. It was now snowing but they had reached the point where the north-east ridge abutted the west ridge, and where it turned south towards the summit.

Along this final ridge they found a great gap into which they had to lower themselves on to the ice-cap but they were almost there. At 4.15 p.m., thirteen hard hours after starting out, they reached the summit of Batian.

At last, in place of the sharp pinnacle we had come to expect, a huge dark-grey mass loomed ahead of us. A few steps cut in the icy floor of a gully, a breathless scramble up easy rocks, and we were there beside our little cairn on the summit of Batian. There was no chance of getting down before nightfall, but no consideration of that sort could stem the flood of my joy and, let it be admitted, relief. I do not know what Tilman thought about it. He did not know the way down the south-east face. If he imagined it to involve climbing of a standard similar to that which we had just done he must have had some misgivings, though characteristically he expressed none.

They had little time to waste. Eating a little meat paste, and taking a short rest, Shipton then began to lead them down the south-east side of Batian. They crossed the Gate of the Mists between the two peaks, wasting time as they had to cut steps in the ice. Nelion was climbed and immediately vacated. 'Things now began to happen,' wrote Bill, laconically.

First, the point of his ice-axe was twisted off, then he slipped and dropped it. Almost at the same time Eric began to suffer a series of violent attacks of sickness, brought on, they realised, by the meat paste.

Fortunately Bill was not affected. They discussed whether it would be sensible to bivouac but a wind arose from the east and they decided to go on. 'Very slowly and cautiously we climbed down, using the rope to lower ourselves wherever possible. The most vivid impression that remains in my mind of this grim ordeal is how S, in the feeble state he was, not only climbed, but led the way unerringly and safeguarded his companion,' said Bill later.

By 9.00 p.m. they had reached the Lewis Glacier and they trudged up to Point Lehana, from where they had a five-hour march back to their camp. 'Now that the tension was over we realised how exhausted we were,' wrote Bill. Eric remembered that there was a hut lower down on the glacier and there they holed up until dawn. They arrived back at their camp at 8.00 a.m. the following day from the ascent and turned in to sleep, well satisfied at what they had achieved.

Eric Shipton later wrote: 'I still regard the traverse of the twin peaks of Mount Kenya as one of the most enjoyable climbs I have ever had – a perfect and wholly satisfying episode, shared with an ideal companion.'

But they still had a week left and they filled it by climbing a number of other peaks, including Point Piggot, from the summit of which they were rewarded by a superb view of Batian. Then, on their last climb there was an accident. They had decided to make one last summit, Midget Peak, and they got to the top around midday. It was very misty and it began to snow. 'What had been pleasantly difficult on the way up would be decidedly unpleasant on the way down,' wrote Eric.

They hurriedly began to descend, reaching a narrow gully. Here Bill, in front, disappeared from view. Eric belayed himself to a large rock bollard and had been paying out the rope to Bill when all of a sudden 'there was a sickening jerk, and the rope stretched down the gully as taut as a wire hawser from a dragging ship.' Eric was uncertain as to what to do. There was no way, had he untied himself and climbed down, that he could reach Bill (with only one rope between them). Neither would he have the strength to pull Bill's unconscious body back up, should that be the problem.

Eric chose to try to lower Bill further down the mountain blind and trust he would come to rest on a ledge. Miraculously, this is what happened, although he made what could have been a bad mistake as he did so. He now took the rope off the bollard, taking Bill's weight round his waist – a mistake as it meant he could not straighten up as Bill's weight came on the rope. But, as he moved down, the rope slackened. When Eric reached a point where he could look down he found Bill staring back up at him.

Bill looked odd but answered Eric's questions rationally enough. In fact he was suffering from concussion and he believed, when he saw Eric above him, that they were back on Kilimanjaro. He was in a dead end and his first task was to climb back to where Shipton was anxiously waiting. 'How he contrived to climb up the rope to the platform above, I cannot imagine,' wrote Shipton.

Their troubles were still not over as they had to make a traverse back across rock covered now in snow. With Bill firmly belayed, Eric finally managed it by diving across. After that it was a question of making about nine abseils of which Bill wrote: 'We were singularly ill equipped for this travesty of climbing, necessary though it was, since we had with us not even a pocket-knife, so that the rope had to be hacked through with a sharp stone' (this to make the slings through which they threaded their rope for the abseils).

Eric could never remember how many abseils (or rappels) they made but he recalled that their 120-foot rope was reduced to forty feet by the end. Despite this near miss, both men had had a wonderful time, and they had discovered each other as a perfect climbing companion. Bill later wrote: 'This was, I think, the most satisfying fortnight either of us ever spent or is ever likely to spend in Africa,' a remarkable statement from a man who, by his own account, spent a fifth of his 'allotted span' in that continent.

It was, however, eighteen months later that they next climbed together, for the last time in Africa. Their target was the Ruwenzori, the mysterious Mountains of the Moon. Even by 1932 these mountains, on the border between Zaire and Uganda, were rarely penetrated by whites. They had been discovered by Stanley in 1888, who was amazed to find there really were snow-capped mountains in Central Africa. After that it was not until 1906 that the Duke of the Abruzzi explored (and named) the peaks. Then, in 1926, Noel Humphreys led two expeditions to the mountains, the second of which climbed both Margherita and Alexandra for the first time since the Abruzzi expedition.

After their success on Mount Kenya Bill and Eric Shipton had decided that these mysterious peaks were to be their next goal. But in 1931 Shipton was away in the Himalaya with Frank Smythe, where they successfully climbed Kamet (thereby further cementing Shipton's own reputation as one of the foremost of the young climbers of the 1930s). Bill, meanwhile, reputedly kept his rock-climbing techniques honed by using the walls of the local farmers' club, and a neighbour's outside house chimney as practice pitches.

Bill joined Shipton on his farm in January 1932, from where they travelled the 500 miles in Bill's car – no mean feat in itself, given the condition of African roads in the 1930s. They had no trouble collecting porters – fourteen in all – because they had already begun to put into practice their ideas of small-scale 'alpine' expeditions by choosing to establish any high-level camps themselves.

The porters were of the Bakonju tribe, who live on the lower slopes of the range [wrote Eric]. They were a delightful people, with a ready grin, even in adverse circumstances, and they were generally cheerful and willing. One of their chief characteristics was the way they balanced up and down formidables slopes, or from one tree trunk to another with 50 lb loads on their heads – a feat to be envied by even the most practised mountaineer.

With their porters arranged they began their marches, three in all, which took them to the forest edge of the Mountains of the Moon, along the valley of the Bujuku River. Shipton wrote:

It was difficult going as the vegetation was everywhere dense and perpetually wet. Sometimes we went for half an hour at a time without touching the ground, walking over thickly-matted branches. The sides of the valley were steep and broken, and progress was infinitely laborious. One afternoon, while still in the forests, the weather cleared, and we saw the great ice peaks of Stanley and Speke – a startling sight indeed, seen from such very tropical surroundings.

At 9500 feet they left this thick dank forest and came to an area of dense bamboo and then a forest of tree heaths – a thick stand of leafless trees about twenty to thirty feet high covered in fronds of lichen.

Beyond the tree heaths we found an even stranger country, where solid earth disappeared altogether under an overburden of moss or fallen and rotting giant grounsel [Senecio]. Thick groves of these grow on every hand; they are pushed over with one hand, so that in the groves themselves there are many more trees lying than standing. So rotten are these fallen trunks that they will not support the weight of a man, with the result that forcing a path through the labyrinth presented by Senecio forest, growing as it does out of a morass, is laborious to the point of exhaustion [wrote Bill].

Over this nightmare landscape a mist hung, and a deep silence completed what Bill thought of as an apt setting for Lewis Carroll's *Hunting of the Snark*. Out of this brooding landscape they emerged, eventually, camping in a damp but welcome cave at 13,000 feet, close by the Bujuku Lake ('a mournful shallow mere') with fetid mud-lined shores. Across from this lake they could see, through the gaps in the writhing mists, the 'grim precipices of Mount Baker, the serrated ridge of the Scott Elliott Pass, and the peaks and glaciers of Mount Stanley'.

They had got rid of two of their meagre number of porters en route; now they sent back another group of six, leaving themselves with the remaining six who were, according to Bill, so daunted by the route ahead that they decided to leave them where they were and to shift for themselves. They left their camp on January 17th, with two porters assisting them in the first phase. They established a bivouac at 15,000 feet at 11.00 a.m., sending their porters back just as it began to snow. Bill and Eric climbed on, with forty-pound packs. By one o'clock they had reached the Elena Glacier and finally, from here, made the Mount Stanley plateau. By now the weather was so thick they were at a loss to know exactly where they were so they pitched their tent.

At sunset, when the weather briefly cleared, they were amazed and delighted to find that they had settled down more or less exactly on the summit of the main divide. Bill wrote:

> A few hundred steps up a snow-slope, and we were brought to a stand as much by a view which held us spellbound as by the sudden falling away of the ground at our feet. Far to the west and below us, through a rift in the driving clouds, we could see the dark green, almost black, carpet of the Congo Forest, upon whose sombre background was traced a silvery design by the winding Semliki River. To the south showed a lighter patch, where the waters of Lake Edward reflected the last light of the day; but in a moment sinking sun and rising mist merged all but the snow at our feet in a once more impenetrable gloom.

What this brief glimpse of their surroundings had also shown was a snow slope leading up to the Alexandra Peak, one of the many which fringed the Mount Stanley plateau. They planned to climb it the next day but continuous snow and the thick mist defeated them. They stayed, increasingly wet and cold, in their inadequate tent. It was three days after they had made their camp that they finally got to the summit (at 16,740 feet). There was a cairn there, with details of both Abruzzi and Humphreys climbs; they were only the third party to attain this and the subsequent summits.

The next day they started for Margherita, again in mist. Groping about for hours they were astonished to come across a set of tracks. 'Such was our bewilderment that wild and impossible conjectures of another party on the mountain flashed across our minds before we realised the unflattering truth that these were our tracks of the previous day, and that we were climbing Alexandra for the second time,' wrote Bill. They crept back to their leaky tent 'with our tails well down' to find their sleeping bags were also now soaked through. Despite this, they were determined to reach the highest peak in the Ruwenzori (again, measured by them at 16,815 feet), which they made on the 21st. From the top they had a moment's glimpse of Alexandra and were able thus to confirm their success.

Their food gone, they now began what Shipton called an 'undignified' descent to their cave Base Camp. There, they allowed a day to recuperate before setting out to climb Mount Speke on January 23rd. Again the weather was bad but it cleared just long enough for them to see they had climbed on to a glacier above the Stuhlmann Pass. 'We roped up, more from ingrained orthodoxy than necessity, and climbed an easy snow slope to Vittorio Emmanuele (16,080 feet), gaining its summit at half past ten,' wrote Bill. After this they climbed on to the Mount Baker Ridge, traversing it to Semper Peak and thence to the highest, Edward Peak. For the first time, here, the weather relented, allowing them a view of the entire range which looked, in the view of both of them, 'mild'.

From this last high spot they turned back to camp, choosing, however, to travel south initially, away from their camp by the lake. On the way back they found the helichrysum both friend and foe, often providing what Bill called a 'Thank God handhold' and then holding back their progress by its toughness. On their descent Shipton sprained a shoulder, Bill lost a wristwatch, both blamed on this plant. On the valley floor they battled against it some more, as well as against the giant grounsel – and the onset of night. They had still to cross the Scott Eliott Pass with 'flagging energies'. Over the pass, with the lake in sight, Bill now lost his camera, with all his exposed film.

They left the Ruwenzori the following day and made their way back. They did double marches, easy now the way was downhill and the trail had been broken. Back at their car they found a swarm of bees had settled in its body. The boy they had left to guard it was, Bill reported, surprised that they did not want to keep the bees, or even the car while the bees were still there. The boy ejected the interlopers and Eric and Bill returned – checking the car for snakes before they set off.

Bill reflected on this expedition that it had taken the Duke of the Abruzzi more time getting from Kampala to the mountains than he and Shipton had spent on them. Later, Bill was often dismissive of modern transport and its ability to decant the explorer out of civilisation and into the wild so quickly; he had a point, even more valid at the end of the century.

Bill returned to England a little later in that same year, 1932. There, in April, he went again to the Lake District with his sister, Adeline, and his friend, Dr John Brogden, a mountaineer with experience of the Alps and Norway. On a dull Sunday in late April Bill set off with Brogden for Dow Crag opposite the Old Man of Coniston. Adeline had decided to go to church so in her place they took Vera Brown, a schoolteacher. It was a cold and windy day.

They roped up for the climb, Brogden leading, and had almost reached the summit when Vera slipped on wet rock. Unbelayed, Bill was dragged after her but they were both held by Brogden, also apparently unbelayed. To today's climbers the idea of the two men being badly belayed or even moving together while roped up is extraordinary and highly dangerous but that is what seems to have happened. Unsurprisingly, Brogden could not hold the two bodies dangling below and all three fell some sixty feet before landing in a gully.

Vera Brown was badly injured and both Bill and Brogden were knocked out. Bill recovered consciousness, as did Brogden but he was, unlike Bill, unable to move. Bill now began an epic crawl to try to get help – his back was badly injured and he could not walk. He went down the crag to try to find some other climbers; failing in this he made his way back to the others to tell them he was going for help. This meant getting across four miles of rough country to Coniston village.

It took him four hours; in the hotel where they were staying Adeline remembered seeing an object crawl in, covered with blood. 'I thought it was a dog to begin with,' she said later. It was Bill, concussed, severely hurt, but still alive and able to tell where the others were. He had to be physically restrained from trying to go back with the rescue party who found Vera alive but Brogden dead. It made Bill a hero in the tabloid press of the day, the *Daily Sketch* headline being 'Heroic journey by injured companion to summon help'.

Bill was told he would never climb again by his doctors and it was well into the summer before he could move very much. It was this injury which was to plague him all his life. Pam Davis remembers vividly his phrase for his back pains: 'Like the poor, always with us,' he would say to her. But Bill, being Bill, that summer he planned a lone climbing trip to the French Alps.

There he hired guides to get him up peaks in the Dauphiné and Mont Blanc group. He is known to have climbed Les Bans, the Meije, the Ecrins and Col des Avalanches, the Aiguille du Tour, the Aiguille de L'M, the Col de la Fenêtre and the Col du Chardonnet.

He returned fit, if not entirely well, first to England and thence post-haste to Kenya where he had been attracted by the gold fever then afflicting the colony. As we have seen, his failure in this new venture may have decided him to leave Africa for good. But he had one last mountaineering trip to undertake there and, early in 1933, he went back to Mount Kilimanjaro to make a solo ascent of Kibo, the highest point that he and Shipton had failed to reach three years earlier. He had been nervous of this, not because of the climb (more of a stiff walk) but because of his recurring problem with altitude above 19,000 feet. However he was not sick and celebrated by sleeping out close to the summit. His climb was perhaps a gesture more obvious now than then: he was saying goodbye to Africa from its highest point.

Bill spent the latter part of 1933 at home in Britain, largely kicking his heels and wondering what to do. Then, in 1934 he wrote to Eric

Shipton to suggest a couple of weeks' climbing in the Lake District. But Shipton by this time had higher ambitions. After his success on Kamet in the Himalaya in 1932, he had been invited to take part in the 1933 Everest expedition, and although they got to within 900 feet of the summit the weather, as so often, defeated them. Shipton, though, had been appalled by the profligacy of the organisers, using an army of porters and over 350 pack animals. He was sure that the big peaks of the Himalaya could be tackled by small, lightly equipped fast-moving teams, living off the country.

He set his sights at Nanda Devi, one of the highest mountains in the British Empire and a peak surrounded, literally and physically, by mystery. When Bill contacted him, he wrote back suggesting that they made a reconnaisance of the mountain. What followed was to lead Bill on to the greatest personal triumph of his climbing career.

CHAPTER 6

Nanda Devi: Prometheus Unbound

By 1934 Eric Shipton had an established reputation as one of the foremost of British climbers, reinforced by his inclusion in the unsuccessful 1933 Everest expedition. But Shipton was increasingly disillusioned with the 'siege' approach to the big Himalaya peaks; he longed to get away from what he called the 'monstrous army invading the peaceful Tibetan valleys, the canvas town that sprang up at each halting place' simply to explore the million square miles of mountains the region offered with 'increased mobility and a greater sense of cohesion and purpose'.

But Shipton was not rich; like Bill he had not made his fortune in Africa and he regretted not having an academic hook with which to make a purchase on expeditioning or adventuring. He decided, however, that he had nothing to lose in trying to make a go of becoming a full-time adventurer; over the years there is no doubt that his decision had a profound influence on Bill. In many ways theirs was a symbiotic relationship. At this stage, Eric would influence Bill; later, at least in choice of territory to explore, Bill would influence Eric.

Eric calculated that it would be possible to mount an extremely small-scale expedition to the Himalaya using a very few local porters, and staying for five months, for the paltry sum of £150. He knew, of course, that Bill would have no problem over that concept; in the end they spent just £286 between them, a remarkably economical expedition for any time or place.

As to where they should go, in his autobiography, *That Untravelled World*, Shipton wrote: 'There was no difficulty about choosing my first objective. Nanda Devi (25,660 feet), the highest peak in the Garhwal Himalaya, was surrounded by a mountain barrier which had never been penetrated. The only breach in this remarkable wall was on its western side, where the Rishi Ganga had carved a gigantic canyon, twenty miles long, to the Dhaoli Valley.'

No one had ever reached the so-called Nanda Devi 'sanctuary' inside the mountain ring Shipton was describing, although Hugh Ruttledge, a well-known climber of the time, had managed to climb the mountain rim to look down into it in 1932. Earlier, Tom Longstaff, another of the foremost mountain explorers of the early part of the century, had managed to get into the Rishi Gorge (in 1907) but had been turned back by the formidable difficulties it set. Shipton went to spend a weekend with Longstaff, who gave him valuable advice, insisting that his own failure could be overcome. But Longstaff laughed out loud when Shipton told him how much money he had allocated for the trip, a sum he was raising by lecturing.

Bill, approached by Shipton, agreed at once that he would come; he also agreed they could manage on the budget Shipton proposed. On April 6th, 1934, they set out on the cargo ship *Mahsud*. Shipton had engaged three Sherpas, Angtharkay, Pasang and Kusang – as equals, it must be stressed, and this was another novelty in this expedition. Indeed, both Bill and Eric 'discovered', if that is the right word, the notion that as the Sherpas lived, worked and died in the highest parts of the Himalaya, in Nepal, they would be invaluable as climbing partners. So it proved, as Edmund Hillary was to attest, nineteen years later. (So it proves to this day, when one Sherpa at least has been on the summit of Everest four times.)

In 1934, much of the Himalaya – including Nepal which was entirely shut off – was forbidden territory to climbers and explorers. The British government writ might run in the sub-continent as a whole but the politics of the northern borders remained, as they had in the nineteenth century, extremely problematic. The decision to try for Nanda Devi was largely because the Garhwal Himalaya lay well within the British part of India. Nanda Devi is part of Hindu mythology, the birthplace of the sacred Ganges River. The physical barrier – the mountain wall of the sanctuary was over seventy miles round and the cliffs rose to 21,000 feet in places – lent much to its mystery.

The Garhwal is a region of about one hundred miles, east to west, fifty north to south. The natives are short and sturdy, and fairer than the natives of the plains. Some even have blue eyes. Nearer to the border with Tibet the natives are Bhotias of Tibetan origin. The three main rivers run north to south, cutting deep gorges and leaving between them three great ridges: the eastern one contains Nanda Devi, the middle Kamet (which Shipton had climbed in 1931), the western the Badrinath-Kedernath range.

In the Nanda Devi group a main ridge runs north to south, with three arms in the south, projecting westwards. At the southern end a long arm contains Trisul (23,360 feet); some miles to the north of this another contains Dunagiri (23,184 feet); and between these two is the shortest arm of all, at the very end of which is Nanda Devi. From Trisul and Dunagiri two spurs project towards each other to form the fourth side of the wall around the Nanda Devi sanctuary, nowhere less than

18,000 feet. The only breach is in the Rishi Gorge, whose river drains the Nanda Devi glaciers.

Nanda Devi – whose name means 'Blessed Goddess' – was a challenge that even Shipton considered might have been too much. Ruttledge, who had looked into the sanctuary, had written:

> In a mood of hopeful anticipation our party, on May 25th, trudged up the narrow glacier which leads from Sunderhunga itself to the base of the wall, of which the greater part is invisible from a distance. One step around it, and we were brought up all standing by a sight which almost took our remaining breath away. Six thousand feet of the steepest rock and ice.

From this wall a huge hanging glacier trembled permanently, letting fly gigantic icefalls at regular intervals. Ruttledge, looking down on this, contemplated what kind of climber would want to endure 'three days and two nights under fire from this artillery . . . The jury's verdict was unanimous; and the Goddess keeps her secret.'

Bill and Eric were undaunted in their hopes. They met the Sherpas in Calcutta, after a bit of a mix-up which Shipton feared would destroy their slender economy; Bill had never seen a Sherpa before and, no doubt, was astonished when they were eventually located after a wild chase: 'clad in shirts and shorts, and crowned with billycock hats from under which glossy black pigtails descended, the three men were distinctive enough,' wrote Eric. There was little common language between them but they managed to get their train – third-class accommodation to save money. The independence and attitudes of the Sherpas was again apparent to Bill and Eric. They had had to split their party and Angtharkay, who came with them, refused to use the 'small cupboard' provided for native bearers. Instead, he slept on the floor of Bill and Eric's compartment 'much to the disgust of our fellow passengers', noted Eric.

Their resourcefulness was apparent later when Bill and Eric were panic-stricken (their term) as the train that should have borne Kusang and Pasang to them pulled out of the station at Bareilly, where they had to change trains, without the Sherpas being located. The two Brits debated returning to Calcutta. They ran to the train due to take them on to Kathgodam, the railhead nearest to Nanda Devi:

> As we ran we glanced rapidly into each carriage trying to spot our gear and, of a sudden Tilman gripped me by the arm. There, comfortably established among their possessions and eating oranges with every evidence of serene enjoyment, were Kusang and Pasang! It seemed a pity to disturb them. We crept quietly

past to our own carriage, horribly conscious that Angtharkay's account of our antics would lose nothing in the telling.

But far into the night we argued about the mystery. The most experienced traveller who had to effect a change of trains at midnight in a country whose language he did not know, might be very pleased with himself if he managed without mishap. Yet two Sherpas, neither of whom had ever travelled by rail, neither of whom even knew the name of their destination, had contrived to get out at the right station and into the right train.

We might smile now at such attitudes, even from the enlightened pen of Eric Shipton; in truth, both he and Bill were drawn to these stout-hearted, tough and resourceful hill tribesmen as to kindred spirits. In the 1930s, though, such enlightenment was remarkable indeed.

They left the train at Kathgodam in good spirits and loaded their gear (1000 pounds of it, even for such a small group) on to a lorry which took them to Ranikhet, where they were able to use a government rest house. Here they took just a day and a half to complete their preparations for the months ahead. 'We had brought from England some biscuits, cheese and pemmican to supplement the local food,' wrote Shipton. 'Our diet, however, was mainly composed of chupattis and tsampa.' They ate a good deal of sugar and Shipton found it a very bleak diet, although Bill did not. Shipton points out in his autobiography that it was this trip which gained them both a reputation for spartan living which Bill never lost. But, he says, they were merely following in the traditions of pioneer travellers the world over.

And there were many advantages, the first and most obvious being the speed with which they moved. From Ranikhet, with ten Dotial porters, they reached Surai Tota, a village in the Dhaoli Valley, in twelve marches. There they engaged more porters to carry supplies to the Base Camp they intended to establish in the Rishi Gorge. Their Surai Tota porters deserted them while they were still trying to get into the Rishi Gorge, the lower part of which was impassable. But the Dotial men stayed, for which Bill and Eric were very grateful.

For two days they struggled high above the gorge in deep snow, sometimes up to their armpits and after two failures they found a way down to the gorge itself. 'It was an astonishing place,' wrote Shipton. 'The southern side of the valley was composed of tier upon tier of gigantic slabs, steeply inclined, which culminated, 10,000 feet above the river, in a host of spires set at a rakish angle, while beyond them stood a range of ice peaks. The northern side, the one we were on, was scarcely less precipitous.' Route-finding up this cleft was a nightmare. They would climb 2000 feet up a buttress and then down the other side, to gain maybe half a mile. Sometimes they had to retreat.

Their problems were now compounded by the hitherto loyal Dotials who were deeply affected by the oppressive atmosphere in the gorge, constantly roaring with the spate of the river. Both Bill and Eric knew, too, that each day using these porters meant that their precious food supplies were running down. The weather, however, remained fine, for which they were thankful. On May 28th they reached the junction of the Rhamani Nullah with the gorge, the furthest point reached by Longstaff and Graham. Here, at the site they had chosen for their Base Camp, they discharged their Dotials.

They found they had food for five weeks; the encampment was a good one, providing snug weatherproof quarters and, with a grove of birch trees, plenty of fuel. They also had a great stroke of luck in that at that point a giant boulder had become wedged across the river, forming a natural bridge.

All of them were now extremely fit. By now, too, they had established a very close friendship with their three Sherpas. Eric Shipton wrote: 'With such colleagues leadership was hardly called for; indeed in more than one tight corner it was theirs rather than ours that saw us through. We owed all our successes to their unfailing staunchness.'

Even so, looking further up the gorge, they saw that only fifty yards from their camp the canyon became perfectly smooth. They found a cleft above where they were, then a gully, and they climbed 2000 feet to find a series of ledges running westwards. These were extremely perilous and it took nine days to find a way along them. They now made an astonishing series of relays back and forth along these ledges, carrying their supplies four miles further up the gorge. The last mile was the worst and the river was now rising below them, cutting off any chance of making this final traverse at that level.

They found their route eventually and, at last, they became the first known group ever to enter the Nanda Devi sanctuary. They had food left for three weeks. 'It was a glorious place, and, of course, the fact that we were the first to reach it lent a special enchantment to our surroundings,' wrote Shipton. It was immediately obvious that they would not have enough time to survey the sanctuary so they concentrated on the northern half, intending to come back in September, after the monsoon had broken. The weather was mostly fine and they slept in the open, on the pastures strewn with wild flowers. They did some climbing, getting on to one peak at 21,000 feet and failing on another at 23,000 feet. They also got to three cols on the eastern and northern rim.

By June the monsoon had arrived and they retraced their steps back down the Rishi Gorge in torrential rain. 'The gorge was even more splendid in foul weather than in fair,' said Shipton. On July 1st, with all their food gone, they reached the Dhaoli Valley, six weeks after they had left it.

For the next two months these intrepid men explored the nearby Badrinath range, and, almost incidentally, made two crossings of it, the first outside Hindu mythology to do so. Thus they effected a direct connection between the three sources of the River Ganges. Their second crossing nearly led them into a disaster when they descended a 6000-foot ice precipice into what they believed, from over a mile above, was a lush valley. It turned out to be a terrible gorge, from which there was now no escape (they had abseiled down into it). It rained continuously and at times they took an hour to cover just twenty-five yards. Their food ran out and they lived on a diet of tree fungus and bamboo shoots.

After a week of this they stumbled into a tiny hamlet where they could get flour, cucumber and a handful of dried apricots. In September they returned from these escapades to the Rishi Gorge. This time, knowing their way, and with local porters, they got through in eight days. Back in the sanctuary, they easily surveyed the southern part. More important, they found a 'practical' way up Nanda Devi, by way of the southern ridge up part of which they climbed.

But they had not brought enough equipment to make a serious attempt and, in any case, their boots were by now, like their clothes, falling to pieces. 'Our ambition was to find a way out of the basin over some part of the encircling ranges which had so long proved impregnable. With little choice in the matter, we determined to concentrate our efforts on the lowest depression (18,000 feet) on the southern wall, which Hugh Ruttledge and his Italian guide, Emil Rey, had attempted to cross two years before.' To do this Shipton climbed a 23,360-foot peak with Angtharkay and Kusang, so they might look down on this col. As a result the entire party got out of the sanctuary in this way, a climb which stretched them to the limit ('more difficult than the precipice we had descended into the Kedernath valley seven weeks before,' wrote Shipton). Bill later chose to write: 'a way out was found . . . a much simpler affair.'

For Eric Shipton this last climb was the best and the most exciting. They had plenty of food and, once more, the weather was kind to them. Two days later they were back in Ranikhet. 'We had achieved far more than I had dared to hope,' wrote Shipton. 'I appreciated as never before not only the joys of unencumbered travel but also the deep satisfaction of exploring an unknown range; and from then on I became far more interested in this than in climbing peaks.'

In many respects, so did Bill. Both of them could reflect on their quite extraordinary efforts over these months, and on their Sherpa companions and their great strengths. Both were delighted they had actually spent £7 each less than their budget, the final seal of success.

Both now made plans to go back and climb Nanda Devi in 1935 but a surprise decision by the Tibetan government to allow two expeditions to Mount Everest – in 1935 and 1936 – threw this plan into disarray. It is worth reiterating at this point that before the Second World War Nepal, from which side Everest was eventually to be climbed, was closed to westerners. Tibet, in the 1930s an independent state, allowed occasional expeditions, usually under strict conditions.

The Mount Everest Committee, in London, had a small balance (£1400) at its disposal from the 1933 expedition. Eric Shipton offered to lead a reconnaisance party to the mountain to set up the intended full assault in 1936. He decided that with six climbers (including himself and Tilman) and at £200 a head they could make much progress. He had his own reasons for wanting to do this, having been part of the circus of 1933, led by Ruttledge. 'I was anxious for the opportunity to demonstrate that, for one-tenth of the former cost and with a fraction of the bother and disruption of the local countryside, a party could be placed on the North Col, adequately equipped to make a strong attempt on the summit. I began to recruit my party, which naturally included Bill.'

By now these two were already being dubbed the 'terrible twins', both known to care more for exploration than summit-bagging. Bill, in fact, was not best pleased when he got Eric's offer for, although he wanted to try for Everest, he thought a party of six excessive. We can legitimately surmise he thought at that time that a party of six *white* men excessive; Sherpas would no doubt be excluded from this objection.

As part of Shipton's determination to keep costs down, he consulted the Lister Institute on diet, who in turn worked out a 4000-calorie-per-day food roster of extreme monotony (it included pemmican, cheese, milk powder, sugar, flour, vegetables, nuts and ghee with tablets to supplement vitamins). The party eventually chosen consisted of Bill, Eric, Edwin Kempson, a teacher at Marlborough College (and a friend of Wyn Harris of Africa fame), Dr Charles Warren, Edmund Wigram, a medical student, L. V. Bryant, a New Zealander, and Michael Spender, brother of the poet and taken as a surveyor.

On the Sherpa side, Angtharkay was a natural choice, so was a younger friend of his, Tenzing Norgay, destined to be the man who finally reached the summit of Everest with Hillary. Pasang and Kusang, from the Nanda Devi trip, were also included. Tenzing was only twenty in 1935 and this was to be his first expedition. It was a fateful expedition in many ways: Tenzing almost did not make it and the New Zealander, Bryant, proved such a good choice that Shipton's report could be said to have influenced the inclusion of Edmund Hillary, another New Zealander, eighteen years later on the 1953 expedition.

They left Darjeeling at the end of May 1935, and crossed the Kongra La, travelling westward along the Tibetan border until they got to Sar. Here they paused and, for two weeks, explored the Nyonno Ri and Ama Drime ranges. Shipton excused this as necessary for acclimatisation but there is little doubt that Shipton was using their proximity to unknown territory simply to indulge his new passion for exploring.

In fact they could see Everest from where they were and the weather was good. At least one informed opinion is that had Shipton not wasted time and headed straight for the mountain he could have climbed it. As it was they did not reach Rongbuk, the jumping-off point for Everest, until early July, when the monsoon had already broken. A clause had in fact been written into Shipton's contract forbidding an assault on the mountain. Would he have ignored it if conditions had been good? One would like to think so. Walt Unsworth in his book on Everest deals with this question at length.

When Shipton saw the weather around Everest was good, should he have made a dash for it, attempted (and maybe succeeded) in climbing the mountain, proving at a stroke that his and Bill's idea of alpine-style Himalaya expeditions really worked? He was short of equipment, as well as men – and time – but, had he done it, all of this would have been forgotten. He would, in Unsworth's words, 'just possibly have pulled off the mountaineering coup of all time'.

As it was, they started from the Rongbuk monastery (now destroyed by the Chinese communists as part of their campaign to wipe out Tibetan culture) on July 6th. None of them was in good health. Kempson reported, for instance, that 'Bill is going slow'. Shipton was doing best out of all of them. They reached Camp 3 (at 21,000 feet) on July 9th and then moved on, 500 feet higher, to where the 1933 expedition had left a food dump which they fell upon with great glee.

It was a very different emotion that passed among them when they found the body of Maurice Wilson, an eccentric mystic who had been determined to reach the summit of Everest solo to prove to the world that his ideas of fasting and prayer could save it from a second world war. He had, like Bill, been in the First World War and it is interesting to reflect on the different paths both these men of the 'lost generation' took, so that they should meet, finally, on Everest. The one, a totally inexperienced climber; the other a taciturn, in many ways equally withdrawn, stoic.

Above Camp 3 rose the steep ice slopes of the North Col; because of the shifting ice, the route the 1933 expedition had used was no longer there. Instead, Shipton's party began a traverse to try to reach Camp 4. All were now ill – Bill too ill even to attempt this part of the climb. Eventually Shipton ordered a return to Camp 3. Nevertheless, on July 12th, Shipton, Kempson, Warren and nine Sherpas made it to the North Col with supplies for fifteen days. The intention was to take a light camp up to the ridge at 26,000 feet and from there recce the upper slopes – even, if possible, to climb them.

Shortly after this the weather broke, and a huge avalanche swept the col; worse, none of the high party had heard it. They came down from what Kempson described as the most dangerous mountaineering trip he had ever been on and abandoned Everest for another year. While this drama had been taking place on the North Col, Bill, with Wigram, had climbed Lhakpa La, the pass between the East Rongbuk and Kharta Glaciers and from there had got to the summit of the unnamed peaks on either side.

When Shipton's party rejoined them, they all then went on an orgy of mountain climbing; all climbed Khartaphu (23,640 feet). They then split into two groups. Bill, with Shipton and Wigram, climbed Kellas Rock (23,190 feet), a 22,580-foot unnamed peak and a couple more 21,000-footers. Later still, Tilman and Wigram went off to survey the route to Everest from the west, up the main Rongbuk Glacier to the Lho La. They found that it held no chance for a descent into Nepal and they thought the West Ridge impossible as well. They made a difficult crossing of the pass north of Changtse and ended up on the East Rongbuk Glacier, near Camp 2 – the first time a direct passage had been made across the northern ridges of the Everest group. Altogether, during these weeks, the pair climbed seventeen peaks of over 21,000 feet.

On August 14th, with the party back together, they all tried for Changtse (24,730 feet) in order to get pictures of Everest (they later said) and to test the snows during the monsoon. Suspicion remains that they really felt like bagging a prime peak while the opportunity presented itself. In this they were unsuccessful although they reached 23,000 feet. They were now frustrated by the Tibetans in their efforts to travel east, back to the Nyonno range, and they beat a retreat, coming out via Sikkim over the Chorten Nyima La. Even so, they did more climbing in the obscure Dodang Nyima range in the north of that country, before returning to Darjeeling.

As a Himalayan expedition this is rated as one of the most successful of all time; between them they had climbed twenty-six peaks over 20,000 feet and, remarkably, they had kept to their very low budget; as well, Michael Spender had managed a great deal of survey work.

Because Bill was deemed to have 'failed' by the Everest Committee in his recurring problems with altitude sickness, he was excluded from the major expedition which left for Everest in 1936; Shipton went reluctantly, because once again it was a siege expedition of the kind he loathed. Bill had nothing planned but he was, by now, a mountaineer of repute and he was approached by a group of young Americans who were toying with the idea of climbing Kangchenjunga (28,160 feet), the third highest mountain in the world.

But Kangchenjunga is on the border between Nepal and Sikkim, both politically difficult countries in the 1930s, something the Americans, led by W. F. Loomis and Charles Houston, appeared not to have considered. Loomis eventually came to Britain early in 1936 to discuss their plans, and Bill suggested that they might like to climb Nanda Devi instead. To this Loomis agreed, should permission for Kangchenjunga be denied.

93

The full party now recruited consisted of Charles Houston, Loomis, Arthur Emmons, and H. Adams Carter on the American side, Bill, T. Graham Brown, Peter Lloyd and Noel Odell on the British. Bill went early to India – in April 1936 – to arrange supplies. When he got there he was told they would not be allowed into Sikkim. Bill, kicking his heels, decided to try and cross the Zemu Gap, on the borders of Sikkim, and on the flank of Kangchenjunga. In this, as with several similar exploits, one can see in Bill a certain egoistical delight – being able to tell his disappointed Americans that he, at least, had been to see the mountain from which they were forbidden. One can also see, equally clearly, the 'bolshie' side to Bill. Having been forbidden to swim in the lake he none the less dips his toes in it to show he is not fazed.

He had trouble recruiting Sherpas – not least because the majority and the best had been snapped up by the big Everest expedition. Eventually he collected four, along with two ponies and they set out. Among the Sherpas was Pasang Kikuli, who had been on the frightful German Nanga Parbat expedition of 1934; he would shortly go to Nanda Devi with Bill and later with Charles Houston on the 1938 reconnaissance of K2.

The Zemu Gap which Bill was trying for was a pass on the ridge between Simvu (22,360 feet) and the most eastern satellite peak (25,526 feet) of Kangchenjunga. A complete map of the twelve-mile-long Zemu Glacier on the side of this mountain had been made by a German party in 1931 but this one pass remained largely unknown, although it was supposed to have been crossed once.

On their way in, close to the glacier, Bill was tempted to climb Pandim (22,010 feet). Although a difficult mountain, he identified a notch in a ridge leading to the summit and he was determined to try. He set off early with Pasang Kikuli and the other three Sherpas. He was high on the mountain: 'There was no warning sound, but some instinct made me look up, and there, coming straight for us out of the mist, were half a dozen boulders. They hit the snow above with a thud and then took the line of the runnel in a series of menacing bounds, some in the runnel itself, some outside.' They had had a miraculous escape and they immediately went back down the mountain.

Now Bill tried for his main objective, the Zemu Gap. He was unsuccessful, being defeated by the icefalls guarding it. They had made their camp at the top of one of these, at about 18,000 feet. Above them was a second intricate icefall, at the top of which was a final 100-foot icewall.

Pasang Kikuli joined in the assault next morning, and together we hacked a big staircase up the 30 foot of steep ice, a job which took two hours. Above that we were able to kick steps, but there were only a few inches of snow overlying the ice, and we realised that when the sun had done its work the snow covering would not hold. A little higher we came to a horribly frail bridge over a deep crevasse.

They went over this, crawling carefully but Bill doubted whether it would hold a man with a pack. They climbed on, however, to inspect the final icewall and there discovered it was as high as he had feared, overhanging as well.

He decided to beat a retreat, choosing to make some hair-raising abseils in the process, contemplating as he lowered himself down that the alleged crossing of this formidable gap had almost certainly not been achieved before. But, like so many elements of his life, Bill stored this failure away, knowing he would be back some day.

He now addressed the problem which he had come to solve: the ascent of the 'Blessed Goddess', Nanda Devi. Back in Darjeeling, on May 21st, he cabled Loomis, who had arrived in Bombay, and they discussed using the time before the rest of the party arrived, at the end of June, in getting supplies up into the sanctuary to save having to carry them all in later.

Part of Bill's problem was with the lack of Sherpas but he finally took Pasang Kikuli and one other of his first four; later he hired four more. For the rest of the porters he recruited Bhotias, the stalwart tribesmen who had helped him and Shipton in 1934, from the village of Mana.

Once again, the starting point was Ranikhet – up a fifty-mile road from Kathgodam, itself a thirty-six-hour train journey from Calcutta. Ranikhet is 6000 feet above sea level and it was with relief, after the heat of the plains, that Bill arrived there. He was further fortified by the sight of a hundred miles of snow peaks in the far distance. There was no time to waste.

Bill had by now met up with Loomis, who did not impress him much, not least because of a mix-up as to where they should meet. 'Loomis is not a fast walker and takes up a good deal of road,' Bill noted in his diary. He was probably grumpy, too, from having lost his pipes at the end of the Zemu Gap failure, and from having a bad attack of diarrhoea. The march up from Ranikhet was hard work.

When reading accounts of travel in Garhwal the peculiar nature of the country should be borne in mind. The whole country is an intricate tangle of valleys and ridges with their attendant ravines and spurs, which, even in the foothills are all on a scale undreamed of in this country. The stages of a march may seem short, but involving, as most of them do, a rise of 3000 ft. or more and an equally great descent, they are quite long enough. It is possible to be in a valley not more than 300 ft above the sea, the home of a vegetation which is almost tropical, and at the same time to be within fifteen minutes of snow-clad peaks, 20,000 feet high.

At Joshimath, Bill and Loomis waited for the Mana porters who duly arrived; some had been with Bill and Eric in 1934. Now they were close to the gorge and Bill, conscious that time was running out, urged the party on. On June 14th, his diary records: 'I crossed the river and threw my axe back for that chump L, who of course has not got one. It hit a stone and bounced back into the river taking his topee with it. And so a third one of mine meets a watery end. Damn and blast it. L did try to stop it by jumping in and got a good wetting. The Sherpas and some of the Mana blokes not very happy on the water.' Shortly after, Bill was calling it 'this bloody trip'.

They had some trouble getting over the natural boulder bridge with their loads, and with the traverses further up the gorge. They were all 'disquietingly dependent' on tree branches and tufts of grass as holds, perilously suspended 1500 feet above the gorge on the traverse above the boulder bridge. Further up they came again to the 'slabs', smooth rock sloping up at an angle which made it hard to stand. Fortunately, these were dry. Loomis and Bill went up to the top where a wall had to be climbed, and they began to haul up the loads dumped by the porters.

As some point Bill went down on the rope to speed things up as he feared rain might hinder them.

> To superintend this I was standing on a narrow ledge about twenty feet above the floor of the gully and, thick-headedly enough, almost under the rope. Things then happened quickly. Gazing at an ascending load I was petrified to see a large flake of rock, probably loosened by the rope, sliding down the wall straight for me. Whether it hit me, or whether I stepped back to avoid it, is only of academic interest because the result was the same, and next instant I was falling twenty feet on to the slabs, head first and face to the wall, for I distinctly remember seeing it go past. Hitting the slabs I rolled for a bit and then luckily came to a rest before completing the 1400-odd feet into the river.

'I thought I was finished,' his diary records, 'but stopped rolling before the slabs. Left thigh and knee bruised. Left shoulder wrenched, ditto neck and hands badly cut. Altogether a pretty mess but might have been worse.' He also found later that he had a cracked rib. This effectively put him out of action and it was Loomis who took the porters on to the spot, in sight of the sanctuary, where they dumped the food loads. Bill lay in the camp above the wall and, in his words, felt sorry for himself. In truth he could hardly move and he was wondering how on earth he could get back to Ranikhet by the 25th (it was now June 16th).

On the 17th they started back. 'I started with P[asang] and went very slow. Blokes [porters] caught us at the rocks and I was lowered down with all precautions. Bad night with my rib which is now beginning to hurt.' By the 19th he was having pains in his legs as well, although his other injuries were mending. They reached Josimath by the 20th; Ranikhet by the 25th, on time. The rigorous walk out had, Bill said, effected the cure he sought.

Here, most of the rest of the party joined them, along with the rest of their supplies, up from Delhi. They had more than they could use, as the plans had been for a party of twelve for Kanchenjunga. This presented a problem to Bill, who had to decide what to leave out. With his spartan attitude to expedition equipment and food, he was surprised to find the Americans, in particular, agreed. The reason was that, unlike the British contingent, they were used to climbing in, for example, Alaska, where a man had to carry his own gear and sustenance, no porters being present. The combing out of all but the essentials took place in a spirit of harmony.

The weight suggested for personal gear was thirty-five pounds; Sherpas, carrying their own twenty-five pounds, could then carry for the 'sahibs' as well, freeing the westerners to walk in unencumbered. Bill, however, found that everyone re-equipped themselves with a further small personal rucksack of twenty pounds or so, very little of the contents of which were used.

Despite this, they were away on July 10th. From Ranikhet they used two lorries to tranport themselves, twelve porters and about a ton of gear and food. At Garul, they abandoned the lorries for thirty-seven Dotials, the same tribesmen whom Bill and Eric had found so willing in 1934. There, the usual argument began between the expedition leader (Bill) and the chief porter of whom he wrote:

> The headman, having successfully palmed off most of his [load] on to the more complacent of his followers, contenting himself with an umbrella and a canvas bucket, perhaps with a view to being prepared for both contingencies – flood or drought. There was some talk of stopping for the night at a dak bungalow two miles away, the headman arguing with some cogency that it was raining (a fact which might have escaped our notice) and quoting the time-honoured rule that the first day's march should be a short one.

Bill pointed out that if they only marched in fine weather they would never arrive and that as the porters had been marching in for two days it was not their first day. Tongue firmly in cheek he told them he would make an exception to the raining rule as far as his own party went.

At Mana they added ten Mana men – Bhotias. Here too the last of their party, Emmons and Adams Carter, arrived. Their passage through the Rishi Gorge was a miserable affair. By now Bill was very familiar with its terrain but it had been raining incessantly and the river was in full spate. His diary records: 'July 26th – Mist which at midday turned to rain when we had reached the ridge above the Rhamani. Got down in thick mist and rain and found river impassable. L and I went out on a rope but it was clear the porters could not get over. Camped by the river. Rather a black outlook.'

In the evening the Dotials went on strike, and the next day they resolutely refused to cross the river using the rope Loomis and Bill had secured across it. Their Bhotia porters, however, did cross: 'their resourceful minds soon hit on the right method for roping the loads over, putting our scientific brains to shame,' wrote Bill. The Dotials were adamant. They took their pay and left – eating the Bhotias' food in the lower dumps as a petty revenge.

They now had sixteen porters, instead of forty-eight. But Bill worked out that if the 'sahibs' took sixty pounds each on their backs, it would be possible, if they also cut the food from sixty days to forty. As a result, it took twelve days of very hard graft to get all this into the sanctuary and then up to their Base Camp on the mountain. Before they could even begin this work, they had to rebag the food into different loads, all in the driving rain.

Up to this time, it was not thought a good policy (to put it mildly) that European climbers of Himalayan mountains should exhaust themselves by carrying in the kinds of loads Bill's party were now having to do – and over the most appalling terrain. 'These preconceived ideas were upset and our policy justified by the event,' was all Bill noted later.

His diary notes meticulously the loads of atta and sattu (staples for their daily diet) carried in each day. Once in the sanctuary they began collecting fuel, Bill mindful throughout that food for their Bhotia porters would soon run out and they would have to be sent back down the gorge. Finally, on August 7th, he notes: 'Paid off 11 Mana men Rs 25.8 each and Carter's two men. Lunch in the sun, very hot. Relieved to be here and rid of all coolies except Sherpas.' He was writing at their Base Camp at 17,000 feet.

Now came the climb up the mountain. They had established Camp 1 at 19,000 feet, having carried up forty pounds each, the Sherpas sixty pounds. After a day off, they were engulfed in a blizzard but on August 11th they restarted. From Camp 1 Bill and Noel Odell climbed on to a ridge and although they were encountering poor crumbly rock and difficult snow conditions they put Camp 2 here at 20,400 feet. Charles Houston and Graham Brown used this as the jumping-off point for Camp 3, set at 21,400 feet. By August 21st all the climbers had been as far as this to stock it with food.

By now, though, they were all ill, the westerners from altitude sickness, Pasang with snow blindness, some of the other Sherpas with dysentery. One, Kitar, died at the Base Camp. The party of

British and American climbers were now to fend for themselves. They elected Bill as the leader of the climb, or, as he puts it in his diary: 'I was given the invidious job of leader, that is to say to decide who goes first.' To add to the foot of his account of woes, Bill discovered that all but a small quantity of their tea, vital to keep dehydration at bay, had been lost over the edge of the precipice, beside Camp 2 – the 'Gite' as they all called it.

They managed to establish Camp 4, but only 500 feet above Camp 3. It was the breakthrough, however. Another blizzard held them up and then, on August 24th, they were able to carry more food up to Camp 4, enough for a fortnight. They knew that if they could get a bivouac established 2000 feet higher, the summit would be in reach. Bill decided that Odell and Houston were the strongest for a summit attempt. They would have two days to do it in and a second pair would have a chance after that.

On August 25th five climbers – Bill, Lloyd, Odell, Loomis and Houston – each set off from Camp 4 with a fifteen-pound load up the snow slopes. On the whole it was a long steady grind but it gained them the height they needed. Lloyd led them up a rock chimney – with his load on his back – and when they all got to the top of this, it was decided to leave Odell and Houston to search for a campsite while the others went back (it was four o'clock in the afternoon). The pair found their camp at about 23,500 feet.

The next day was a slack one with Bill worrying about how he could get a second pair up to Camp 4. Loomis now complained of frostbite and he was counted out of any summit attempt, at least solving that problem. Then, on the 27th, they heard Odell yodelling from above. Carter and Brown had by now joined them at Camp 4 and it was Carter who announced that the yodel had been followed by the news that 'Charlie is killed.' Bill wrote later: 'As soon as we had pulled ourselves together, I stuffed some clothes and a bandage into a rucksack and Lloyd and I started off as fast as we could manage, to be followed later by Graham Brown and Carter with a hypodermic syringe.'

It was, Bill said, not a climb easily forgotten but when they got to the tent they found, to their relief, that what Odell had been trying to shout was 'Charlie is ill,' the result of eating some bully beef. They all roped up and started down, meeting Brown and Carter on the way. At this point, Bill and Noel Odell turned back to the high bivouac, Bill laconically noting in his diary that 'fortunately had some extra clothes with me'.

The weather held on the 28th and they made a higher bivouac, guessing it to be at 24,000 feet. By now Trisul was well beneath them and even the top of East Nanda Devi (24,379 feet) was looking close. The next day, August 29th, Bill's diary reads:

> Up at 5 and started at 6.15. Cold and miserable. Interesting rock
> arete and then followed N's track to snow hillock arriving about

7.30. Followed a desperate grind up about 500 ft of snow. Very doubtful about getting anywhere. Noah's [their nickname for Odell] suggestion of sleeping till evening. Reached foot of final rocks 1 pm. Self weak and defeated by first pitch. Noah led. I took over. A steep snow gully landed us just below final ridge. Avalanche escape. Summit 3 pm. Air temp 20°[F] warm in sun. Left at 3.45. Down by 5.45. Tea. No food. No sleep.

The avalanche Bill noted could have been a complete – and very final – disaster. Later, he wrote: 'There was a sudden hiss and, quicker than a thought, a slab of snow, about forty yards long, slid off the corridor and disappeared down the gully, peeling off a foot of snow as it went. At the lower limit of the avalanche, which was where we were sitting, it actually broke away for a depth of a foot all round my axe to which I was holding.'

Of the summit, at 25,645 feet, he later wrote:

It was difficult to realise that we were actually standing on top of the same peak which we had viewed two months ago from Ranikhet, and which had then appeared incredibly remote and inaccessible, and it gave us a curious feeling of exaltation to know we were above every other peak within hundreds of miles on either hand. I believe we so far forgot ourselves as to shake hands on it.

Although a very few men had climbed higher on the slopes of Everest, this mountain was the highest any man had ever climbed to a summit. It made Bill famous back in England when the news got out, putting him on the front pages of many newspapers. They had climbed it without oxygen, or any modern aids, using nailed boots, crampons, ice-axes, ropes and immense fortitude and courage.

As a final fillip, after they were all down from the mountain, Bill, with Charles Houston and Pasang Kikuli, made a first crossing of Longstaff's col. It was while he was engaged on this that, back in England, his father died, not knowing of his son's triumph on Nanda Devi. Never more could Bill have reflected more ruefully on the impossibility of ever fully pleasing his father; now, he never could.

Bill later wrote an encomium of praise for every member of the Anglo-American team, ending his book on Nanda Devi with the quote: 'The game is more than the players of the game, And the ship is more than the crew.' He would remember this expedition as his greatest ever mountaineering triumph. Despite his friendship with Shipton, it must have been sweet, too, to know that he had done it without his more experienced friend. His other friendships, notably with Peter Lloyd and Charles Houston, lasted all his life.

CHAPTER 7

Titanic Days

When Bill returned to England in the autumn of 1936, now a justifiably famous mountaineer, he discovered that he was also a very rich man, with no need to work in a conventional sense at all. While the bulk of his money had been put in a trust fund in favour of his nieces, Bill and his sister Adeline could enjoy the interest from it.

What Bill thought of this arrangement, he never said. He never publicly said much either about the death of his mother, six months after his father. With her death Bill was left with a sister (Dearest Adds) and two young nieces, one of whom, Pam, was in many ways to become as near to a daughter as he might ever desire.

Even so, the death of his mother in April 1937 did not prevent him from continuing with his well-advanced plans to go to the Karakoram, in the region of the north-west Himalaya, with Eric Shipton, on what was to prove to be the greatest exploratory journey ever made in that immense mountain arena.

The Karakoram, in what is now Pakistan, is the greatest concentration of really high mountains in the world. Shipton, while fuming over their lack of progress on Everest in his tent in 1936, had begun to plan out a journey which, he later said, was to change the entire course of his life.

'The most obvious objective was the exploration of the unknown region, several thousand square miles, surrounding the basin of the Shaksgam River, immediately beyond the main continental divide. Represented on the map of the Karakoram by a challenging blank, it lay across the undemarcated frontier between Kashmir and Sinkiang.' In short, it was perfect. Shipton, back from Everest, went to the External Affairs Department of the Indian government and got their permission to go into this region, having first secured the interest of the Indian Surveyor General.

His plan was no doubt aided by the fact that, in keeping with the Shipton–Tilman theory of exploration, there would only be four westerners: himself, Bill, Michael Spender and John Auden. The budget, another masterpiece of economy, was £855 and Shipton had little difficulty raising this from bodies such as the Royal Geographical Society. Part of this sum included supplies for four months for fifteen (themselves plus seven Sherpas and four local Baltis).

The four British arrived in India towards the end of April and they met the Sherpas on April 27th in Rawalpindi. The Sherpas included Angtharkay, Sen Tenzing (who became known as Foreign Sportsman), Lobsang, Ila, Lhakpa, Angtensing and Nukku, the last as strong as an ox if somewhat slow of learning. As before, the Sherpas proved to be good friends as well as stout companions and incredibly tough load-carriers. With twelve pack animals, this party of eleven marched up the Sind Valley, and on to Skardu, the capital of Baltistan. Here they bought further supplies.

They crossed the Indus, marking the geographical boundary between the Himalaya and the Karakoram, and travelled up a difficult valley to Askole, reaching this last outpost on May 24th. This was a critical moment. Everything now depended on their ability to get across the immense mountain ranges ahead, and, moreover, to get nearly two tons of food and equipment across with them.

Shipton faced an extraordinary logistical problem: to keep his tiny party of fifteen alive in the fastness of the far Karakoram for the length of time he had set aside for the survey, he had calculated on using 104 porters. All these had to be provisioned for, on the march in and their march out once they had dumped the equipment and supplies. The supply question meant buying two more tons of flour.

To begin with, the local tribesmen were reluctant to have anything to do with this scruffy band, unlike any other expedition they had dealt with; not only was their appearance odd, they clearly had little money to spend, few exotic supplies with them to loot. Worst of all, Shipton noted, they were clearly being expected to undertake a much more arduous journey than the climbing expeditions they had been used to. It was only when they realised that Shipton's team was, however poorly financed, a bird in the hand, so to speak, that they agreed to work as porters.

They finally set out from Askole on May 26th. Bill's diary entry reads: 'Still raining 6 am. S and A [Spender and Auden] left at 9 for the Biafo [glacier]. Paid out Rs286 for 50 Mds. Picked some fresh blokes. Tipped Chuprassi Rs15. Roll call and allotting of loads. Left at 1.30 in slight rain. Two and a half hours to Biafo. One and a half to Korophon glacier. Rain until 4pm, arrived 5.30. Last loads at 7pm. River water. Fuel. Rain at night.'

Two days later Bill went down with a fever, along with Sen Tenzing. This, combined with heavy rain, snow falling on the passes ahead, and the daily consumption by the porters of two hundredweight of flour, had

Shipton near to despair. He decided that Auden should remain behind with Bill and Sen Tenzing, while he and Spender pressed on. They were now dragging increasingly reluctant Balti porters behind, afraid that the mad Englishmen would lead them to a place from which they would not be able to find their way back. Shipton contrasted their sinking morale with that of the seventeen men from Skardu who, with the Sherpas, managed to keep the whole show going. A few days later Shipton paid off the porters and they returned, leaving his party with the Sherpas and the Skardu men.

Bill and Sen Tenzing had now recovered. Bill's entry for June 3rd reads: 'Left at 8.45. Blokes heavy loads. Self none. Tensing 101bs. Felt weak. Approaching the glacier met the army [of discharged porters] on the way down. In a hurry and not interested in us. Barely a salaam.' He caught up with the rest of the party, a week after they had left, and all four established a Base Camp nine miles from the Shaksgam River. They kept four of the Skardu men, paying off the other thirteen. Shipton's expedition to survey the Karakoram now may be fairly said to have begun.

Shipton wrote about this 'threshold' later.

> No doubt the sheer happiness of these moments is later enhanced by the retrospective knowledge of the success they preceded but certainly that evening, warmed by the unaccustomed luxury of a blazing camp fire, I was blissfully aware of our position. To the east and west stretched an unexplored section, eighty miles long, of the greatest range in the world. We had food enough for three and a half months, and a party equipped and fully competent to meet the opportunity.

Nor did they fail. In nine weeks of surveying, mapping and climbing in these 18,000 square miles of mountain and glacier they achieved everything they could have hoped for. If the 1935 expedition to Everest had indulged in an orgy of climbing, the expedition to the Karakoram similarly indulged in an orgy of surveying and exploration for the sheer joy of it. Never again in this region was so much to be done. They all emerged in tatters and rags as a photograph of Spender towards the end shows; they were all totally happy.

Their first task had been to survey the pass across the Aghil Mountains between the Shaksgam and Yarkand Rivers. This pass had been crossed by the great Victorian explorer, Sir Francis Younghusband, in 1887, but had not been seen since by travellers from the west. Now Bill and Eric and their party located it.

With Spender, the surveyor, working out exactly where it was, John Auden now explored to the west and Eric and Bill set off with some porters to search for the Zug (false) Shaksgam. To do this they climbed a 20,000-foot peak to get a good view.

They found this river, followed it down to where it joined the Yarkand, and then they all recrossed the Shaksgam (just in time – it was now in spate). The next ten days were spent in exploring some of the huge number of glaciers in the region, in this case those flowing north and west from K2, the world's second highest peak. 'At the foot of its northern face we found a huge amphitheatre with a slender buttress rising from the level floor in one prodigious sweep of 12,000 feet to the summit dome. The air was clear and very still as we watched ice avalanches break from a hanging glacier so far above us that no sound broke the silence of the cirque,' wrote Shipton.

There were still many puzzles to solve, the most intriguing of which was the question of Snow Lake. This had first been discovered by Sir Martin Conway in 1892, who named it. It was a huge snow basin with a series of mountain islands rising out of it, and he thought it might be as large as 300 square miles. Ten years later Hunter and Fanny Workman had rediscovered it, and believed it to be an ice-cap – unknown outside the poles. This was the question to answer: was it?

The party now worked its way up a huge glacier, the Skamri and on August 1st, Shipton's birthday, they broke through the upper basin. Their direction, helped by Spender's theodolite, was towards where they believed Snow Lake would be. Through the upper part of the glacier they now found a vast fan of routes. They were at the hub of the Karakoram, glaciers radiating from it. Shipton divided his party into three, expecting each third to find its own way back to Kashmir. It was an inspired decision, brought on by the cornucopia of unknowns set out before them.

John Auden and the four Skardu men crossed one of the passes they had surveyed, getting into the Panmah Glacier system and working their way thus back to Askole. Eric, with Michael Spender and five Sherpas, went north-east. They spent a fortnight exploring the complex mountain range between the Skamri Glacier and the Shaksgam, eventually crossing the Shimshal Pass and there meeting the first 'outside' people they had seen for four months.

Bill, meanwhile, with just two Sherpas, had travelled further west. After crossing a number of passes they reached Snow Lake and crossed it. In so doing Bill found that it was not an ice-cap but one of seven contiguous glaciers. He also explored the Cornice Glacier, found by the Workmans who had convinced themselves that it was a unique geographical feature – a glacier with no outlet. Bill, no lover of science, had believed this story, probably because it appealed to his sense of the romantic. He was disappointed to find that it had an outlet, like all other glaciers, just as he had been disappointed to find that Snow Lake was not an ice-cap.

Finally, he and his two Sherpas broke through the great rock wall south of the Hispar Pass and got out to Arundo in Baltistan. On their journey Bill, Sen Tenzing and Ila came across the footprints of some kind of animal. They were able to follow the tracks for a mile: '16 inches apart and about 6–8 inches diameter. Blokes say it is hairy like a monkey,' Bill noted in his diary. This was Bill's first sighting of a Yeti track, with the question of whose existence Bill was to be heavily involved down the years. The 'ASM' (Abominable Snowman) file in the archives is a thick one, with many letters and poems, many of them by Bill. Whether he ever really believed in it is not recorded, but his love of mystery, of romance and of mischief (the sheer fun of arguing against po-faced and strait-laced science) suggests strongly that he wanted to believe.

The expedition emerged, in their three parts, in September 1937, and Shipton was now so taken by the Karakoram that he was already making ambitious plans for a return, involving over-wintering, by acquiring a herd of yaks and living like the natives. Whatever Bill might have thought of this plan, it was shelved because the Everest Committee, in London, had been able to find enough money to send a small team to Everest in 1938.

The background to this is of interest. Bill had been invited to discuss a small-scale expedition to Mount Everest by the committee, a combination of Royal Geographical Society and Alpine Club 'elders', in February, along with Eric Shipton, Smythe and Charles Warren. The committee had begun to believe there might be something in alpine-style assaults, compared with the costly (£10,000) failure of the 1936 expedition. The result of the talk was that Bill was asked to lead the next Everest attempt. What Shipton, the more experienced climber, thought of this is not recorded. No doubt the Everest Committee believed Eric to be more interested in exploration than bagging the long-sought-after Everest summit. His natural anarchy, compared with Bill's (at least surface) military manner, may also have affected their decision. This was finalised by March 1937, just before Bill left for the Karakoram. The problem was that the committee, having at long last given in to the climbing lobby, were hopelessly underfunded.

A £2000 advance from Hodder and Stoughton, the publishers, for the 1936 expedition story, had cleared their debts but the committee felt unable to ask for money from a public grown sceptical at successive failures. At the last moment Tom Longstaff, the well-known climber and the doctor on the 1922 expedition, offered £3000, as long as either Bill or Eric were confirmed as leader. To this the committee had agreed and this was the situation awaiting the pair when they returned from the Karakoram.

Longstaff had laid down some conditions for underwriting the expedition. These included that there should be no advance publicity, and that anyone selected should be willing to pay whatever they could afford for the honour of being invited. With these rules, much as he might have devised himself, Bill set about putting his team together. Eric, naturally, and also Smythe. Charles Warren was taken on, although Bill took him as a climber, not as a doctor. The last three were Peter Lloyd, Peter Oliver and Noel Odell. Bill used Shipton to help devise a budget: this came to £2360.

Bill was persuaded to take oxygen, against all his principles: the politics of the pro-oxygen lobby were one thing; perhaps he also had in mind his own poor performance on Everest in 1935. Only four sets went, though. For their diet, the team were subjected to the by now standard Shipton/Tilman ration of two pounds per man per day, mainly of the plainest kind. Bill's emphasis on sattu and atta, a high-carbohydrate diet, may have been an accidental discovery that such fare is a much better antidote for altitude sickness than medicine. If so, it was a discovery that has been confirmed more recently from scientific study.

He refused a free crate of champagne from a well-wisher although he did accept a case of tinned tongue. But Bill included porridge and soup among his definition of luxury food. Noel Odell never forgave Bill for their rations, in part blaming their failure on its inadequacies (they suffered a lot from flu, which could have been attributed to the weaknesses in the food rations). Food, Odell reasonably argued, helps morale.

Food was a dominant issue of this expedition. Bill had decided to use pemmican as the high-altitude ration – holding the mugs of soup down at all was one problem, allied to the taste of this exotic dish. Bill said later that he thought that the pemmican soup he and Peter Lloyd managed to hold down at 27,000 feet on Everest in 1938 was a feat unparalleled in Himalayan climbing. The trouble was, as on many other occasions, Bill extrapolated his own experience to make a general case. With food this was one thing; but his fearsome response if he thought any in his party was not up to scratch was because he was desperately hard on himself.

He gave no quarter but frequently displayed indifference to others' weaknesses which, in many cases, were mere mortal desires to live a little less on the edge, and a little less frugally. Bill isolated himself in this way, and collected a number of enemies. He was a frightful man to be on an expedition with in this one sense. Yet his strengths, unshakeable leadership among them, were such that men wanted to go with him. If anyone would get a team on the top of Everest it would be Bill, his tough-minded certainties overcoming any obstacle.

He had built, and continued to build, this hard crust in his life to protect himself. Bill fought himself and, each time he did so, he simply had to win; losing would have led to his complete moral collapse. Like the drunk who cannot afford to have even one drink, so with Bill, it seems, was the overt display of emotion. Let a little out and the dam would burst. Much of this can be ascribed to the First

World War; some, unquestionably, came from his relationship with his Victorian father.

The party arrived in Sikkim on March 3rd, 1938. From there, they marched up the Tista Valley, through the Gangu and over the Sebu La (at 17,000 feet) into Tibet. Their intention was to reach the Rongbuk Glacier early in order not to miss the clear period before the monsoon broke. But this meant they faced heavy snow up the Tista Valley and the Tibetan high plateau was terribly cold. They were all ill, mainly with flu, including Bill, and this may have weakened their resolve. Their poor diet would hardly have helped.

Rongbuk was reached on April 6th; the Everest summit was clear, but swept by violent winds. They had collected a fine team of Sherpas – Angtharkay the magnificent was the sirdar, but there were also Pasang, Kusang, and Tenzing Norgay. When the porters arrived they set immediately to work, establishing the Base Camp.

Camp 3 was in place below the North Col by the end of April. By this time Bill had already had flu. His diary entry for April 18th reads: 'Camp II – Left one man sick and went up with 32. Even so had to leave 6 loads. Left 1 Bell tent standing. Felt rotten at starting and got worse. Bed on arrival with cough, headache and stiffness, probably flu.'

He still felt 'fairly weak' but they had established Camp 3, they had lifted a month's food supply to it and although everyone was remarking on how cold it was, the question in Bill's mind was what to do next? The decision not to try for higher camps was dictated by illness – afflicting nearly everyone, including the Sherpas. Bill did not want to retreat to Rongbuk so he decided they should instead cross the Lhakpa La and so into the lush Kharta Valley on the east side of the mountain. The Kharta Valley was only 11,000 feet above sea level and a good place in which to convalesce. They spent a week there. Even so, Bill's diary is littered with comments about feeling 'bloody'.

When they got back, very early in May, they found Everest covered in snow; the monsoon had broken. This was hard to take. In 1936 Ruttledge had cursed when the monsoon had broken on May 25th. On May 18th they returned to Camp 3 and established a new one slightly higher. Bill wrote: 'Bit above here to new camp nearly killed me,' but they all found it hard work. The next day Odell and Oliver made an attempt to get higher. When they got back Shipton and Smythe had arrived; these were always seen as the pair who were most likely to summit. Bill had worked hard at ensuring that they were not overtaxed to this point in order that they would have the best chance.

They waited until May 24th; the slopes above had now been secured with fixed ropes to within 300 feet of the North Col. Shipton and Smythe easily overcame that; everyone, except Lloyd, now down with flu, along with twenty-six porters, managed to get on to the North Col, dumping their loads on the site of the 1936 camp. They all then returned to Camp

3. The following day Tilman and Smythe went back up but they could see that the peak was covered in soft deep snow and there were clouds piling up around; they descended once more.

Back at Camp 3 they had a discussion: 'Decided to occupy IV with 4 of us on 29th. FS [Smythe] and E [Shipton] to go I [Camp I] and come up when mountain clearer. Is it going to get any better? Perhaps it's not so bad as it looks,' wrote Bill in his diary. They were still debating whether the monsoon had in fact broken, but on May 29th a foot of snow fell. The day before Bill, with Odell, Warren and Oliver had climbed up to Camp 4 on the North Col. On the 29th they pushed on up the North Ridge, the trail through the deep snow being blazed by Tenzing Norgay (then just twenty-four years old). By one o'clock Bill and Tenzing had reached 24,500 feet. Bill wrote: 'Tenzing and I went on till 1 pm. Last bit a steep and soft snow slope. Stopped under a bulge at about 24,500. Self no windproof or gloves. Pleasant day, good cloud effects. Down by 2 pm. Snow started 3.30 and is still going on 5 pm. Can do little now but have not given up hope of doing something even in snow.'

While this was going on Shipton, with Lloyd and Smythe, had set up a camp on the Rongbuk Glacier. In the conditions they now faced, a new approach was mooted. This was to leave the East Rongbuk Glacier and to try a new line. The first camp which Shipton established at 18,000 feet was called Lake Camp; a second camp was then made at 19,000 feet, two and a half miles further up the right side of the Rongbuk Glacier, at a point where a subsidiary glacier joins the main one. This is the approach to the North Col. Bill, with Shipton, Lloyd and Smythe, now occupied this camp. The next day they came round the corner of Changtse and began to work their way up. Although the slopes were very exposed to avalanche they established another camp a mile up this glacier on top of an icefall, at 21,500 feet.

The following day, June 5th, they came across the debris of a huge avalanche. Even so, they pressed on, now horribly aware of how exposed they were, reaching the North Col again at 11.00 a.m. and reoccupying Camp 4. On June 6th they started up the ridge, and were pleasantly surprised to find the snow had hardened. But this happy state did not last, two porters with them becoming exhausted, and it was a chastened group who made it to Camp 5. Here Smythe and Shipton stayed, while Bill and Lloyd returned to Camp 4. The real heroes of the day were the Sherpas, Pasang and Tenzing who, having reached Camp 5, went down 700 feet to collect the loads from the two stricken porters and then carried them back up to Camp 5.

On June 8th the party from Camp 5 moved up again, this time to establish Camp 6 at 27,200 feet on a gentle scree slope below the 'yellow band'. But on the day after that the snow was deep and powdery and the route above was looking impossible. Shipton and Smythe tried to make for the First Step, but it was clearly suicidal to go on. When they reached Camp 5 on their retreat, they met Bill, with Peter Lloyd, coming up. Despite what they had been told these two continued up to Camp 6 and beyond, this being the highest point on any mountain that Bill ever reached – just 1800 feet below the summit (at about 27,400 feet). But then he and Lloyd came back down to Camp 4.

The best comment on the problems of the last 2000 feet of climbing Everest, now of course summited by 500 and more people, many without oxygen (which Bill did not use on his climb), is probably from Eric Shipton, quoted by Bill in *Everest, 1938*.

There can be no doubt that one day someone will reach the top of Everest, and probably he will reach it quite easily, but to do so he must have good conditions and fine weather, a combination which we now realise is much more rare than it had been supposed by the pioneers on the mountain. It is difficult to give the layman much idea of the actual physical difficulties of the last 2,000 feet of Everest. The Alpine mountaineer can visualise them when he is told that the slabs which we are trying to climb are very similar to those on the Tiefenmatten face of the Matterhorn, and he will know that though these slabs are easy enough when clear of ice and snow they can be desperately difficult when covered in deep powder snow. He should also remember that a climber on the upper slopes of Everest is like a sick man climbing in a dream.

Perhaps showing his acute disappointment, Bill's diary ends on June 8th, the day he climbed to his highest point on a mountain. This was the last expedition to try for Everest from the Tibetan side for many decades; war was returning to Europe and beyond; while after the war the Chinese invasion of Tibet would cut that country off from climbers for a generation. The as yet closed country of Nepal, home of the Sherpas, would be the base for the final conquest, still fifteen long years away when Bill left the slopes of Everest that summer.

He did not return to England, however, choosing instead, and maybe as a relief from what had just happened, to go back to the slopes of Kangchenjunga to try once more for the Zemu Gap. He had by now convinced himself that no one had ever climbed it. This time, he decided to try to cross it from the other side. He took two Sherpas with him, Renzing and Lhakpa Tenzing. On their way in and close to the gap itself, he found more Yeti tracks.

This time, they had no trouble climbing to the summit (at 19,200 feet). Now their problem was getting down the other side.

From our visit in 1936 I knew of the steep ice-wall on the south side, and had taken the precaution of bringing 240 feet of Alpine line. Even so on first looking over the top I got a shock. There was a wall, over 200 feet of it, and overhanging sufficiently to prevent one from seeing where one would land. We could not use the rope down this. However, search revealed a very steep and narrow gully descending from the junction of the crest of the pass and the precipitious shoulder of Simvu. Between two runnels of ice was a thin ribbon of snow.

Loose and wet though this snow was, they made their way down. It was nearly vertical. Bill went first, hacked out a platform and the Sherpas followed. In this way they descended, a rope's length at a time.

They reached the icewall which had caused Bill so much grief before; it had changed out of recognition, a great chasm having opened up. By now they had, as Bill put it, 'burnt their boats'. They had to go on. The only way was to descend into the chasm and climb out the other side. At one point, asked to trust the rope by Bill, Lhakpa said, 'Do you want to kill me?' but, after this difficult and dangerous moment, they were clear of any further major problems. Bill had made what was clearly the first crossing of the Zemu Gap.

It was very misty throughout, and the mist continued down into the valley; by now they were wet, cold and heartily sick of the adventure. But, quoting Bill:

> We had climbed a mountain and crossed a pass; been wet, cold, hungry, frightened, and withal happy. Why this should be so I cannot explain, and if the reader is as much at a loss and has caught nothing of the intensity of pleasure we felt, then the writer must be at fault. One more Himalayan season was over. It was time to begin thinking of the next. 'Strenuousness is the immortal path, sloth is the way of death.'

The rest of the world's affairs were now catching up with Bill. He had rather hoped, after 1938, that they could keep on going back to Tibet until Everest had been climbed, but the feeling was that the Tibetans might well not allow any more expeditions in. Eric Shipton, meanwhile, had plans for a return to the Karakoram, in which preparations he wished to include Bill.

In early 1939 many people in Europe believed war was inevitable – and soon. Bill was among them and he turned down Shipton's expedition on the grounds that he wished to be in closer touch with events, in case the international situation got much worse. He choose to go to the Assam Himalaya, to climb Gori Chen (21,450 feet) for which he finally received permission in February. In March, Germany invaded Czechoslovakia; the British government, finally shamed into action, guaranteed the integrity of the Polish frontiers, Hitler's next target; war became inevitable.

The expedition to Assam was a bad one. Bill recruited three Sherpas, Nukku, Thundu and Wangdi, and began to trek into Assam. Almost as soon as he was over the border, news came of the Italian invasion of Albania and he wondered if he should turn back. He pressed on but he and his Sherpas contracted malaria. He left two in a village and struggled on with Wangdi. Foolishly, but typical of Bill in this regard, he had only taken 100 quinine tablets for all four of them. 'I assumed we should not be in malarious country for more than two nights,' he wrote.

He and Wangdi struggled on, getting tantalising glimpses of Gori Chen as they did. But now Bill had malaria.

> I meant to lie at earth next day, but it was such a wonderfully fine morning that I went to a point across the river to do another 'fix'. This was a liberty which the malaria parasites in my blood seemed to resent, and for the next seven days, when fever and headaches allowed, I had leisure to reflect on the absence of our quinine and the fearful virulence of the Assam breed of malaria.

He did not know it at the time but he had *falciparum* or cerebral malaria. This was, shortly, to kill Nukku. After this unhappy event, Bill was finally moved to order a retreat. 'So ended my 1939 journeying, and a more unqualified failure has seldom been recorded. Here we got nowhere . . .'

Bill returned to England and to the army, where he re-enlisted as a gunnery officer. For the next six years his life was to be settled for him by the ebb and flow of the Second World War. His climbs were few and far between; that he managed any is a tribute to his determination to ensure that at least part of this second global conflict in his lifetime would yield some, if only spartan, fruit.

By 1945, when the war ended, Bill was forty-seven and his thoughts turned immediately to exploration in far-off places.

The final chapter of his true climbing career now has to be written. It lasted just five short years but it took him once more to the edge of Everest, this time from the other side – in Nepal.

CHAPTER 8

The Final Frontier

When the war in Europe ended Bill had added a DSO to his Military Cross and he retained the rank of major, a title he liked to keep about his person, so to speak. His initial reaction to VE Day was to try to get into the war in the Far East, still dragging on; in this endeavour he was unsuccessful. Meanwhile, while waiting for demobilisation, he climbed an Italian mountain, Presenella. This may well have convinced him that he was back on course as a mountaineer. He had no instinct for staying in the army; as a career, it offered him nothing and he had very effectively burned his boats as far as promotion went.

But there were other reasons not to stay in; in the beginning of *Two Mountains and a River*, published in 1949, Bill says: 'Just as after the first war, when one took stock, shame mingled with satisfaction at finding oneself still alive. One felt a bit like the Ancient Mariner; so many better men, a few of them friends, were dead: "And a thousand slimy things lived on; and so did I."' The last time out he had headed for Africa; now he had a single goal – the Himalaya.

Demobilised, however, he found that the post-war world was not quite the same as it had been in 1919. Restrictions were, if anything, increasing in the austere conditions that Britain found itself in. 'In 1946 England could be compared to the married state,' he wrote, 'those who were out (most of the Services) wishing frantically to get in, while many who were in wished as much to get out and found it devilish hard.'

Frustrated entirely in his efforts to get abroad, Bill had gone to Scotland and climbed Ben Nevis in the spring of 1946. There he had slipped, fallen on scree and broken his arm and was extremely embarrassed to find that his rescue party were a group of Boy Scouts. This fracture led to a typically Tilmanesque episode with the specialist Adeline insisted that he saw when Bill stormed out, no doubt leaving the consultant railing to his colleagues about the pig-headedness of ex-army majors. Still, Bill had recovered enough to get a short climbing trip to Switzerland that summer.

Early in 1947 currency restrictions were temporarily eased, and Bill set about arranging a trip to the Karakoram: he had booked a passage, ordered equipment and engaged three Sherpas. His long-time favourite Sherpa, Angtharkay, now a transport agent in Darjeeling, was setting up the porters. While the final details of this expedition were being finalised, Bill received an invitation from two Swiss climbers, Hans Gyr and Robert Kappeler, to go with them to climb Rakaposhi, a 25,550-foot peak near Gilgit. This presented Bill with a dilemma: on the one hand mountain exploration, on the other grand-scale mountain climbing.

He was helped by the failure of the authorities in what was still (just) British India to provide him with the necessary passes for Kashmir; he accepted the Swiss invitation – whereupon, of course, permission came for him to go through Kashmir. But Bill, ever a man of his word, went to Rakaposhi. He reached Karachi on May 1st and the Swiss joined him a week later. They started for Gilgit from Abbottabad, working their way up the valley of the River Kagan, arriving on June 4th.

A famous Chinese curse is that the recipient may live in interesting times. Bill, in joining the 1947 Rakaposhi expedition, was starting on four years of interesting times. They pose a question for a biographer, still difficult to answer: in these four years Bill travelled along and around the frontiers of India, Pakistan, China, the Soviet Union and Afghanistan – the central players in what was always called the 'Great Game'. This was largely an intricate chess match between Imperial Britain and Imperial Russia, and it concerned the trade routes of central Asia.

Because the frontiers in these remote and mountainous regions are so difficult to mark and to patrol, there was a constant insurgency among the local tribes, whose loyalties could be bought by either – or both – sides. The game generally fell the British way but it was never fully put to the test. But in the post-war world of the late 1940s Russia was the communist Soviet Union, China was falling to the communist guerrillas of Mao Zedong and India and Pakistan were about to be cast adrift as independent states. The conditions of these regions, and who was engaged in what kind of espionage – or worse – would have been of great interest to the British (and their American allies).

To the question: was Bill Tilman acting for British intelligence for all or part of this period, the answer has to be yes but, as with many things to do with Bill, equivocally. The facts are these: he was one of the most experienced Himalayan travellers of all time. He had a tremendous capacity for survival off the land; he was able to slide in and out of tribal regions, using local people as support. He had demonstrated, time and again, his capacity for absorbing immense amounts of information – particularly surveying but also what, in a more innocent context, could be called gossip.

He had just come back from two years behind enemy lines, for which he had been highly trained, and he wanted – as ever – something interesting to do. He got his passage out of Britain in circumstances which might have defeated others; that is, strings were pulled. At the same time, because of his reputation as an eccentric traveller, all this could easily be passed off as the innocent passage of a man obsessed by wild and lonely places. Finally, and best of all, Bill kept his own counsel – and was well known for it. Taciturnity was the greatest asset he possessed in this regard. No doubt it would have appealed no end to his sense of himself as a largely lone adventurer.

In this context, his acceptance of the Swiss offer to climb Rakaposhi takes on a different meaning. Simply put, by allying himself with a group of well-established mountaineers from a neutral power, he could more easily slip off after the expedition. This is exactly what he did.

The Rakaposhi expedition has a footnote in British Imperial history: it was the last attempt to climb a major Himalayan peak under the British Raj; when Bill and the Swiss left Gilgit the Raj had a month to run.

They failed on the mountain, defeated in all their attempts. For Bill, this was a great disappointment. Perhaps he was already aware that his age was beginning to tell, and that he would have few more chances at the high peaks of the Himalaya. He could still enjoy the atmosphere, the surroundings:

> I felt uncommonly happy at trekking once more behind a string of mules with their bright headbands, gaudy red wool tassels, and jingling bells, over a road and country new to me with the promise of sixteen such days ahead. I felt I could go on like this for ever, that life had little better to offer than to march day after day in an unknown country to an unattainable goal.

When the attempt on Rakaposhi had been abandoned Bill turned to the north – to Kashgar and to an unlikely meeting with Eric Shipton who had been the British consul there since 1940. If anything gives away what Bill was really up to, this trek, across the border from what was about to become Pakistan, into China, is a crucial sign.

The British consulate in Kashgar was established by Younghusband in 1888. The reason given for it was to foster the age-old trade across the Karakoram Pass from Kashmir and to protect the interests of a small and prosperous Indian community. But the underlying motive was the growth of Russian influence on this remote province of Sinkiang and to be able to engage in the web of espionage, intrigue and manoeuvre that was at the heart of the 'Great Game'.

The ostensible reason for Bill's visit to Kashgar in 1947 was an invitation from Eric Shipton to climb Mustagh Ata (24,388 feet); what better excuse than that these two veteran climbers of the 1930s should meet again to climb together?

He left Kashmir on a day of destiny – August 1st. 'On this day . . .

the Gilgit Agency was being handed over to the Kashmir State and, although British rule had ended, the Subadar in charge of the fort [on the border] appeared to be in no hurry to haul down for the last time his Union Jack,' he wrote. He met Shipton, with his wife, Diana, a little later in the town of Sarikol.

From here he and Shipton made their attempt on Mustagh Ata. They were accompanied by Diana as far as a camp at 17,000 feet and also by a Sherpa, then settled in Kashgar. Bill's own Sherpas had refused to travel with him into China, Bill believed in part because of what had happened to this man, Lhakpa, who had settled there and married a local girl. Despite the fact that all three of them had been on the 1938 Everest expedition, their attempt failed, Bill's second failure that summer. They had managed to establish a camp at 20,000 feet and, finding the snow in good condition, decided to push for the summit from there. Bill went down with altitude sickness along with Eric. Lhakpa became exhausted and although they thought they might have a second attempt, Eric and Bill discovered their feet were becoming frostbitten. As a result of this, they all descended as quickly as they could.

In Kashgar, whither they had travelled from Mustagh Ata, Bill spent a congenial three weeks of diplomatic socialising – including with the Russians. He then set out for Pakistan, choosing to travel west through China, thence through a part of Afghanistan and back to Pakistan. He said: 'no conscientious traveller turns homeward on the route by which he came if a reasonable alternative offers itself,' and went on to say that this did mean going into Afghanistan for which he had no visa.

> But I argued that Wakhan is a pretty remote part of Afghanistan where it was unlikely that I should meet any Afghan officials, that any Wakhis I had so far come across had seemed kind accommodating folk, and that by nipping smartly back into India . . . I should almost certainly avoid being caught up in the spider's web of passports, visas, and inquisitive officials.

His route took him close to the source of the Oxus, one of the most sensitive areas in the whole region as the Oxus was the boundary between the Soviet Union and Afghanistan. Either Bill was more naïve than he is normally given credit for, or he was deliberately probing this border to see who would take notice of him and his little caravan – if anyone.

He travelled with a Turki from Kashgar, Yusuf, who had no passport at all. He had a father who he thought kept a shop somewhere between Gilgit and Srinagar and he believed that Bill's documents would suffice for them both. They left in early September and it was bitterly cold. Finally they made it to the frontier with Afghanistan and crossed it without challenge. Passing on through the Wakhjir Valley they finally reached the pass which led into the Hindu Kush, the Pass of Khora Bhort.

At this point the local headman insisted they could not leave Afghanistan by this route and directed them to Sarhad, forty miles away. Bill's translator also left him at this point. Astonishingly, Bill now contemplated 'eliminating' the yak herdsman sent with them by the obdurate headman. 'I had got as far as pondering the questionable wisdom of this step and whether Yusuf would be either a willing or a useful accomplice in crimes of violence, when a party of men and yaks appeared coming up the gorge. As omens were evidently unpropitious, with a troubled mind I gave the order to go on.'

Close to Sarhad they came across

two men on foot – a dirty unsavoury pair, one of whom seemed to be wearing some semblance of a uniform. Their manners were no better than their appearance. They shouted at me truculently and unintelligibly, so I waved them airily in the direction of my followers and passed on. This would not do. They came after me shouting still louder at which I turned round. One of them bawled out questioningly 'Russi?'. To which I, not caring much what they might think, made a gesture indicative of assent.

Bill must have known, despite his dismissal of this encounter, that it would be as a red rag to a bull. On this frontier, at this time, to claim Russian (i.e., Soviet) nationality was to court instant arrest. He had his way: under open arrest in Sarhad they were sent on, with an escort, to Iskashim, a further 100 miles away. There Bill was told he might be allowed to go to Chitral in Pakistan. The by now unhappy Bill left Sarhad on October 5th and reached Iskashim on October 10th. He and Yusuf were immediately gaoled.

At this point, Bill confessed later, he was in some despair. His diaries had been taken away, along with his exposure meter, assumed to be some kind of radio. All his kit was thoroughly searched, his tent slit open to check for anything hidden. Yusuf's gear had similar treatment, Bill being astonished at what this man had carried with him for trade in Pakistan. In an earth-floored ten-foot-square cell, he kept himself sane by playing patience with cards eventually provided by the local commissar who, although friendly when Bill met him, offered no immediate hope of release.

Finally, he and Yusuf were let out of their prison but, on the road again, Bill was now dismayed to find that they were travelling west, by no means the route for Chitral. Now they arrived at Faizabad, about 135 miles away from Kabul and connected to it by a good road. Here the military commander had a son who spoke Hindustani, so communication in earnest could begin again. Bill and Yusuf were allowed better quarters while they awaited a telegram from Kabul, which they hoped would let them go. Nine days after they arrived in Faizabad, it came. They finally reached Chitral where Yusuf found he could not go on to Kashmir as the war of partition had broken out. In the end Yusuf managed to get back to Kashgar, although Bill felt very guilty about the way he had misled the man in all their adventures together. Does that guilt include Bill's thoughts about his clandestine mission? We cannot know, although we may suspect.

Analysing the latter part of his journey, Bill dismisses it all as a failure; it is a good cover for what he had achieved. For he had established that the Afghans were extremely suspicious of the Soviet Union but much more kindly disposed to the British still – a happy state of affairs to report back to his masters in London.

In 1948 Bill made another great journey to the east, this time again travelling out to China to meet Shipton, whose removal from the Kashgar post had been delayed. Because of the war in Kashmir Bill had to fly to China, a mode of travel he heartily despised. Shipton arranged to meet Bill in Urumchi, 1000 miles from Kashgar, and close to the Gobi Desert. Eric was making the most of his last months as the Kashgar consul; he and Bill planned to climb the Bogdo Ola Mountains, close to Urumchi. Fortuitously, the Americans had set up a wartime consulate in Urumchi and it was there that Eric based himself; but it was all fairly fraught as by this time the Chinese communists were sweeping through the Nationalist lines right across China.

Bill flew first to Shanghai; then on by air again to Lanchow on the Yellow River; there, finally, he boarded a postal bus for a twelve-day journey to Urumchi; the cost was 28 million Chinese dollars, a sign of the collapsing Nationalist currency, along with their military fortunes. Eventually, he reached the vicinity of Urumchi.

At last, 10 miles from Urumchi, I saw a familiar truck and by it a familiar figure. Two familiar figures, in fact, for Mr Shipton had with him his Sherpa servant, Lhakpa who had been with us in our disastrous attempt upon Mustagh Ata the previous year. Ready hands took charge of my scanty luggage, and as the Dodge trundled onwards towards the now setting sun the gratitude I felt was only tempered by the regret that the old ways of travel had been almost extinguished by the truck and its kind.

They stayed at the American consulate; once more, however, they failed to summit any peaks although they did have four days in the mountains together. It was almost the last time they climbed as a team. Remote peaks in a far-flung land are a fitting setting in which to remember these two men and their career as mountaineers. Bill, at fifty, Eric at forty-one, both soon to have their lives changed completely.

From Urumchi, they returned to Kashgar and more diplomatic entertaining. Bill left Eric for a while to look for a mountain called Chaka Aghil (22,000 feet) at the edge of the Hindu Kush, taking a local British doctor with him. This time, Bill not only failed to climb the peak, he and his companion could not even find it. Back in Kashgar he talked this over with Shipton and they decided to have another try. They succeeded in finding it but the porter they took with them went down with altitude sickness and they turned back when they had reached 17,000 feet. This was the last time they ever climbed together.

On October 1st Bill left Kashgar and travelled west with the mail-runners to Tashkurghan. From there he travelled on his own to Chitral, this time making no attempt to cross the Afghan border. He arrived in Chitral via the Boroghil Pass. He returned to England once again – this time not to the old family house in Wallasey but to the house his sister had bought for them in north Wales, Bodowen near Barmouth, which was to be his base for the rest of his life.

He was now about to embark on his last great mountaineering journeys – all to Nepal, the home of the Sherpas with whom he had worked so amicably down the years. Between 1949 and the end of 1950, Bill made three journeys within Nepal, the last the nearest to a conventional holiday trek Bill would ever do. Almost as a footnote, it is worth recording that on this farewell to the Himalaya, Bill became the first Briton to see the Nepal side of Everest, that aspect from which, just three years later, it was to be climbed.

Nepal had remained closed to ousiders until the 1940s but the changing politics of the region had forced its rulers to relax their strict rules. By 1949 China was on the edge of its communist enslavement; Tibet would shortly fall to the same brutal regime. India was now independent. In these circumstances Nepal – home of the Gurkha tribe who have served the British so magnificently down the years – began to offer a more relaxed prospect. By this time the British had established a full embassy in Kathmandu, an unusual move but one justified by the involvement of the Gurkhas: in effect the embassy operated as a recruitment agency for these men, and as a place where British army pensions for retired soldiers could be paid out.

The opening of Nepal meant a quickening interest in British mountaineering circles over an approach to Everest by this southern route. It is worth quoting Bill (from *Nepal Himalaya*, his last mountaineering book) as he gives a concise picture of the situation in 1949.

> There can be no other country so rich in mountains as Nepal. Apart from Everest and Kangchenjunga and their two 27,000 ft satellites, there are six peaks over 26,000 ft, fourteen over 25,000 ft, and a host of what might be called slightly stunted giants of 20,000 ft and upwards, which cannot be enumerated because they are not

all shown on existing maps. It should be understood that, except for Everest and those peaks on the Nepal–Sikkim border, most of which (except Kanchengjunga) have been climbed, this enormous field has remained untouched, unapproached, almost unseen, until this year (1949) when the first slight scratch was made.

It was this prize – the whole of the mountainous part of the country – that Bill now saw as a goal. In 1948 a party of Indian scientists had been allowed in to investigate the upper part of the Kosi River. There, they climbed Nangpa La, a 19,000-foot pass west of Everest. Then, in the winter of 1948–49 a party of Americans had been allowed in to collect birds in the foothills of central and eastern Nepal. Encouraged by all this the British ambassador in Kathmandu, Sir George Falconer, asked permission for a British climbing party to go in 1949. Conditions were attached by the Nepali government, however: the climbers, including Bill, who had wished to go to Gauri Sankar (23,440 feet), close enough to give them a good look at the south side of Everest, were instead confined to the Langtang Himal. They were enjoined, also, to do some serious scientific work, a prospect which filled Bill with great gloom.

The party from Britain consisted in the end of four: Bill, Peter Lloyd, the botanist O. Polunin, and a geologist, J. S. Scott; among the Sherpas was Tenzing Norgay. The expedition 'shuffled out of the Legation compound on May 29th', into what turned out to be a prolonged investigation of the Langtang, Ganesh and Jugal Himalaya. Although they were faced with persistent rain (and the attendant leeches for which the area is renowned) they managed to achieve a great deal.

They surveyed the Langtang Valley and the mountains that backed it. They found Gosainthan (26,291 feet) and they discovered the 'fluted' peak, named by them after the snow fluting on its west face. Bill and Peter Lloyd subsequently tried to climb it but were beaten back around 20,000 feet. They found a forgotten pass into Tibet – territory now forbidden to them. Bill, in his descriptions of the countryside through which they travelled, excelled himself in providing these first western portraits of a country which has become so very familiar in the past forty years.

For instance:

On returning from this damp excursion I went on to Langtang to check the food, where I was astonished by the swift growth resulting from the recent rain – by the many new flowers, the masses of white Erica which had suddenly blossomed, and the dwarf Rhododendron whose resinous fragrance filled the air. Kyangjin, too, had suddenly come to life. The long bamboo poles of the gompa and the roofs of the now occupied stone huts carried small flags of red and yellow, and the long, grass flat was thick with yaks and horses.

The leeches plagued them in parts of this journey.

Walking along a leech-infested path one is usually fully occupied with home affairs, but it was interesting to note how the weight of the attack upon different men varied. The Europeans were easily the most acquisitive, and if one of us suffered more leech bites than another, it could be attributed to carelessness or to walking along with nobody behind to give a warning of an impending stab in the back.

Bill noted that the Sherpas were distinctly less affected but, more astonishing, the tribes local to any one leech patch were seemingly totally immune to their bites.

They returned to Kathmandu in late September; despite his dislike of science Bill had made a record of trees, shrubs, flowers, even some insects he had come across. He and Peter Lloyd had managed to climb only one peak – Paldor, 19,451 feet – although they had had the excuse of poor weather. But he could not help adding in *Nepal Himalaya* that

the killing of two birds with one stone, however desirable, is seldom achieved intentionally and never by aiming consciously at both. I am not implying that the presence of the collectors or the strong whiff of science which pervaded the party impaired our aim, but that a lot of luck will be needed if the climbing of a good peak is to be included in the exploration of a large, mountainous area.

Bill, no doubt rueing this overall failure, approached the Maharajah of Nepal at the moment of their departure in 1949, asking for permission to return the following year. This permission was granted, but very late. What Bill had in mind was the Annapurna range. Bill, typically, had rather planned on a small (i.e., probably two or three) party; the Himalayan Committee of the Alpine Club had other ideas; the British party consisted of six which, for Bill, was excessively large.

He was more successful in keeping the scientists out; there was only one, a botanist, Lowndes. Emlyn Jones was then a young surveyor, just into his first job, but he managed to get leave. Bill had no intrinsic objection to surveyors and, in any case, Jones was a first-class alpine mountaineer. Apart from these two, Bill took Dr Charles Evans, Major J. O. Roberts and W. P. Packard from New Zealand.

Lowndes and Jones oversaw the ton of baggage across India by train. On the way these two saw their compartment go up in smoke when an axle ran hot. Bill, typically, wrote: 'This caused more delay, and the loss of some kit which was borne with equanimity since most of it belonged to Roberts.'

They reached Kathmandu on May 5th and they were looked after by the ambassador's wife, Lady Falconer, leaving for the Annapurna range five days later. There were four possible peaks, numbered I to IV, between 26,492 feet and 24,688 feet. While Bill and his team were in the range a French group made the first ascent of Annapurna I, the highest summit yet achieved, but Bill did not know this at the time. Bill finally selected Annapurna IV as their objective. They established four camps, up to 22,400 feet.

From Camp 4 they sent Evans and Packard on a first summit push but they were defeated by bad weather, the same storm which was afflicting the French team on Annapurna I in much more dramatic circumstances. On June 19th Bill made a summit attempt with Evans and Packard. Bill got as high as 23,400 feet.

> The sun shone bleakly through a veil of high cirrus which it had painted, as upon flimsy canvas, an iridescent halo. Climbing even at that height, which was by no means extreme, our pace seemed fully as slow as that of a glacier; unhappily, one feared, without the glacier's inexorability. Having climbed for nearly two hours we paused at a small rock outcrop to take stock and to compare our height with that of Macha Puchare, whose fish-tail seemed to make a rude gesture at us from above a bank of cloud. It is difficult to judge by the eye alone, but the most helpful among us dared not affirm that we were much, if anything above it; which meant that we had risen only 500 feet. After another hour, during which we gained height quicker owing to the steeper slope, the altimeter put us at a height of 23,400 feet. Packard was going strong, Charles Evans panting a little, while the combined effect of age and altitude threatened momentarily to bring my faltering footsteps to a halt. In fact, my goose was cooked.

He reflected later that he would be unlikely ever to get above 20,000 feet again.

They retreated from Annapurna IV without incident and went on to explore the region around it. On a side exploration with two Sherpas Bill had an accident, again falling backwards about fifteen feet on to his much afflicted back; it took him five days of lying still before he could move, unable even to sit up without help. Back in Kathmandu this annoyance was compounded by the refusal of the embassy staff to allow any of them back in until they had been de-loused and tidied up – including having haircuts – on the lawn.

Bill had now been in Nepal that year for nearly five months (it was late September) but one more trip in Nepal was to present itself before he was played out. In Kathmandu he met Oscar Houston, the father of Charles Houston with whom he had been on Nanda Devi. Charles Houston had presented his father with a trek to the south side of

Everest; now, Oscar invited Bill to come along. Only Bill's words can tell this part of the story.

At Kathmandu, where we were lapped in comfort at the Embassy, we did not take long to wind up our affairs. I felt I could safely but perhaps undeservedly murmur: 'Now my weary eyes I close, Leave, ah leave me, to repose'. But it was not to be. I there met Mr Oscar Houston, the father of Dr Charles Houston a companion of Nanda Devi days, who had everything in train for a journey to Solu Khumbu, the district on the Nepal side of Everest and the home of the Sherpas. He invited me to join his party, and a refusal to do so would have seemed ungracious. Moreover the journey would be of supreme interest; apart from viewing the south side of Everest there was the fun to be expected from seeing Sherpas, as it were, in their natural state. Mr Shipton and I had often discussed such an unlikely happening, and here it was offered to me on a plate. In 1949 the Himalayan Committee had asked the Nepal Durbar for permission to send a party to reconnoitre the south side of Everest, but this had been refused and the Langtang Himal offered in its place.

Despite having to wait for Charles to turn up, Bill agreed to go. 'After all, I thought, if Charles Houston is prepared to fly from New York for the sake of five weeks in the Himalaya, I ought not to grudge waiting a fortnight for the sake of a memorable experience in such good company.'

He went on: 'Besides the Houstons, father and son, there were two old friends of theirs, Mrs E. S. Cowles, an American climber of note, and Anderson Bakewell who was then studying at the Jesuit College of St Mary's at Kurseong near Darjeeling. Hitherto I had not regarded a woman as an indispensable part of the equipage of a Himalayan journey but one lives and learns.'

We are fortunate in having Bill's diary for this trip, and Betsy Cowles', as well as their respective published accounts. The latter are each about twenty pages long; Bill's diary is as usual, laconic; hers is gushing and informative.

Bill has no entry for the day they met; Betsy writes: 'We all awaken as Gyalgen says we're at Jogbani. Then there appeared Andy and Bill Tilman, Sherpas (plus Sherpette!). We load up a big bus and pile in to the jute mill's guest house, have tea and get settled.'

The walk in to Namche Bazar and the Thyangboche Monastery was the first by westerners. A car and a lorry had taken them to Dharan, at the foot of the hills, forty miles away. There, the little party found eighteen coolies and three ponies. They had to climb 2000 feet on a loose stony track to get started, all under the midday sun, 'a rather brutal first day for those new to Himalayan travel,' thought Bill. Already Betsy was saying to her diary: 'I don't know what we'd do without Tilman. He stands calmly overseeing loads.'

The journey in was magical for all of them, conscious of the privilege of being the first westerners to go in since the border had reopened. For the Nepalis, too, it was a new experience. They had some of the usual troubles with the porters on the early part of the trek but this was resolved. Now, they were approaching the Khumbu, where the Sherpas lived. 'On 14 November we reached Namche Bazar,' Bill wrote.

The track crossed and recrossed the clear, blue river, here hurrying along like a mountain torrent, by wooden cantilever bridges which in no case had to span more than twenty yards. For a river which drains what is perhaps the grandest thirty miles of the Himalaya it is surprisingly small . . . We were welcomed to the village by an inquisitive but friendly crowd. Namche Bazar, of course, has never ranked as a 'forbidden city'. It is far from being a city, and has remained unvisited not because of any very serious difficulties in the way, but because no one has thought it worth the trouble of overcoming them. Nevertheless, it had for long been my humble Mecca. As we rode in I shared in imagination a little of the satisfaction of Burton, or of Manning when he reached Lhasa.

Bill and Betsy Cowles were slowly making friends, a condition in which they continued for the rest of her life (she died in 1974). Charles Houston and his wife, who both knew Betsy very well, say she did ponder out loud over whether she might have married Bill, although she thought him too set in his ways at fifty-two to have been a good prospect (she was divorced). If Bill was in a private rapture over his penetration into the land of his long-time Sherpa companions, Betsy was in her own reverie.

T warms up at times (gave me a piece of his orange, peeled a while ago) smiles cutely when making one of his dry jokes. Like 'Trouble with America is you are all package minded'. I think he is quite a man and will be happy if we end by being friends. Tonight was wonderful; the early arrival in camp, everything aired and dried and washed (incl ourselves). Then a good dinner and we sat around after, writing by the big lamp (worked this time) – then a big fire and Bill telling about his 2 disappointing seasons. All that went wrong and why. One senses real sorrow there ('my ceiling is 24,000 feet – just too feeble'). O talked interestingly about S America. C cute and gay as always. Stayed up until after 8!

A little later in the trek, she was writing: 'Last night we sat around the fire, Bill telling of his war experiences. Dunkirk, then dropped by parachute into Albania and Italy. Stayed a year in Albania,' followed a few days later with 'B warming up, sang a little song at tea!' It was not all sweetness and light. Betsy was beginning to work out when Bill was liable to bite her – or anyone's – head off. 'I irk HWT sometimes, but must not try to be too pervasive; or 'HWT's abysmal pessimism is a real load for everyone to carry,' and 'HWT in a bad temper but I feel better about it now he is mad at everyone and not just me.' Part of this was Bill's annoyance with the porters, part his natural reticence which Betsy was having a hard time with. When he really could not face any more of the exuberance of his American friends, Bill simply strode on ahead. According to Betsy's diary he had told Oscar that their trek was harder than getting into the Nanda Devi sanctuary but it is likely that this was to help the elder Houston feel better.

From Namche Bazar Bill and Charles Houston set out to investigate the Western Cwm of Everest. They had only six days to do it in, being due back at Jogbani on December 6th. However they all went to the Thyangboche Monastery, Bill and Charles reaching it first. 'Mrs Cowles, of course, stole the show, and soon had them all, urchins and lamas alike, eating out of her hand,' wrote Bill in *Nepal Himalaya*.

The short visit to the south side of Mount Everest did not inspire either Bill or Charles to believe Everest would be more easily climbed from this side. Betsy recorded on November 19th: 'At about 3 Bill and Charley return. Everest unclimbable from the S they say. They feel fine about their job, feel it's been done right. Look weary.'

The expedition was nearly over. Bill bought Betsy a Tibetan bowl in Ghat on their way back. Now it was friendship; Bill told her of his time in Africa, of the early climbs he had made. No doubt Betsy related her own very illustrious climbing career in the States. They were making up silly limericks, too, some of which Bill noted in his diary (and which appeared in the published account which is unusually skittish for a standard HWT text). At one point they all had a hunt for fleas and lice. 'Bill has them; I haven't. Much laughter,' Betsy notes.

On November 29th Bill and Betsy together cooked a cake for the Thanksgiving Day celebrations the Americans had planned for the 30th. There was a minor problem over finding supplies of spirits; they had already drunk their own brandy.

Nevertheless, in the Aran valley of 30 November, the pilgrims had their Thanksgiving Dinner – table decorations by Mrs Cowles, heating and lighting by Danu, solid fare by Gyalgen, fruit cake by Himal Bill, and bottled lightning from the jemadar's private cellar. For my part I gave thanks for past Himalayan seasons, few without their missed opportunities and frustrated hopes, but all of them good, and of which this, I thought, should be the last.

125

Betsy wrote: 'All such fun; gaiety from everyone and great interest in the undertaking. Sense of group loyalty and affection. HWT so nice today. We decide we Americans are too gullible, he too suspicious. He agrees!'

In *Nepal Himalaya* he concluded his account of this trek with:

The best attainable should be good enough for any man, but the mountaineer who finds his best gradually sinking is not satisfied. In an early English poem attributed to one Beowulf we are told:

> Harder should be the spirit, the heart all the bolder,
> Courage the greater, as the strength grows less.

If a man feels he is failing to achieve this stern standard he should perhaps withdraw from a field of such high endeavour as the Himalaya.

Bill Tilman never returned to the Himalaya, though he flew over them on his way to Australia in 1964. He returned to Bodowen in the winter of 1950, just short of fifty-four, a man who had decided not to go on climbing the highest mountains. He had been a soldier and a writer but those hardly constituted a basis for anything else, certainly not for a middle-aged man with a bad back. The next three years were to become a kind of interlude in his life, a swerve away from the exploring past of the great land masses, until he discovered a new life, that of a sailor explorer; as just that, an interlude, I have included this part of his life at the end of the account of his Second World War exploits.

The Second World War splits Bill's career as a climber. When it began he was still young – he even looks much younger than his years. When it ended, six long years later, he had become middle-aged. Before the war he is palpably successful on the high peaks; after it, he never has a summit success. If the First World War had aged Bill prematurely, turning him into a man who would always walk alone, the Second World War reshaped him. Although he would have seen it coming from afar, its opening would have been the shocking realisation that this was no ordinary foe. For most of those fighting the Nazis in 1939, this was a crusade as stark as any medieval fight to the finish against pure evil.

In the six years of fighting, especially the last two, Bill's earlier hardness turned into the epic stoicism for which he is most famously remembered today. It retempered his soul, and went a long way to create the legend.

PART THREE

A Warrior's Tale

CHAPTER 9

Distant Guns

'The business of trying to adapt a war to one's own ends can be over done. At least such was my own experience in the first two or three years of this war. It is better to lie passive, neither helping or hindering the current, but drifting with the stream of events as directed, or so one likes to think, by Higher Authority.' So wrote Bill in *When Men and Mountains Meet*, published in 1946.

Bill was already back in the army when war broke out on September 1st, 1939, having returned from Assam, anticipating what everyone was beginning to realise: war with Germany was inevitable. His rank, despite his age (forty-one) and experience was as lieutenant, the same he had held in 1919. His regiment was 32 Field Regiment, Royal Artillery and he joined it the day Poland was invaded, at Brighton.

Bill had spent the early part of 1939 in the Assam Himalaya, on a nightmarish expedition. Bill had been lucky, luckier than he perhaps knew at the time, and he had returned to England, almost certainly not all that well – but for Bill, overcoming any latent effects of malaria would have been a secondary consideration.

His regiment was sent to France in the autumn of 1939 as part of the British Expeditionary Force, and there it waited, dug into its position, while the long weary months of the 'phoney' war slid by, the Germans being occupied with mopping up Poland and lands to the east. Bill, meanwhile, had been promoted to acting captain in November.

The German Wehrmacht opened the war in the west in April 1940, invading Norway. Then, in May, they began their blitzkrieg into the lowlands of the Netherlands and Belgium, a repeat of 1914, before sweeping into France. In the north they attacked Denmark and Norway. Bill remarked, somewhat ruefully, that 'in Norway the campaign was over before the mountaineer, who felt that here at last was his opportunity, had had time to send off his first appeal: "Sir, I have the honour to forward this my application for transfer, etc."' In France, the BEF was overwhelmed within a few short weeks, retreating to Dunkirk where, along with hundreds of thousands of others, Bill was taken off the beaches.

Along with the remnants of the BEF Bill now found himself involved in the desperate efforts made by Britain for home defence in the clear expectation that the country would shortly be invaded by the Germans, now triumphant over most of western Europe. He served with 120 Battery, in his remustered RA regiment, in Suffolk. They were armed with twelve-pounder quick-firing guns, appropriated from the Royal Marines. In September 1940, while the invasion threat was still very real, Bill was promoted to major, the highest rank he held, and took over command of 120 Battery.

The invasion threat lessened during the latter part of 1940 and the war settled into the slog it was to become over the next five years. Bill, sensing the way things were going, and no doubt relieved that this fight was not going to be a rerun of the trench warfare of 1914–18, now applied to be sent to a theatre of operations where he could be useful. 'I moved heaven and earth to get myself sent to East Africa, a country about which I knew a good deal. The result was that I found myself in a regiment earmarked for Singapore, of which I knew nothing. I had the very greatest difficulty in extricating myself from this ill-starred unit only twenty-four hours before it embarked.' (They were all taken prisoner by the Japanese, a year later.)

In a letter to Adeline, of March 20th, 1941, he wrote:

We got on board today and am settling in. I have a cabin to myself, presumably thanks to field rank, and shall be pretty comfortable. Judging by the dinner they gave us tonight, we are going to live extremely well . . . One course tonight was duck and tinned peas. If you have never tried them together do so when you come by a duck and a tin of peas. Mrs Howard, from where I wrote you this am [by this means Bill circumvented the censor for Adeline would have known he was leaving from Liverpool], wanted you to move into the top floor of a big house across the road from her. It is unfortunately unfurnished and in an area almost as likely to get a packet as Grove Road . . . I didn't think you would be interested but had a look at it to please her . . .

Shortly after, the family house at Grove Road, Wallasey, was badly affected by a landmine and Adeline moved out for a few months to the Wirral until it had been repaired. She was, at this time, working as an air-raid warden, as well as being in charge of the local Red Cross. Bill ended this letter to her: 'It will be a longish time before you hear again so don't expect any news for months. Love to Pam, remember me to Edith and Gladys [the maids].'

This voyage was to take him first to India, then Iran and Iraq and thence on to the desert warfare of the North African campaign. He left for India on the day he wrote, and the convoy sailed right round Africa to get there, avoiding the death traps set by the Italians and Germans in the Mediterranean. En route Bill suffered badly from sinusitis, a complaint which put him in hospital in Poona – but only after he had settled his men in.

In a letter to Adeline of May 16th he wrote:

I'm writing this in the hope that it will go some day soon but of course there is no regular mail nowadays. I sent a deferred cable the other day just to let you know I was all right.

I'm writing this in hospital in Poona but am leaving it tomorrow for Kirkee and the regiment. About 2 days before reaching Bombay I got a foul earache which was the beginning of a foul disease called, I think, sinusitis; probably due to bathing in the rather dirty swimming bath on the boat. I held out as long as I could but a week ago was driven in here with violent headache. They took an X-ray and found my whatnots in the head were full of pus, punctured my nose and syringed the atrium and today I feel almost right but a bit weak.

On May 25th, he wrote: 'This is a most demoralising existence. Waited on hand and foot by silent slaves; barbers, tailors and bootmakers in attendance at one's bungalow; a bungalow with a large luxuriously furnished living room, a verandah to sleep on, a bedroom, a dressing room and a bathroom.' He wanted to move out because he thought he was paying too much, as he was still only on English rates of pay with no foreign allowances. On the positive side he had discovered a small local hill with '20ft of climbable slabs. The rock is rotten, but in rubbers one can get some exercise and amusement of an evening.'

From India his battery were now sent to Iraq – in late May 1941 – equipped with First World War equipment. Since the end of that earlier war Britain had a mandate in a large part of the Middle East (granted by the ill-starred League of Nations), inheriting colonial responsibilities from the collapse of the old Ottoman Empire, which put it in Egypt, Iraq, Persia, Jordan and Palestine. The French held Syria and the Lebanon. This area was of great importance for two reasons: the Suez Canal and access to India, and oil, shortages of which plagued the Germans. On both counts, the Germans were expected to attack – as they were to do along the North African coast.

Despite their poor equipment and thin numbers, the British army presence in this region was vital to the overall strategy at this stage of the war. Bill's job was containment.

They landed at Basra, after a trip up the Persian Gulf in which Bill lent a hand in stoking their troop transport. To Adeline he wrote, explaining:

> Several of the men of my battery are giving a hand in the stokehold.
> The lascar firemen are rather a scratch lot and require assistance.
> I amused myself last night by doing 6 hour spell with them. 10pm
> to 4am. It was not as bad as I expected but then I didn't have to
> work as hard as they did. It was grand working with nothing on
> but a pair of shorts with the sweat streaming down and washing
> off the coal dust.

After a week in Basra, they drove in three stages up the valley of the Tigris to Mosul. 'The march was notable for the mortality rate of the tractors due to overheating by day, and for the number of Arab rifle thieves in the night . . . On this march two men with a Bren gun buried it and slept on it, and the next morning were facing a charge of "losing by neglect" one Bren gun rifle.'

On July 27th, he wrote to Adeline: 'No change here. We seem to be taking root. I hate to think we shall be left to garrison this part of Irak for the duration . . . Did I tell you I had a flip in a Blenheim the other day? Pam would have enjoyed it but I can't say I got much kick out of it.'

They were involved in the tail end of the Syrian campaign to eliminate the Vichy French forces and to secure the region against any possible immediate threat, an impossible task in reality because of the thinness of their forces against the enemy, now in possession of nearby Crete as an invasion platform. The attack did not come, however, and Bill's unit settled down, so much so that Bill had, by the autumn, planted a garden around his tent in Mosul.

> We certainly lived very well. A Syrian contractor, efficient but of
> imperfect morals, looked after the mess and the men's canteen.
> Every Sunday he put on a chicken curry for which guests used to
> come in from far and wide . . . The Syrian wished me to go into
> partnership with him after the war in the turkey export business,
> but whether this was a tribute to my honesty or gullibility I never
> decided . . . For special occasions we imported a superb walnut
> brandy from a monastery in the hills.

The work was routine – the kind that Bill hated more than anything else. In these circumstances he believed he was rotting away, and certainly not doing his duty, other than by his men, whom he looked after fiercely and protectively. His superiors, who would have no doubt been aware of the contents of his letter of November 11th via the censor, might well have made another mark against Bill's promotion prospects.

In part, this letter said: 'The men have a grudge, and a legitimate one too, in that they have had no green envelopes since they have been here. A green envelope is not censored in the unit and so these are much appreciated by men who naturally dislike putting all their private feelings in letters which will be read by their officers . . .'

In the same letter he expressed his fury that the regimental HQ had tried to get him to detail his men to help build a mess for the officers, work he considered to be outside their duties; this, too, would have prejudiced his chances of promotion. In this regard Bill showed distinct 'bolshie' tendencies; his later career as a guerrilla is the best illustration of where he was heading.

Back home Adeline – who was getting mail about two months after Bill wrote it (as he was from her) – had moved back to Grove Road. Bill wrote: 'Touching to see the familiar address . . . I admire your guts. Still I think it's no more than one should do and I dislike those people who go to the country and stay there; it will not do the moneyed people any good after the war.'

In the relaxed circumstances of Iraq, it was not surprising that Bill's thoughts turned to climbing. 'In Mosul I had met a friend from India who had thoughtfully come to war with his ice-axe and I was able to borrow that essential implement.' Bill's ostensible reason for sloping off was the soaring price of charcoal (used for heating), supplied from out of the hills to the north of Mosul. 'An official inquiry into the charcoal business at the source was as good an excuse as any for a week in the mountains.'

Bill took two of his men with him and they set out in February 1942 in a fifteen-hundredweight truck. Apart from the borrowed ice-axe, Bill had bought a thirty-foot clothes-line for use as a climbing rope. Their destination was Amadia but they had to leave the truck well short of this village and, using mules, which Bill borrowed from a priest, they walked on. 'After a tiring march we camped about four miles short of Amadia in a spot which had few attractions other than its proximity to the shapely snow and rock peak on which I had had my eyes all day.'

The next day, leaving his men in camp, Bill climbed this peak 'of almost Alpine standard'. Later, he took the men up it as well but they declined the 'spectacular summit ridge'. There is a hint of contempt in Bill's account of this, along with his determination to let the reader know he climbed this peak twice, the first time on the day his two companions had had to stay in camp to rest after their long march. Bill, whilst usually careful not to boast sometimes, and perhaps understandably, cannot help but make his point.

But, apart from this diversion, life in Iraq was becoming very dull. It was with some relief, then, that Bill took up the offer of a brigadier to inspect the defences in Persia (modern Iran). While on this excursion Bill found another mountain, Bisitun, a 10,000-footer, and he climbed it, the last part alone and in the dark. 'There is no more satisfying ending to a climb than to spend the night on the mountains, preferably on the top. The bond between man and mountain, forged in a day-long struggle, never seems so strong as when at its close you seek the meagre shelter of some rocky overhang near the summit with which you have been striving all day to get on terms.'

On his way down Bill had what he called a 'memorable' bathe. As these are scattered throughout his life here is his full description, from *When Men and Mountains Meet*, of what ingredients they must contain.

To qualify, the first essential is for the bather to be really hot and tired. Then, if not sea-water, the water must be clear, deep, and cool (or otherwise have some unusual compensating feature), so that as it closes over one's head the whole body seems to absorb its clean, refreshing goodness. To make this clear, a bathe in the Dead Sea, for example, would not be refreshing but might qualify as unusual. Lastly, and this is important, one must be stark naked, with no clinging costume to impair the unity of body and water.

By May, Bill had moved with his regiment to Habbaniya, the RAF station west of Baghdad. Meanwhile, in the North African desert the British 8th Army were to suffer their disastrous defeat in the desert and at Tobruk. Almost every day field regiments were leaving the 9th Army (of which he was a part) for the North African campaign. And so for Bill's regiment too, came orders to move south and then west.

Seven days after quitting Habbaniya we joined an Indian Infantry Brigade near Mersa Matruh over 1,000 miles away. In two days we had crossed the Syrian desert, the Jordan and Palestine. After a much needed halt of one day on the coast for rest and maintenance, we carried on southwards through the Sinai desert to the Canal, jammed in a stream of reinforcements moving down from Syria.

Bill noted, 'There are no mountains in the western desert.' For the next few months, until the defeat of the Germans at El Alamein, it was to be all fighting.

At first, Bill was ordered to form a 'Jock' column, an ad hoc detachment of modern twenty-five-pounder guns with two-pounder anti-tank guns for protection, along with a battalion or company of infantry as support. The British army was in full retreat after the fall of Tobruk on June 20th, pursued now not by the Italians but by Rommel and his Afrika Korps. The 'Jock' columns were a desperate stop-gap measure while the Alamein line was being prepared. Bill and his 'Jock' column found themselves 'swanning about' in the desert west of the undefended minefield which ran from Mersa Matruh to Siwa

Oasis. Their orders were to stop at any cost approaching enemy tank columns.

'The first shots fired came as something of an anti-climax,' he later wrote.

Although there was a thin screen of armoured cars a few miles to the west between us and the enemy, whenever we halted we invariably brought the guns into action ready to fire. During one of these halts, a vehicle, apparently a British 2 pr *portee* [a gun carried on a three-ton lorry] was seen approaching. An officer drove out to exchange news and promptly had his truck (an armoured OP) holed by the 2pr. The whole battery of eight guns incontinently opened up, but the stranger escaped untouched. Our difficulty was that the Germans had captured so many of our vehicles that we could never quite believe what we saw.

The next day, from a safer position behind the minefield they were attacked by artillery and thirty tanks, the latter standing off and shooting 'hull down'. After three hours of this they had suffered forty casualties although all the British guns were still in action. Despite earlier orders saying they were not to retreat, at sundown they were given permission to withdraw. All around them British batteries were being overrun. Even so, their problems were not over. On the retreat they lost a gun. 'It was all the more galling to lose one of them during the subsequent night march when it parted company with its trailer. The surprise and chagrin of the sergeant of the gun when, at the first halt, he discovered there was nothing behind his tractor, would in other circumstances have been funny.'

Their next serious fight was two days later at Fuka after the fall of Mersa Matruh. This time the whole brigade was involved. The Germans attacked towards dusk, with the sun behind them, and they quickly overwhelmed the British lines. They captured both the regimental HQ and the infantry brigade defending it, but Bill managed to get his own guns clear, the result finally of his 'higher authority' realising that the guns were, at that stage, far more important than losing local battles.

Bill's little group of guns went back to being a 'Jock' column again.

Alarms and excursions at all hours of the day and night, retreats and advances, shellings and being shelled, with on the whole never a dull moment, was the order of our existence. One can laugh now, but at the time the laughter was a bit hollow. I remember driving up to within two hundred yards of a tank, in response to a beckoning figure on the turret, before spotting its black cross; and at another time approaching on foot a ridge which we had intended using as an observation post and hearing an enemy vehicle coming up the other side, obviously with the same intention; and I recall how we lay in close leaguer on a dark night watching an enemy column pass a few hundred yards away.

But it was warfare that suited Bill: all fast movement with small mobile columns; plenty of action and loads of initiative, the kind of getting out of tight spots he had long known and understood in mountaineering. It meant working closely with his men, too, and must, in that respect at least, have felt like the First World War, when as a young subaltern he had lived and fought alongside his troopers. He wrote, glowingly, 'all felt like members of a family; so that when we were having a bad time, or in retreat, there was, as there always should be with good troops, a more comradely helpful spirit abroad than the "devil take the hindmost" air of a successful advance.'

Even better for Bill was the lack of control from the top.

At no time, to descend to a more material plane, did the battery ever live so well as during the days on column. There was no interfering HQ to blunt the edge of initiative, to ask silly questions, and to demand irritating, tell-tale returns. Wandering about as we did in a more or less trackless waste, here one minute and gone the next, it may seem odd that we fed so well, or that we were able to draw adequate supplies of petrol, water and ammunition; but so it was, and the Supply services of the Indian Division with whom we served were always able to meet our requirements once we had established contact.

He added that they were blessed by having a battery captain with a Falstaffian mind, a man constantly on the lookout for supply points from which he drew freely. It was easy in these circumstances to raid these supply points because no one at HQ knew who was operating or where. 'We no longer wondered whether we had enough milk or sugar for tea with each meal. The amount we drank was limited solely by the amount of water available, and every halt which seemed likely to last longer than twenty minutes was the signal to "brew up".'

All good things have to come to an end. In Bill's case it was when they finally dug themselves in on Ruweisat Ridge, 'connected ourselves by telephone to various inquisitive and interfering headquarters from division downwards'. This was then at the start of the first phase of the battle of El Alamein, the defensive positions the British held at the end of July 1942. Rommel failed to break through these and in November the British counter-attacked. Now, Bill's unit was in the devil take the hindmost advance which would sweep the Germans finally out of North Africa.

He was still managing his letters home to Adeline. In August 1942, he wrote: 'I had a letter from Odell y'day. The previous one was written on his way out to India, this one on his way home. He doesn't say why but I suspect it may be due to his having reached the retiring age. Eric [Shipton] I believe has left his post of Consul at Kashgar but I have not yet discovered what he is doing. Love to Joan and Pam.'

Pam and Joan, Adeline's daughters, are a constant reference in Bill's letters home. He always much preferred Pam, whom he saw all through his life as a woman after his own heart. Of Joan he is often dismissive, as he is, too, of her husband. In September 1942, in the thick of the North African advance of the 8th Army, he wrote home: 'I had a letter from Joan from Blackpool dated June 29th. Neither of them seem to be doing anything of much use. I suppose they think you are doing enough for three.'

The 8th Army was now in hot pursuit of Rommel's Afrika Korps. The end of 1942 would see the Allies finally triumphant in North Africa and, in every sense, it was a turning point. Perhaps partly as a result Bill could write: 'Only once, immediately after the breakthrough in early November, did we come near to recapturing that "first fine careless rapture". But our share in the pursuit was short-lived, and we spent a bleak, cheerless winter at El Adem, near Tobruk, clearing the old battlefield of Knightsbridge.'

From here they moved steadily westwards, mopping up the remnants of the Afrika Korps, until, finally, they reached Tunisia. Here Bill found something he had yearned for ever since the year before, in Persia – a mountain, Zaghouan.

We dropped our trails more or less where we stood. My choice of site for Regimental HQ was possibly influenced by the presence of two German field kitchens, one with its copper full of a stew ready for dishing up, the other containing a slightly overdone rice pudding. By late evening the Germans in Zaghouan had come to heel, but the French Commander mistrusted them, and insisted on our remaining at half-hour's notice. Naturally, since coming into those parts from the 8th Army front near the coast I had had my eye on Zaghouan, the only mountain I had seen since Bisitun. Many long broken limestone ridges help to form a striking mass which, on the north and west sides, rises abruptly from the Tunis plain.

Thinking it was now or never, he set off with one of his battery commanders, promising the CO, from whom he had obtained permission, that they would be back before dawn. They took with them a German equivalent of a Verey light pistol: 'the big idea behind this was to have a Brock's benefit on the mountain summit to celebrate the victory.'

Climbing an unknown mountain in the dark was as hazardous as Bill had suspected it might be, even when the peak in question was a mere

4000 feet. Stumbling up (and occasionally down) they found their Verey pistol most useful for firing off red and green flares to show them the way.

Some of these broke into pleasing clusters of stars, but these were not of much value as pathfinders. I have since learned all about German light signals. By a simple system you can tell by touch, in the dark, the various colours and types . . . The 'Fallschirm', or parachute flare (which would have been just the thing for us), has a parachute in relief on the top. There is also a 'Pfeifpatrone', or whistling flare, which has a point on the top. Unluckily we had none of these. A shriek of dismay from the light as it hovered over the chasm (which they had nearly fallen into) would have been an artistic touch.

On the top, near to dawn, they ate some German rations, of which Bill approved. To the east a battery was firing the last shots of the North African campaign; Bill's lyricism at such moments wished to soar like an eagle and describe the scene below but his sharp sense of the absurd forced him to admit, when he finally wrote about this climb, that 'unluckily a blanket of cloud hid everything.'

This anticlimax was followed by disillusionment. The truck by which they had arrived at the site of the climb had been pillaged by the local French mercenary troops, the Goums. Their driver had slept right through this assault. Among the items missing was one of Bill's last pipes. As Bill wrote: 'One might say of the Goums, as Stonewall Jackson said of his Texans: "The hens have to roost mighty high when the Texans are about."'

The African campaign was over; the invasion of Italy was being planned. Bill, now forty-five, was still a major while many of his contemporaries had been promoted to brigadier, colonel or even major-general. Bill, with his long distinguished fighting career and with his wide experience of warfare in a number of theatres, never achieved a higher rank. Why not? is the obvious question.

The answer, according to Bill, was simple:

It may be an odd view, but I think one drawback to the army is that promotion is almost inevitable. No one is allowed to remain where he is; once having set foot on the slippery slope of promotion he must either go up or down. That is possibly why so many good men refuse to accept a stripe, and prefer to remain in a position of important permanence at the bottom. In the Artillery the command of a battery is the best that life affords. It is a post a right-minded gunner would wish to hold for ever; once beyond that he feels that it is a case of 'farewell the tranquil mind, farewell content'.

Even at the head of a battery he still has both feet on the ground, in close contact with men and the seamy side of war; he is still on the right side of the gulf which separates those who plan from those who act, and which is crossed immediately he becomes part of a Headquarters – even the modest headquarters of a regiment.

From the throne to the scaffold is a short step; short and equally decided is the transition to Second-in-Command of a regiment – the ultimate end of a Battery Commander. Though the appointment carries with it an extra 6d a day, it is the equivalent of the Chiltern Hundreds so far as any active responsibility is concerned. It is a stagnant pool, from which in the fullness of time and chance he may be fished up to command a regiment itself, but the unlucky or unworthy may float there for long enough gathering seaweed or barnacles.

Bill had been 'promoted' to Acting CO of his regiment in November 1942, when his CO had been posted to the division, temporarily. He hated it, and bombarded his seniors with requests to be allowed to return to his battery. No doubt that, as a result of this odd behaviour, he was (according to him) marked as 'not recommended for promotion'.

There were other odd things, too. He wrote to Adeline, on December 27th: 'I am still defying dress regulations by wearing shorts instead of Battle Dress.' He continued, in a heavily humorous vein which might well have escaped Adeline: 'We had an inspection by the Corps Commander, one Horrocks, before Xmas. There was the usual upheaval and stirring of muddy waters which brought many queer things to light so it does that much good. Now the waters are still and the mud is settling again. This, by the way, is metaphorical.'

Earlier in that month he had had leave, in Alexandria, where he had spent a lot of time at the dentist's having a new plate made for his false teeth. 'I still cling to my own teeth below,' he told Adeline, 'but on top only have one survivor. The dentist I went to was a Russian and so was the woman who ran a peculiar sort of Turkish Bath place, only they were vapour baths, and one sat up to the neck in a cabinet like one used to have long long ago.'

There now came a hiatus in his wartime career and one which must have given him much pause for thought. The issue remained his promotion – quite possibly to command his regiment. On March 1st, 1943, however, he believed he had solved this problem. He wrote home: [I have] signified my intention of remaining as Major for the duration, and am now listed as "not recommended for promotion".'

Under normal circumstances, then, he might have remained where he was, in an RA unit, as a passed-over major, commanding his battery as it fought its way through Italy and the rest of the war. Legend now plays a part in the story but it is such a good legend that I pass it on without comment. The suspicious biographer has to add, however, that this is a story thought to have come from Bill himself.

The story goes like this. While acting as CO of his regiment Bill one day in 1943 received two signals. One asked if Major Tilman could be recommended for promotion to command a regiment. The other asked for volunteer officers who could be put forward for special training, involving their being dropped behind enemy lines.

According to legend Bill wrote about himself that no, he could not recommend Major Tilman as fit for any job other than commanding a battery; to the other he replied that yes, Major Tilman was the man for parachute training and, with his mountain experience, perfect for operating behind enemy lines in mountainous terrain. Normally, such a suggestion would have been endorsed by his commanding officer; here Tilman could follow a true Catch 22 situation and endorse (and condemn) himself. True or false, he sent in an application for special forces training.

Or, as he wrote:

Having drawn my 6d a day in such an uncongenial post for several months I was prompted to answer an advertisement in General Routine Orders, which, in the Army, corresponds to the Agony Column of *The Times*. Volunteers were wanted for Special Service of a kind which involved almost complete independence. Better to reign in Hell than serve in Heaven, I thought, as I wrote out my application.

At forty-five, Bill might well have been thought too old for such derring-do as was likely to be required. But special forces are just that; above all the obvious qualities (like super fitness, on which ground Bill had no trouble), the requirement was for resourceful loners, who could very much make do and mend, who could suffer great privation for long periods. In the two theatres Bill was to operate in, up to the end of the war, Albania and northern Italy, one other quality was desirable: mountaineering skills. Bill, far from being past it, was a perfect choice.

CHAPTER 10

Albania

Bill's goodbye to his regiment came in August 1943. Before that he had had to endure the arrival of a new CO. In July he wrote home: 'The new CO is beginning to show his hand now that my restraining influence is removed. Turn-up of shirt-sleeves to be exactly 3 inches, shorts to touch the upper knee-cap etc. What fun they will have.' He asked Adeline to pass on his commiserations to Pam who had failed to get into the ATA on the grounds of height – what nonsense, he wrote, no doubt thinking of his own short stature.

Before he was sent for special training he had some leave in Cairo. On August 1st he wrote from Heliopolis: 'I am sitting this sabbath afternoon, on the verandah with nothing on. A cricket match, which I can't see very well, is in progress across the road.'

The training that Bill underwent for his new role as a member of the special forces took place in Haifa. There, he found he was the oldest, by far, of the group. The training was tough but he enjoyed it. By August 1943 he had passed the course and he was sent to Libya, from where Halifax aircraft made the journey into occupied Europe. His mission, codenamed Sculptor, consisted of himself, and two NCOs, one expert at bridge-blowing and the other a wireless operator.

They left Derna on August 9th, taking four hours to reach the dropping zone. At this stage of the war Italy had been invaded and, to quote Bill, 'was already on its knees and appeared likely to throw in the towel at any moment'. It was Italy that had invaded Albania and Bill, glad though he was to be on this mission, feared that there would be little for them to do other than stop the Albanians from massacring the Italians. How wrong he was proved to be.

We had an uneventful flight, but if there is any charm in flying at night, which I doubt, it is quite spoilt if you know that presently you will have literally to take a leap in the dark. At the energetic prompting of an efficient dispatcher we dropped through the large

141

hole in the floor and, shortly after, we had all landed safely but rather wide of the target.

We had a warm reception, and having walked from the dropping ground to their village headquarters, we sat down to fried eggs and sweet champagne at three in the morning. My principal feeling was one of intense satisfaction at having at length got back to Europe, even though it was enemy occupied, after so long in the wilderness. I could almost have hugged the ground.

Bill had not been home on leave since March 1941 and he was not to go home to England until after it was over, an absence of six years. One may here pause to wonder why this should be so. Apart from ideas of duty – which Bill had in abundance – it does seem curious that he chose to fight out his war in this rather lonely fashion. The answer would appear to be that he was afraid of going home, afraid of what he would find, and afraid that he would not want to return to the fray. Bill's psyche had a fragility in it, a soft side, against which he constantly armed himself. Here, in part, lies his reason for never getting emotionally entangled with women. Its origin, apart from its owner's genetic make-up, may be found in Bill's experiences of the First World War. He found it much easier all through his life to communicate by letters – hundreds, thousands of them, sent like clockwork. For Bill, a written word provided that degree of distance he needed and, unsurprisingly, he was able thus to communicate with considerable affection.

In Albania, though, in 1943, Bill found emotions aplenty; chiefly, these revolved around the internecine disputes between the various factions ostensibly fighting the invaders.

If it is true that 'happy is the nation that has no history', then Albania must be one of the unhappiest. Her history is an unbroken record of invasion, oppression, and wrong by the Turk, Greek, Austrian, Serbian, Bulgarian and German. Few countries can have been so ravaged and so subjected to oppression at the hands of its stronger neighbours, and yet have retained its will for independence unbroken as did the Albanians for 500 years.

This fierceness, however, meant that 'tribal' arguments were everywhere to be found, a Balkan nightmare. The country was mountainous and feudal – a feudalism blended in an unholy mixture with tribalism. Bill was dropped in the south of the country, where the mountains followed a simple plan with two wide open valleys running from south-east to north-west. This gave easy access, particularly to Greece, and in this region Greek influence was strong. Muslims outnumbered Christians, but they were, Bill thought, 'philosophical' rather than religious Muslims and, as he discovered frequently, had no imperative against strong drink.

His problem was far more intractable. It was that the guerrillas were utterly divided. In the first place was the LNC, the Levizja Nacional Clirimtare, or National Liberation Movement, run by the communists and embracing 'all classes, all political opinions, all religions, and a good three-quarters of the people of south Albania'. The objective of this worthy force was simple: the defeat of Nazism and Fascism and the establishment of a free independent democratic Albania. For these aims, Bill noted, they were prepared to sacrifice everything.

But, being the Balkans, there were other groups in the arena, the principal force being the Balli Kombetar, or National Front, who regarded their chief opponents as the Yugoslavs and the Greeks. 'Under an outward show of resistance they were prepared to temporise with the Axis powers, and were not willing to incur suffering by an unnecessary display of zeal in a cause which would probably triumph without the aid of Albania.' A third group, not so important at the time Bill arrived, but becoming more so, was that of the Royalists, supporters of the exiled (in London) King Zog. 'Both these latter parties took Mr Facing-both-ways as their model,' wrote Bill.

Official British policy, as with so many other countries' partisans they were helping, was to supply arms to any resistance movement, and not make what were thought to be political judgments. The problem was that, all over occupied Europe, the most effective resistance was being organised by communists, who were far more dedicated and ruthless in their pursuit of the enemy, not least because the Nazi and Fascist ideologies were so acutely in opposition to their own beliefs.

Bill, whose interest in politics remained vague all through his life (he was, naturally, a British Conservative voter), merely wished to prosecute the war and, both in Albania and Italy, later, backed the communist partisans because they clearly were the best soldiers. After Albania, this soldierly simplicity towards the political situation was, in his own words, to get him the 'sack'.

In Albania, the British had positioned liaison officers with each group. Bill wrote later: 'It was the peculiar tragedy of Albania that this well-meaning policy was persisted in after it had become clear to most observers that these differences were fundamental, and even when only one of the parties was fighting and suffering while the other two were either actively hostile or feebly neutral.' It also meant at one absurd point that arms dropped to the Balli Kombetar were handed over to the Germans by them.

After a week getting to know all this, and much more besides, Bill decided that the LNC were the people to back and, accordingly, he elected to go to the Gjinokastre area, not far from the coast and from the Greek island of Corfu. They travelled cross-country, using mules and taking three days. They were well received on their journey and ate well. There was no sign of a war until they reached Permet, garrisoned by the Italians.

Close to Permet they were challenged.

With one exception they seemed suspicious of our *bona fides*. The exception was a voluble little man, not unlike Charlie Chaplin, who had once owned a restaurant in Tirana, and who now attached himself to us, unbidden, in the role of chef to the mission. Though not unmindful of his own wages and trade perquisites, he filled this post very satisfactorily for three or four months. His pastry was ethereal, his soups substantial; the mission at Shepr, where we lived, earned a well-deserved reputation for good fare.

Disaster came when various bits of parachute silk were found in his house. Condemned to be shot, it took all Bill's skills to save him. Bill wrote to Adeline about this sequence of events:

I have got a new cook. The last one left under a cloud and has been sentenced to be shot (not by me) but I got him off, perhaps an error. The new one has cooked for Royalty but I don't think he will have the opportunity for doing that again. I'm thinking of bringing him home with me and opening the — Restaurant in Soho with a special cheap lunch, the 'partisan lunch'. I'll receive them in a dinner jacket, you can sit behind and take the cash.

Have you done anything about Lent this year or has it been done for you by a loving Govt? Tobacco very nearly gave me up had not a supply arrived in the nick of time but I have given up drinking saki which was a considerable sacrifice when one considers its cheapness, palatability, alcoholic content, the long evenings, the lack of company . . .

Love to Joan and Pam – ever yours – Bill

The letter, the only one to get out of Albania, is dated January (1944), when Bill had been going through a very bad patch fighting the Germans, who had swept in to replace the Italians. In Shepr, where Bill had finally settled his mission, they had rented a house for one gold sovereign a month. They found the local partisans to be willing but weak in organisation, and badly armed. 'Nearly every man had a rifle, captured, stolen, or inherited, which might be of Italian, German, Greek, Russian, Austrian, or French origin; but except for a few Italian light machine-guns there were no automatic weapons.'

But what they lacked in guns, the Albanians made up for in spirit: 'Even in those early days I was impressed by the camaraderie and *esprit de corps* of the various battalions and "chetas", the easy-going relations between men and leaders, and the severity of the discipline. For immorality, theft, looting, or even failing to put into the common pool what had been captured from the enemy, the penalty was death.' There was, though, little action at this stage.

I first saw the partisans in action in a night attack on Libohov, a small town on the opposite side of the Dhrino valley to Gjinokastre. A garrison of fifty Italians lived there in the Citadel, and it was the home of many prominent Balli. My part in the action was to prevent the arrival of reinforcements from Gjinokastre by mining the earth road which connects Libohov with the main road, but from what I had heard of the Italians in Albania, the last thing which the garrison of Gjinokastre would be likely to do was to stir from the barracks after dark.

It was a bold but futile effort, Bill wrote. Six partisans were killed, largely because of the huge quantity of rifle and mortar fire in the dark; but the result, apart from a few burned houses of the Balli, was that the Italian garrison remained in their fortress. This was the only action of its kind that Bill took part in before, on September 8th, they heard news of the Italian collapse.

This posed a serious problem for Bill and his mission; they now had a very short period in which to get, or if necessary to buy, as many arms from the Italians as possible before the Germans arrived, as they inevitably would. The Gjinokastre area was garrisoned by the Perugia division, commanded by a General Ernesto Chiminello; he had 5000 men and a mule battery of eight 75 mm mountain guns under him. Bill sent him a letter, asking him to come to Cepo, six miles down the valley from Gjinokastre, to discuss surrender terms.

It was, as Bill admitted, a very cheeky offer. The partisan group with which he was operating had about 200 lightly armed men and the Italians could, in reality, do what they pleased. So it turned out, a complication for Bill being that the Balli Kombetar were also instructing the Italians to surrender their arms to them.

At length our patience was exhausted and on the 14th we all marched by night towards Gjinokastre. The partisans, whose numbers had swollen to 500, took up positions in a ravine about 1,000 yards from the northern perimeter of the barracks, and Badri [the partisan leader] and I with a small escort climbed up to the fortified outpost ridge and passed through the wire under a white flag. From the ridge, which was strongly held, we looked down on the fine modern barracks, the vehicles and guns neatly parked. Our mouths watered, like Blucher's at the sight of London. The company holding the ridge were bewildered but friendly.

145

Negotiations with the general were protracted but largely fruitless. Mindful of how close the Germans now were, Bill tried to put pressure on the Italian officers; tempers were frayed, even though the Italians provided lunch for Bill and his partisans, while they argued among themselves. Eventually, though, Bill received a 'terse' note saying the Italians would not give up their arms. 'Feeling rather foolish, we left, and we had not got back to our lines before heavy firing broke out on the main road.' This died down and the partisans were left to wonder what to do.

Finally Bill decided to cut off the garrison water supply and left to return to Shepr to get a more general situation report. Then, on his return to the Italian lines, he found the worst had happened: the Italians had burned what they could not carry and marched to the coast, to the port of Saranda, which they had reached unhindered.

Before he chased after them, Bill made a diversion to the Greek frontier, across which the German army would be likely to come, and blew a bridge he found there.

The piers were 6 ft thick, but the builder had thoughtfully provided holes in them for demolition charges. With my six partisans acting as a covering party I hastily rammed 35lbs of powerful explosive into each of two piers and connected the charges with a length of detonating fuse. Just as all was ready some Greeks from the nearby village appeared, took in the situation at a glance, and launched an indignant protest on behalf of the doomed bridge. It was of no particular value to them, they said, but if the Germans found the bridge blown they would certainly burn the nearest village, which happened to be theirs. I quite saw their point, but war is war.

Bill blew the bridge, noting, 'I ran back to survey the work of my 'prentice hand with the modest pride becoming to an amateur in crime. The bridge had "had it in a big way".' It was the first act of sabotage he had committed. On the way back to Gjinokastre he celebrated this success by burning a wooden bridge they had crossed, although, in both cases, he knew it would hardly stop the coming German onslaught.

Later, in Saranda, where Bill found his Italian general still hoping to get away, the reopened negotiations over arms were more successful. The Italians now agreed to surrender all but their small arms and to defend the town against any German attack, although Bill was doubtful if the demoralised Italian squaddies would have fulfilled this obligation.

It hardly mattered. Two thousand of the 5000 troops had been embarked when the newly arrived troopship for the rest was bombed and sunk by German Stukas. Later, Bill heard that General Chiminello and his officers had been captured by the Germans and shot. A curiosity, for Bill, was that the Albanians took pity on the many Italian troops left behind wandering in the countryside, starving, and took many of them on as farm labourers over the winter.

Meanwhile the Germans, after a delay, were pouring into Albania and Bill and his partisans had to move from Shepr. He moved to Cepo, knowing the Germans would soon take Gjinokastre, briefly 'liberated' by the partisans. There, he discovered that most of the Italian arms handed over to the partisans had fallen into German hands. Badri had decided to fight it out with the German advance columns at Tepeleni, a few miles to the north, a futile but brave decision.

On the morning of 1 October, I watched the long-expected German column drive past. From the monastery spur several miles of white ribbon of road were in sight before it disappeared round a corner just short of the bridge about to be blown. Headed by motor-cyclists and staff cars, sixty troop-carrying vehicles and two 115mm guns crossed the bridge at the bottom of the Cepo valley.

After the bridge had been partially blown and battle had been joined down the valley, Bill noted with great sorrow the way the Germans took their reprisals.

A small cluster of houses at the foot of our valley was wantonly burned by men from the vehicle park. Although they were a bare 500 yards from our outposts, the partisans held their fire. It is possible to write calmly enough about burning villages, but when we actually see men at work setting fire to one peaceful, familiar little homestead after another, the rising flames, the roofs falling in, and the labour and loving care of years dissolving irretrievably in a few minutes, it is impossible not to experience a hot wave of dismay, revulsion and hate. To watch fires caused by bombing and shelling is bad enough, but guns and planes seem impersonal and their effects do not rouse the same intense feeling.

Winter was now coming on and the months that followed were confused, dangerous and difficult for Bill and his mission. During September and October 1943, the partisans were getting about three or four plane-loads of equipment a month. The dropping ground was close to Shepr and the squadron of Halifaxes undertaking these difficult missions drew the highest praise from Bill. 'One night we had three planes over the target at the same time, their headlights full on to avoid colliding. The valley looked like Croydon on a busy night, and I wondered what the Germans in Gjinokastre thought of it.'

Between these air drops, Bill reported that life had become indecently dull and placid. He and his two men were eating three good meals a day,

147

visiting neighbouring villages, helping train partisans in explosive use and 'argued more or less amiably with various people who came to see us'. Most of these arguments revolved around the policies of the Allies in indiscriminately supporting the other factions in Albania, and when the British intended to invade.

Bill took to making long journeys, 'travelling fast, living hard, and always returning with increased zest to the masterpieces of Cesio our cook'. On these trips he dispensed with the large escort the partisans liked to provide, taking only one guide, Mehmet, of whom Bill was to say that 'he was uncannily clever in the dark and could follow the faintest of paths on the blackest of nights. He was intelligent, active, stout-hearted, cheerful, good at driving a bargain, a good mixer and a good walker,' adding to this account that most Albanians were not good walkers.

Bill believed one of the reasons for this was their great love of the fresh spring water which gushed out of the limestone mountains. 'In summer it is quite impossible to get an Albanian past one of these springs. They are great water connoisseurs, and will distinguish between the excellence of one village and another solely by its water.' He also noted that they rarely shed any clothes so that, again in summer, a walk of any distance left them sweating and exhausted. Even Mehmet followed this tradition: 'I don't think I saw him with his shirt off more than once. I believe he thought it indelicate.'

On one trip with Mehmet, to Valona to send a signal as their own wireless had broken down, they had a number of adventures. One was with the Vlach (gypsy) dogs which chased them. The stones Bill and Mehmet flung they simply tried to catch; in the end Mehmet had to use his sten gun to chase them off. Bill, the dog lover, was pleased even so that the results were not fatal. In the villages they passed through where there were no partisans, Mehmet would go to the headman 'who either took us in himself or sought out for us the best accommodation'. It has to be remembered that, in doing this, these villagers risked their lives. The Germans, had they heard of these acts of kindness, would have certainly burned the village and killed its inhabitants.

It was on this trip that they came across thousands of Italian soldiers, abandoned by both their own command and by the Germans, but looked after, in a fashion, by the LNC. Later, close to their destination, they had to pass through strongholds of the Balli. Such was the animosity between the LNC and the Balli that Mehmet only got Bill safely through by pretending he was a German officer.

We finally ran the mission to earth in a leaky hut on the summit of the high ridge which separated the Shushice valley from the sea.

In an area where sympathies were so mixed their position was unenviable; after doing his utmost to work with both parties, according to instructions, the officer concerned eventually elected to champion the cause of the Balli. This had unfortunate results for everybody. He established a sea base in some caves on the rocky coast of the Karabarun peninsula, known later to us as Seaview, where in time a good many tons of arms and ammunition were landed. As in the meantime the Balli had become so flagrantly unfriendly, the distribution of these arms to them was banned; but since they held all the land approaches to Seaview, the arms could not be issued to the LNC. So they lay there uselessly until in the end the base was betrayed to the Germans, who stepped in and took the lot.

By the end of the year, however, despite these setbacks, five mobile brigades were in being in the region and Bill was being exhorted to establish a sea base in the territory controlled by these partisans. He lighted upon Grava Bay, whence a track led to the town of Kuc, from where supplies could easily be distributed. To get to the bay Bill and Mehmet had to undertake another long journey. On the way they passed the steel bridge at Tepeleni 'upon which I should very much have liked to have tried my hand', Bill wrote. But the bridge was the only link between Gjinokastre and Kelcyra where there was a large grain store on which the people of Gjinokastre depended. Bill stilled his explosive desires.

Reaching the village of Brataj, he discovered that a state of war now existed between the local Balli and the LNC. The local commander, another Mehmet, and an ardent communist, was not pleased when he found out where Bill intended to go and he doubted, in any case, whether they would get through the village of Dukati where they intended to pick up a guide for the rest of their trek.

He himself talked at length but he was far outdone by a young woman on the Brigade staff. Her manners were offhand, her appearance was a 'check to loose behaviour', and she poured out an incessant stream of parrot-like propaganda until after midnight. There was only one bed in the room the brigade staff occupied, and I made no bones about accepting when they offered it to me. The woman slept under it. At dawn next morning Mehmet and I stole silently away without so much as a 'Goodbye' to avoid reawakening that terrible tongue.

In Dukati they were politely received 'though there were black looks when they heard with whom I was working'. The leader of the Ballis was, Bill reported, quite candid in his attitude. They were close to the main coast road (and thus German reprisals) and he had no intention of doing anything which might provoke them. Their ambition, he said, was to keep themselves alive and unburnt in their village until the war ended, when they had hopes of a British mission arriving to sort out

149

the factions. Meanwhile, as the Germans opposed communists, it was obvious why they gave them an occasional hand against the LNC.

None the less, Bill got his guide to Seaview and they found the mission they sought, although 'a disinterested listener in the cave that night might have thought that representatives of the Balli and the LNC in British uniform were telling each other a few home truths.' Bill was careful not to condemn his fellow British officers in this regard but, as he says, 'I have found it difficult to exclude a preference for men who fought on the same side as ourselves' (i.e., the LNC).

On their way back from this encounter, Bill and Mehmet ran into the battle for Dukati, now joined between the Ist Brigade of LNC partisans and the Balli.

We were too tired for any more detours so we pushed on recklessly over bare grass slopes, hoping to get within speaking distance of the partisans before they shot us down at long range. Suddenly a shout rang out and we found ourselves covered by a machine-gun and several rifles 100 yards off. In spite of his parched throat and some excusable nervousness Mehmet waxed loud, eloquent and convincing. We were not known to them personally, but they sent us under escort to Mehmet Schio with whom we had a few recriminatory words for not having warned us more explicitly of his intentions.

Bill eventually found Grava Bay, but the landing site became 'pie in the sky' as the Royal Navy judged it to be too open to the prevailing southern wind. Stores, meanwhile, kept on piling up at Seaview, under Balli control, and it was not until May 1944, months later, that supplies were landed at Grava. Bill made a sortie to Grava Bay in January, where he waited for three days but, as always, he was anxious to get back to Shepr. It was at Shepr that he learned that the head of the British missions to Albania had been captured; this was a great blow, for Bill had hoped that he would have been able to influence Brigadier Davies to stop the even-handed policy and to throw whole-hearted support behind the LNC.

While all this was going on another signal came: 'a trifling sum new added to the foot of Bill's account' to paraphrase one of his own favourite sayings. This was to the effect that a party of ten American women nurses and twenty orderlies who had made a forced landing near Berat were on their way to Shepr for evacuation. 'They reached Shepr in charge of a British officer, the nurses in good heart and looks, the orderlies – big stalwart men – tired bedraggled, and depressed.'

Bill tried to get them away from the airfield at Gjinokastre but the Germans arrived at the wrong moment. Then, to Bill's utter astonishment one day, while they were still waiting, eighteen Lightning fighters, a Wellington bomber and two C47 transports came roaring down as if to land. Fortunately the British officer in charge refused to give the landing signal.

Later Bill found out that the officer in charge in Italy had got bored and had simply sent the planes without reference to Albania.

> Since there were a couple of armoured cars on the main road just across the river, he [the British officer] rightly refused to give the signal for the planes to land, in spite of the hysterical pleading of his flock. A subsequent attempt to get away by sea was successful. Thus after two months of more or less painful wandering, for the most part patiently borne, they landed in Italy and were made much of.

The winter of 1943–44 in Albania had proved to be a hard time for the partisans. As the weather worsened so the Germans stepped up the level of their activities, helped in many cases by the Balli. Permet was attacked and taken; Shepr, though not burned badly when the Germans came, had been totally ransacked. 'Everything movable had gone, as had all the animals, which were used to carry away the swag. For this, the Balli, who followed the Germans like jackals, led by a man called Ismael Golem, were mainly responsible.' In a village nearby thirty-five old men had been shot as a reprisal for a local ambush.

The radio equipment had been missed but it hardly helped Bill's temper when, receiving the first signal from headquarters after this débâcle he found that its author was expressing a 'considered' opinion that the partisan brigades were expensive to maintain, militarily useless, and politically objectionable. No doubt this signal was one of the items Bill had in mind when he told his superiors, once safely out of Albania, what he thought of their tactics.

The situation got worse, the Germans and the Balli everywhere attacking the LNC and their positions.

> We crossed a high snow pass to the even more miserable village of Progonat, where either through fear or changing sympathies, we met with an indifferent reception. We were not thrown out but, on the other hand, no one would take us in. Cold and wet, we tried one house after another until at last we imposed ourselves almost by force on an elderly couple. Mehmet stuck his foot in the door to prevent them shutting it, while behind it a man and wife almost came to blows with each other on the question of whether we should be admitted or not.

Still later they had a very lucky escape when they were both challenged in dense mist.

Both our Marlin automatics were slung and any attempt to use them would have invited a shot. It was a ticklish problem for Mehmet to solve. If they were Balli and he confessed who we were we should get shot, while if they were partisans and he did *not* say who we were we should likewise be shot. A tense staccato dialogue, which I could not follow, ensued; with Mehmet apparently sparring for time and a clue as to who they might be. The tension gradually relaxed. We walked forward, rather dry-mouthed, to be welcomed by the partisan patrol leader.

But by the spring of 1944 Bill and his mission were having to keep much more alert, even though the improved weather meant that they could move around more easily: 'unrestricted freedom of movement, the *sine qua non* of guerrilla warfare, was once more restored.' By now the Germans were constantly on their tail. In part it was his own activities, small though they might be, which had induced this. For example:

We also started laying mines on the road south from Gjinokastre by which the German garrison brought supplies from their base at Jannina.

I attended the first mine-laying exploit in the capacity of safety officer and umpire. It was chiefly remarkable for the smallness of the bag and as a demonstration of how unlucky a man must be to get a hit at night. About three in the morning a large ten-ton lorry came along and was duly wrecked, whereupon our machine-gun party, carefully posted in a ruin 50 yards away, opened up. The gun, which was Italian, was on its best behaviour that night. For nearly five minutes by the clock the night was rendered hideous, and then in a silence that could be felt, three trembling figures emerged unscathed from underneath the lorry – a German NCO and two Balli. The lorry was empty.

Bill had been ten months in Albania and although he said he was by no means tired of it, he was wearied by the anomalous situation of British support all round. Although the British command had realised, belatedly, their mistake as far as the Balli were concerned, they had now taken to supplying the Royalist Zoggists. For Bill, this was to become academic. On May 18th, 1944, Bill said goodbye to the partisan leader Radowicke and on May 22nd he was evacuated from Grava Bay.

Of the Albanian missions he wrote:

For my part I returned convinced that our policy of giving moral, financial, and material support to the LNC was just and expedient. Unhappily the goodwill thus earned and deserved was offset by the dislike we incurred for supporting the other two parties. At first all were treated equally, but even after two of the three parties had shown themselves to be useless and untrustworthy, we continued to sustain them morally by sending them missions, by refusing to denounce them by name, and by making only obscure references to the deeds and sacrifices of the LNC.

Bill believed that, despite their communist background, the LNC were the only people to back in Albania. 'The resolution they showed through many months of hardship, danger and disappointment, the will to win, their faith in themselves and in their cause, all seemed to me to establish their claim to leadership and to manifest that in them lay the best hope for Albania's future.' It was this view, forcefully expressed back in Bari, that got him the sack. 'I have parted company with my late employers on a matter of policy,' he wrote to Adeline during this mid-summer period, just after D-Day, 'and am now trying to find another job. If everything else fails I shall go back to the Army. Even CO/2 of a regiment would be preferable to rotting in Bari.'

During the summer here he began to go sailing: 'I was surprised to find I did not feel sick the first time,' he told Adeline. 'I went out although it was quite rough.' He also went to the cinema, a rare indulgence, watching *This Happy Breed* with Noël Coward although he complained he could not hear a word said. He had not been to see a film for seven years. 'I also had to go to a party at a FANY mess (there are a lot of them in the office of this firm). There was dancing but I hadn't the nerve to take to the floor as I have forgotten my brief lessons.'

He tried, and failed, to get himself posted to the Special Operations Executive in the Far East, writing to Adeline:

I had hoped to be able to tell you, this week of being on the move again but today, I got the answer to my application for a similar job in the far east – refused on the grounds of age and rank – 'Othellos, occupation's gone!' However I have one if not two, other irons in the fire. If both these fail I shall find myself washed up high and dry at some RA Base Depot with precious little chance of any active employment – even in the despised role of CO2.

In the end, early in August, he was offered a chance to fight with the Italian partisans in northern Italy where, despite the Italian surrender (and change of side) the Germans were holding on. Perhaps someone had noted that Bill got on with communists; the Italian partisan movement was largely communist-inspired.

CHAPTER 11

Italy

'It was my good fortune to spend the winter of 1944–45 in the mountains of north-east Italy,' wrote Bill, adding a rider that, really, it was for the mountains he went. In this case, the mountains were, or became, secondary to the life of a partisan that he led. Bill's time in Italy was formative; although in his late forties, and set in his habits, he could still alter in subtle ways. The Italian campaign of liberation affected Bill and, for example, he remained in contact with his Italian translator, Victor Gozzer, for the rest of his life. He also kept up correspondence with John Ross, his second-in-command, and with many other people involved, particularly the Italians, who have never forgotten him, or ceased to revere his memory.

This aspect is the most significant. Bill was highly honoured by the Italians in this region of the Veneto, and to this day. In 1993 the Veneto and the city of Belluno, in whose liberation Bill played a prominent part, were still honouring his name (and that of John Ross and Victor Gozzer) with medals, certificates and more. Although some of this may be put down to an Italian love of ceremony and feasting, the rest is genuine enough.

The ostensible cause of this latest celebration was the opening of an *alta via*, a trekking path through the Dolomites, a composite of the routes Bill and his companions made in 1944–45 from their dropping zone to the Cansiglio forest to the east of Belluno. The Alta Via da Tilman is a testimony to the affection that people of the region feel for this Englishman, as was the granting of the freedom of the city of Belluno to him in 1945, an event and an award he always treasured.

The reasons why British (and American) missions were being dropped into this region of Italy behind enemy lines was fairly clear-cut. The German resistance in Italy had proved far more stubborn than the Allies had anticipated and the Wehrmacht had fought tenaciously range by range, valley by valley, in their retreat. There were sound reasons for this as the Germans had realised that the more Allied divisions they

155

could tie up in Italy, the fewer there would be for the campaign in France and the Low Countries. Moreover, this region of Italy had historically been part of the old Austro-Hungarian Empire and it had, once more, been annexed into Greater Germany.

It was not bad country for guerrilla fighting on the whole, although the mountain groups were isolated from each other and the infrastructure of roads and railways intersecting these ranges sufficient for easy defence. The Germans were well dug in, as in Albania, but fortunately not quite so intractably; there were political divisions among the partisans with the communists often leading the opposition. The recent switch by Italy to the side of the Allies also complicated the situation on the ground.

The Simia mission in which Bill took part was some time coming to fruition. The plane taking them in left first from Brindisi on August 26th but failed to find the drop zone. On August 28th Bill reports: 'We . . . watched with interest the lights of Trieste appear on the starboard side and those of Venice to port.' They were picked up by searchlight and shot at but continued on their way. 'As I stood in the door, holding hard to either side and glaring fixedly at the red warning light, waiting for it to change to green, time passed unnoticed. I began to wonder if I had gone suddenly colour blind, incapable from distinguishing green from red, while Ross, in a moment of aberration, suggested I should jump and hope for the best.'

They had been standing at the door for an hour when the pilot announced he could not find the drop zone again and turned for home. Then, on August 31st:

After the first wild whirling moment, when you sense the grateful tug of the harness, the first emotion is one of satisfaction, not unmingled with surprise, that the thing has actually worked once more. Then you feel you would like to shout with exultation and pride in being such a clever fellow as to float there so delightfully in the moonlight; you wish you could float there for ever. But this pride and exultation does not last.

Bill made a bad landing, so bad indeed that he badly hurt his back. John Ross recalls that this was because Bill had stuffed the pockets of his Sidcot parachute suit with books to read for the coming months, handing over all their (forged) Italian money to Ross. In *When Men and Mountains Meet* Bill says that 'even the packet of two million paper lire stowed away in the seat of my Sidcot suit failed to mitigate' (the blow he was struck on landing). Either way it meant he was *hors de combat* for several days, writing that even 'for an "actual necessity" I had to crawl away into the forest on hands and knees.'

In some ways worse, none of their kit had followed them down and for four months there were to be no successful follow-up drops. They had landed on the Altopiano d'Asiago, high above the valley of the Brenta and, as it happened, close to Victor Gozzer's home and family. Apart from Gozzer (codenamed Gatti), there was John Ross and the radio operator, Marini. In the drop, John Ross had had a lucky escape, having landed in a tree; Marini had sprained his ankle but his heart was not in the task. An ex-submariner, he was eventually to be captured by the Germans.

His replacement, Benito Quaquarelli ('Pallino') was described by Bill at some length.

He was young, and his service in the Italian Air Force had not only failed to quell his natural exuberance, but had instilled in him a violent dislike of control of any sort. He was a gifted operator. With the most amateurish aerial, which the experts would view with derision, he would in a few moments make contact with Base several hundred miles away, and pass and receive messages singularly free of corruption. But his other virtues he hid under a bushel.

He was idle, insubordinate, temperamental, mindful of his own comfort, and extremely touchy if any of his shortcomings were pointed out to him. He was like a desert sore, always there, always irritating, and quite incurable. Many times we sighed for Marini. Many times we were on the point of having Pallino shot. But good operators were irreplaceable, and when he was working, pounding out messages with frozen fingers by the light of a guttering candle, we forgave him all; indeed we almost loved him. But when he had finished his schedule and started crooning, probably the 'Internationale', for he was an ardent Communist, murder would again raise its snaky head.

Of Victor he wrote:

the interpreter . . . who was an ex-officer of Alpini from Trento, with a short but varied career. During the early years of the war he had been, for an Alpini, in the seemingly anomalous position of subaltern in the Italian Camel Corps, somewhere on the south-west border of Tripoli. Having come back to Italy, he was caught by the Germans at the time of the Italian surrender and put in a train bound for Gorizia but, since he was a man of resource, he jumped off and made his way to Rome, where he joined the Allied Army, serving for a time as interpreter with the Long Range Desert Group [forerunners of the SAS]. He was not long and weedy but emphatically lean, with features so clean-cut as almost to resemble the 'hatchet-faced' men of American detective stories [of which Bill

157

was inordinately fond]. He spoke excellent English and presumably impeccable Italian.

John Ross was a young English officer, but he had close Jewish relatives and to have himself dropped behind enemy lines as he did was an act of considerable courage; he later went on to become an eminent medical consultant, a career from which he has only recently retired.

These were the men who got to know Bill Tilman better than almost anyone else in his life, apart from those who fought with him in the First World War. These months in northern Italy were to throw these few men together in a closed and dangerous environment. To be with a man under these harrowing circumstances, for the Germans proved to be very active indeed, was to see a man totally exposed, totally reliant on his comrades.

For Bill, these months represent the best in his fighting career. And not just for the fighting. Although he began by dismissing the Dolomites as mere hills, he managed to climb a fair number while he was there and, finding that there was a permanent glacier on Marmolada, his opinion was modified all round. He had started out, too, with a fair degree of contempt for the Italians, not least for their having switched sides; when the war ended he had changed his view of them, too – at least of those with whom he fought.

The men – Ross and Gozzer – who got to be with him the most, liked him immensely. Victor Gozzer says simply, 'He changed my life.' Ross found him tough, utterly reliable, a formidable leader and organiser. Both had their differences with him. For Victor, one abiding memory is of a long night trek, helped as always by local guides. One of these told Victor to give him his pack; when Bill saw this, later, he assumed that Victor had asked the man to carry it and he went into a towering rage. Officers should always be seen to be willing to shoulder their own burdens, he argued, otherwise how can you expect the men to follow your lead.

For Ross, Bill could sometimes be terribly harsh in other ways, failing, for example, to hand over some of their admittedly forged money to help the starving local people; or not intervening when the partisans led 'offenders' away to be shot on some misdemeanour or other. Bill was, in these and other ways, as typically hard as all the stories ever told about him relate. But his integrity in these matters was never in question, just, at times, his humanity.

John Ross writes thus:

I began to wonder why he should have chosen me as a companion and whether his choice throws any light on him. I had come from a rather sheltered urban background and had a rather unexciting war record with anti-aircraft in the Middle East before joining SOE. I was not particularly tough and physically my only qualifications were fitness, persistence and being a good beast of burden. Maybe I showed more interest in literature and music which may have appealed to him. There were certainly many tougher young men in the base camp in South Italy where we were gathered.

We were a rather hearty crew with few commitments but plenty of swimming, basket ball, drinking and singing, etc. Bill did not join in much but was usually around watching. His swimming consisted of going far out into the Adriatic and floating around for hours. The outside of the harbour wall at Monopoli (our base) consisted of huge blocks of stone piled chaotically and Bill enjoyed diving into the narrow gaps between them. I was expected to do so also when with him – it scared me stiff. We were together quite a bit then.

I remember being interested that he came to a recital in Monopoli with me, a quartet, and enjoyed it; I can't remember that we ever discussed composers or his likes and dislikes but I do remember his literary preferences; Jane Austen was a great favourite. I do recall upsetting him by singing the Cole Porter number 'Oh, I'd love to climb a mountain and scale the highest peak, but it would not thrill me half as much as dancing cheek to cheek.'

Everything was a challenge to him – to do things better, quicker and with minimum fuss, equipment and time. If the partisans said a climb or march took a certain time he was then determined to do it more quickly, if necessary with his own improvised route. If we had walked overnight to a new situation the suggestion that we rested before prospecting for a dropping ground or going on to look at enemy positions was instantly dismissed and we did our recce straight away.

We were of course in a strange situation – not leaders or organisers but 'liaison officers'. This perhaps explains why I was never conscious of Bill making careful plans ahead, and I felt that so much of what we did depended on day to day decisions or what was suggested to us by the partisans. We were unfortunately in a very 'one down' position from the start. Owing to the bad conditions on the night we were dropped, we arrived without any supplies for the partisans. We did not even have our own weapons except for revolvers and it was four months before we managed to organise a drop of arms etc. There was little we could do to assert any authority being so dependent for everything.

Our advice to hit and run instead of standing up to German attacks was thought to be a policy of cowardice and was disregarded until the series of German attacks in the autumn did destroy the resistance organisation and notice was taken of our ideas. I have vivid memories of Bill arguing with partisan leaders one evening when we were surrounded on our mountain top and we urged them to fade away – it was in a barn by the light of a wood fire and carbide lamps. The partisans were bearded with red Garibaldini scarves around their necks – like Act Three of *Carmen*.

I certainly did not distinguish myself in any particular way except to survive in pretty awful conditions and I always thought that Bill felt I had let him down in the last few days of the war when I was isolated some way north of Belluno trying to organise more drops and got back to the scenes of great activity almost too late to be of any help. I was therefore surprised that he must have recommended me for an award and that we continued our friendship.

That went on after the war and I saw quite a bit of him in London and he visited me in Cambridge where he joined in various activities such as rowing to Ely and back and on cycling expeditions. He seemed to enjoy the company of undergraduates but, as always, was mostly an onlooker. Conversation never flowed easily and it was usually a matter of dragging information about himself from him.

His intolerance has been commented upon and I suppose that it was a manifestation of his inability to think that anyone could carry out a task without throwing themselves wholeheartedly into it and without sacrificing everything towards achieving it. He allowed himself no sympathy and gave others little; one could certainly suffer from this. I was often surprised, when we were in Italy, that he did not seem to appreciate fully the fears and the poverty of the peasants with whom we worked. For example, we had money and could easily have rewarded those who sheltered us at considerable risk but he could not be persuaded to do this.

When we had been 'liberated' we returned to our HQ in Siena. I found a letter there telling me that my father had gone bankrupt, my parents had separated and that we no longer had a family home. Bill was most sympathetic and this was one of the occasions when he did talk about his family, telling that his sister had had her husband walk out on her.

When the Simia mission arrived a breakthrough on the Italian front by the Allies was expected. Their primary task, therefore, was to make contact with the local partisans, in the first place the Nino Nannetti division, and to get them to co-ordinate sabotage attacks on bridges and roads with the coming breakthrough.

As they had arrived without their equipment, Bill's first order had John Ross and Victor Gozzer scurrying off to make contact with the divisional

Above left, the young explorer with his bucket and spade. *Above right*, Bill on a climbing holiday in the Lake District with his sister, Adeline.

Below, at an officer cadet training camp, Bill (far left) with comrades, in the summer of 1914.

Above, the original Nanda Devi recce team: in the front row the three Sherpas, Pasang, Kusang and Angtarkay, behind Eric Shipton (left) and Bill.

Below, the very grand start of the successful Nanda Devi expedition in 1936. L to r: Eric Shipton, sister, Adeline, niece, Pam, the chauffeur, Mrs Tilman (in car) and Bill.

Above left, the appallingly difficult terrain of the Upper Rishi Gorge, pathway to Nanda Devi. *Above right*, camped in the Nanda Devi basin with the West Peak towering above.

Below, the successful Nanda Devi team: L to r, Bill, W. F. Loomis, T. Graham Brown, Charles Houston, Peter Lloyd, Noel Odell, Arthur Emmons, H. Adams Carter.

Above left, John Ross and Bill somewhere in Italy, before their Italian adventure. *Above right*, Grandine, one of the Italian partisans, ready for any eventuality.

Below, Bill's and Eric's camp on Bogda Ola.

Above, Nepal, 1950: Bill in funny hat (left) with monks and the two Houstons, Oscar, centre foreground, and Charles, bespectacled right, photographed by Betsy Cowles.

Left, Elizabeth Cowles, Betsy, noted US climber. Bill had written 'lady explorer' on the back of the photograph.

Below, the Nepal recce party: Anderson Bakewell, Oscar Houston, Betsy Cowles, Bill, Charles Houston (of the Nanda Devi expedition of 1936).

Above left, *Mischief*, Bill's first Bristol pilot cutter, bow on somewhere in the Atlantic. *Above right*, haircut time on *Patanela*, en route for Heard Island. *Below*, off watch on *Mischief*. Like all his yachts, *Mischief* was very basic indeed down below.

Above, *Mischief* aground in Angmagssalik harbour in July, 1964, after being holed by ice while following larger ships in through the pack. *Below left*, *Sea Breeze*, lying alongside the Berthon yard in Lymington. She was wrecked on the Greenland coast in 1972. *Below right*, *Baroque* aground off Spitzbergen in 1975 after Bill had made a navigational error. The ballast is being offloaded.

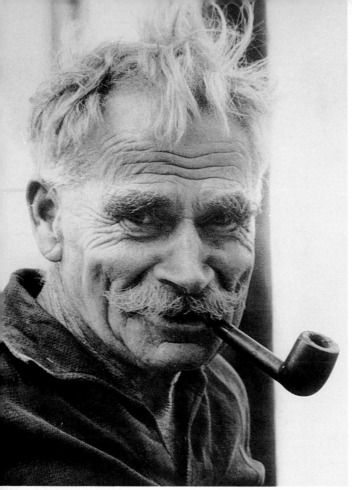

Left, Ancient Mariner, (photo: W. G. Lee).

Below, the last voyage. Bill lost in his own thoughts, stares at the water as *En Avant* leaves the port of Southampton for the far south, in August 1977, (photo: *Southampton Evening Echo*).

EN AVANT
SOUTHAMPTON

HQ. The British major who had received them, Major Wilkinson, was living in a pine forest with about 200 partisans, using old parachutes as tents. 'The smell of the pines and the air, for we were about 5,000 ft up, set my blood tingling,' said Bill later. Wilkinson lent them some equipment – and the new radio operator, Pallino, and they set off to join the others. Bill now caught up with Ross and Gozzer. Their objective was the forest of Cansiglio, to the east of Belluno, where the Nannetti division were based.

On the way they learned that the Germans were conducting a *rastrallamento*, combing out, in the forest. The divisional HQ had been dispersed and there was no means of knowing where they had gone. Bill decided, in the interim and until they received definite news, that they would go back to the mountains to the north-west of Cesio, through which they had just passed, and join the Gramsci Brigade to wait on events. Having crossed the Piave River they now recrossed it and joined the Gramsci Brigade on a plateau mountain called Le Vette.

On their way in, Bill and his party were surprised to be challenged by a British soldier. He was part of a small contingent of escaped prisoners who had formed themselves into the Churchill Company, part of the Gramsci Brigade Bill sought. 'Naturally they were surprised and pleased to see us, and questioned us closely, particularly as to the probable duration of the war, for they were undecided whether they should or whether they should not try to get through to our lines.' Bill told them to hang on where they were.

On the top of Le Vette he found about 300 partisans with a numerous HQ staff living in a long stone-built, tin-roofed cow-shed (a *malga*). They were well organised and discipline was good – most of them, too, were communists. They included, as well as the British, some Russians.

Of the latter Bill wrote that they were also good soldiers who took life seriously. Nothing funny about them, he added, except their names: 'Borlikoff, Orloff, Shuvoff'. The commander of the brigade was a man called Bruno, happily still alive in 1993. Bill described him as a man of strong personality and respected as well as liked by his men. Fifty years on, Bruno is still of the belief that Bill's description of him as 'headstrong' was an insult. All of them were keen to fight, for which they urgently needed arms and ammunition. Still the expected drops did not come.

'In spite of our fervid signals, couched in language which became ruder as time went on, nothing came except our signal stores and kit which were eventually dropped at Monte Grappa, where they were either stolen, or lost in the "rastrallamento".' The partisans were upset by this failure to deliver the equipment they so badly needed. Bill thought that they attributed this failure to British incompetence, allied with a dislike (by the British authorities) of their politics. 'In spite of our shortcomings they accepted us as one of themselves. They supplied bedding, for we still had nothing but the clothes we wore, toilet kit, bowl and spoon; they saw that we got our cigarette and tobacco ration, and even supplied a tame Fascist, whom they had not yet shot, to bring our meals from the kitchen.'

There was little to do, apart from eat, sleep, send their increasingly strident signals and explore the plateau, which Bill began to see as a trap should the Germans decide to attack. They made one hair-raising journey north to visit another brigade; the winter was coming on, meanwhile, and their position at Pietena, on Le Vette, was impossible to maintain during that season. Bruno, however, insisted they held on, hoping the arms would still be dropped. Finally, on September 29th, the Germans came.

About five o'clock on the evening of 29 September we were startled by a distant burst of machine-gun fire. The Churchill Company block-post reported that a German patrol had attacked the post and the store in the valley some 2,000 feet below. The store was in flames . . . Bruno, who was something of a fire-eater, had only one thought, or plan – to fight to the last man and the last round.

With this policy Bill profoundly disagreed. He adhered, correctly, to the view that to stand and fight as a group of lightly armed partisans was to throw away their great advantage. This was, as with all well-organised guerrillas, to be able to move in and out of a situation, a kind of hit-and-run warfare. Their mere existence, even as a pinprick in the side of the Germans, meant that the latter had to use up valuable divisions to keep a lid on their activities, divisions that would normally be used in the advancing front line. To get annihilated, as they surely would on Le Vette, was crazy.

Bill's arguments, translated by Victor, were to no avail. Bruno persuaded his men that the honour of Italy, as well as that of the partisan movement, was at stake; despite their lack of weapons, ammunition and even food, they would stick.

Bruno suggested to Bill that he might like to withdraw his mission at this point but Bill declined.

It was a question of what interpretation would be put upon our action if we agreed. Would they take the commonsense military view that the safety of the mission with its wireless set and all the possibilities of future supplies which this implied, should not be hazarded uselessly, or would they think that we were running away? Not that this should have mattered much to me, for in common with the rest of the British Army I had spent much of the war running away in order to fight again; but it might adversely affect the future by impairing what little influence we had.

162

After Bruno had assured them that if they stayed he would ensure they escaped, come what may, Bill decided to stick it out.

Although the Germans were slow in coming, they were, as usual, very thorough, blocking off all the possible escape routes as they 'combed' their way upwards. The brigade were in a classic trap, and although they had the advantage of height, they were completely surrounded. As the Germans advanced, so the partisans moved back up the mountain. Bruno had mounted a machine-gun on a ridge, high above the HQ in the *malga*, by now (the afternoon of the 30th) being hastily abandoned. Bill climbed up to find him, with Victor in tow. There a famous exchange took place. Bill wrote: 'Bruno, with the light of battle in his eyes, paid little attention to my question of what he proposed doing . . . Most of the partisans in the vicinity, except Bruno, looked decidedly and, I thought, justifiably, scared.' Bill suggested they withdraw. Victor Gozzer remembers that Bruno then replied, 'Tell the major I am going to show him how an Italian patriot dies for his country.' Victor's reply, which found its mark was: 'It would be better if you showed the major how an Italian patriot can survive for his country.' Bruno abandoned, not without sorrow, his machine-gun. John Ross says to this day that this was less of a loss than it might have seemed as it rarely fired without jamming.

Bill left Bruno and returned to the camp, where all was confusion. He sent off a man to tell the Churchill Company that an order to withdraw had now been agreed. While most of the partisans understandably tried to sneak past the Germans and get lower, Bill had decided on an altogether different, and much more daring plan. He chose to lead his small party up, on to the north face of Le Vette.

We might even find a way down, but at the worst the Germans were not likely to remain up there for more than a couple of days. This plan they agreed to. The Churchill Company, in a body, asked to come with us, and the Italian cook from Pietena, who was a friend of ours, offered to carry the wireless set. This made a party of sixteen (11 from the Churchill Company) instead of the four or five I would have preferred. We left the path, shook off some would-be adherents, and struck straight up to the crest, carelessly leaving our tracks in a patch of snow close to the path. As we gained the crest we saw below us the fires of the enemy pickets in the valley the partisans hoped to cross.

They found a gulley – which proved to be a dead-end – and settled down for the night. They had one blanket between them, they were 7000 feet up and it was late autumn. Even Bill admitted they were potentially in great trouble. The next day they watched while the Germans, a few hundred yards below them, continued to search the ground. On the night of October 1st a blizzard engulfed them, blowing from the unprotected quarter, the north. It blew all the next day. They could not light a fire, of course, but they decided to stay a third night, as the Germans could still be heard, now firing below.

By the end of the third day we had to move whether or no. No one had eaten for seventy-two hours, some had frozen feet, and all were stiff with cold. The start was not auspicious. Having gone to the top of the gully at dusk to reconnoitre I was recalled by wild cries from below. Since for three days no one had dared to raise his voice above a whisper, it seemed something important must have happened – perhaps they had found some food. In fact, one of the ex-prisoners-of-war had slipped. I found him lying dazed with a severe gash in the head, on a ledge 60 ft below our 'gite' on the lip of a straight drop of a like distance. His hands were lacerated too, but securing him to the tail of my coat, I eventually dragged him to the top of the gully where the remainder were now waiting.

It was the last incident of a trying time; the small group of frozen men, led by Bill, walked down Le Vette. They met no one and by daybreak were close to a farm which one of the British soldiers knew to be 'safe'. They went down after him and enjoyed their first meal for days. At the farm they learned that the Germans had burned all the *malgas* in the valley, along with a few farms. The Gramsci Brigade, although most of its members had, like Bill's party, slipped away, ceased to exist. The ease with which this had occurred shook confidence locally, among both partisans and supporters; the Germans were still engaging in reprisals – burning farms, hanging those they suspected of being a partisan.

Bill and his party now found themselves holed up in Cesio for three days while partisan leaders came in for discussions. Among them was 'Deluca', a businessman in the fur trade, and a dedicated communist.

He used his business as his 'cover' when bicycling through northern Italy on partisan affairs, as he continued to do untiringly until the war ended. He always carried with him as corroborative details a couple of moth-eaten marten skins to give 'artistic verisimilitude to an otherwise bald and unconvincing narrative'. Deluca was an able, active and influential man, and the greatest help to the mission and the partisan cause; among his many accomplishments were the ability to skin, dress and cook anything that walked. His spiced kid, spitted and roasted, was perfection.

They moved from one location to another, at one point to a farm near Cesio, 'where we lay hidden . . . for a week. Though we were comfortable the strict confinement was irksome. Ross and I shared a double bed with sheets, but we were not obliged to remain in this all day.' John Ross recalls Bill being worried that the farmer and his family would think them homosexuals, as each morning they had left only one impression on the mattress. The reason for this was that this mattress was so uncomfortable they had taken it in turns to sleep on the floor which was less lumpy.

The Germans began an exercise nearby, using 88 mm guns and they moved out of the farm for two days and lived in the woods. It was during this gunnery practice that Bill astonished John Ross by pulling out his Royal Artillery cap and, putting it on his head, standing up and 'observing' the enemy guns. For Ross it was a totally unnecessary piece of bravado; for Bill, perhaps, it was to relieve the tension by pretending, if only for a moment, that things were in some way 'normal'.

One of their meals in the woods was provided by a local woman who found them there thinking, perhaps, that they were escaping prisoners. 'It consisted of a magnificent minestrone, cream cheese, peaches, and unfermented grape juice.' Bill was constantly amazed at the bravery of the people among whom he and his mission moved. All of them risked their lives to shelter and feed them, and often they were turned out in the middle of the night to do these onerous and dangerous tasks. From Cesio they moved to the edge of the Cansiglio Forest where, finally, he joined the HQ staff of the Nino Nannetti Division. Among many of the characters they found there was one man they named the 'Animal Man', another they called the 'Second Murderer', for their appearance, another named the 'Bird Man' for his behaviour.

During the next two months in the Cansiglio many attempts were made to send them supplies by air drop but none got through. General Alexander had broadcast to the partisans, pointing out the obvious, that the Allies would not be advancing through the winter months and suggesting that they lie low until the spring. Bill's own HQ had warned they might not expect much in the way of air drops. 'This, indeed, was a glimpse of the obvious, for we had already been in the field nine weeks without receiving so much as a pair of socks or a spare shirt, and we were to pass yet another eight weeks before this happy event occurred.'

Only one letter got out from Bill to Adeline during his whole time in Italy – a testament to conditions. It is dated December 15th.

I sent off one note about six weeks ago. I wonder if you have received it? I hope you are getting the regular fortnightly messages [see below]. Have had no mail, or anything else, since we arrived last August. A lot of mail was sent but unluckily it fell into enemy hands. I expect there were books and possibly a pipe amongst it.

Life is a good deal harder and more harassed than it was in Albania, but I have no doubt we shall get through the winter all right if that should be necessary. There is a lot of snow here now.

A few weeks ago I had half an hour on skis and fell about all over the place. It seemed to me to be worse than skating. Hope you are battling along and that Joan, Pam and Anne are all well.

The regular messages Bill mentions were sent from HQ to relatives. They were designed to allay fears. For instance, Captain A. N. Maughan-Brown wrote to Adeline: 'Once again I am happy to inform you that the latest information I have of your brother, Major Tilman, is that he is fit, well and in the best of spirits.' Adeline took these official notes very seriously, writing back to the captain on each occasion. 'No doubt he was astonished to get them,' says Pam today.

Later in 1945 Captain Maughan-Brown was superseded by a FANY, Lieutenant Nora Galbraith, who had rather more imagination, writing in consecutive letters about the wonderful warm weather and beautiful spring flowers Bill would be enjoying while remaining – as always in these missives – fit and well.

In the Cansiglio in early 1945, meanwhile, the British and their partisan allies endured another, less threatening *rastrallamento* and Bill and his little group had to move again. They kept up a series of visits to other missions. Travelling by night, these 'visits' can be made to sound routine; they never were and Bill and his companions were in constant danger. On one occasion Bill and John Ross were placed in 'coffins' under a load of wood, and driven down the Agordo–Belluno highway through German checkpoints. John Ross remembers: 'I can still remember seeing through cracks a German at one of the checkpoints standing on top of our wood pile prodding with a rifle.'

This was after the air drops had begun and long-awaited supplies had been delivered. They had enjoyed a good Christmas, during a spell of good weather. They had eaten well, as well as drunk freely on wine and grappa. After the usual toasts Bill, John Ross and Victor, along with the 'more educated' divisional staff, had begun what Bill described as 'a long and exciting discussion on "What is art?"'.

Then, on Boxing Day, came the event they had long awaited – the drop of arms and ammunition. Bill was free to move to the Belluno Division, with whom they eventually established contact on January 9th, 1945. Here they found there had been little activity against the Germans, the main preoccupation of the partisans being to deal quietly with spies and informers. Paralysed in their military activities by lack of arms, they were constrained by their proximity to Belluno's SS HQ, as well as by deep snow.

Partly for this reason, Bill decided they could not risk drops so close to Belluno and he moved accordingly to the Forno area, in the mountains to the north-west of Belluno. During this time Bill was able to do some climbing, including Mount Serva (7000 feet). He reported that it took him seven hours and although he dismissed the climb as not even difficult for winter he was satisfied by the astonishment it caused among his Italian companions.

The drops, made in difficult circumstances, were successful and by February, when the snows were melting, Bill moved back to the neighbourhood of Belluno, where he attached himself to the zone HQ staff, leaving John Ross with the Belluno group, in anticipation of the great events of that spring. At the divisional HQ the problem of being surprised by night-time *rastrallamentos* had been removed by the digging of bunkers, in which everyone went to ground to sleep. Each night they were sealed into one of these by the local farmer, whose buildings they used by day, and unsealed the next morning. Bill, who thought a dog would have been able to scent their presence, was pleased that his fears were never tested while this system was in use.

Although the war was nearly over, dark deeds were still casting their shadow. One day the chief of staff of the division, a man whose *nom de guerre* was Shining Dawn, had placed a picture of Hitler on the local German rifle range with the instruction (in German) to shoot straight. When a group of officers had seen this exhortation they had furiously gone to tear it down. The sign had been booby-trapped and four of them died; many more were injured. The reprisal consisted of ten men hanged on the range and four more hanged in the town square in Belluno.

Bill's comments on his decision to attach himself and Victor to zone headquarters are revealing, as they display the same attitude he had to getting promotion in the conventional army he had chosen to leave.

> I was loathe to leave the division – the more so as we now had some arms and explosives to use. Though to a less degree, it is the same with partisans as it is in the army, the higher the formation the more it loses touch with realities – a loss which no amount of visiting can replace. However true it may be that a looker-on sees most of the game, I have not yet outgrown the preference for being in the thick of it, rather than be relegated to a seat in the grandstand, which is how the headquarters of a formation appears to me.

It was now March and the zone HQ had been established in a farmhouse at the southern end of the Alpago district, an extensive area of rich, hilly farmland north of the Cansiglio Forest and east of the San Croce Lake. Among the people Bill found here was the Italian climber Attilio Tissi, with whom he enjoyed many conversations about climbing. This was a period of lull and Bill took full advantage by climbing all the local peaks. Still covered by a liberal amount of snow they were 'a lot of fun', Bill recorded.

> These jaunts were of necessity solitary. For although the par- tisans lived among these mountains, sang beautiful songs about

them, and liked hearing themselves called mountaineers, they would nevertheless have been dumbfounded at the thought of climbing one. Tissi was too busy, and in any case these could not have been of much interest to one of 'sesto grado' calibre.

The Allied offensive finally opened but the Germans contested every inch of ground and it was not until the third week in April that the Americans broke their line and raced through to Verona. This was decisive as it held the key to the Brenner Pass, through which the Germans would have to retreat. Immediately the partisans moved to block the roads. By the end of April all the small garrisons south of the Piave River had surrendered but Belluno was holding out. By now Deluca was in touch with the German general in Belluno, trying to get him to surrender. Many alarms and excursions now followed with the partisans trying to prevent the Germans from blowing bridges, of no further use to them but of vital importance to the advancing Allies.

Bill and Deluca were finally to be found on the Belluno road on April 30th where they discovered that the Germans in that city were still unhappy at surrendering to the partisans but might be willing to give in to the British, now pushing their way up from the valley. Eventually a British column arrived, meeting the Germans at the T-junction where the road from Vittorio Veneto met the road from Belluno. After a short fire-fight which could have turned into something much worse – many of the German officers were, in Bill's words, 'truculent', 'the affair . . . took on the proportions of a battle', which only ended when the British artillery brought up to support the first column accurately shelled the German HQ.

By eleven o'clock on May 2nd over 4000 Germans had surrendered and the rest, still in Belluno, had given up too.

That morning three of us went on another of Deluca's motor-cycles into Belluno, for so long the goal of our ambitions. I should like to report that we were wrenched from the cycle by an enthusiastic crowd, borne shoulder-high to the Piazza del Duomo and there crowned with laurel leaves to the prolonged and deafening 'Viva's' of the assembled multitude. We were too soon for that. The streets were nearly empty, most of the people wisely remaining indoors until after the situation cleared.

Three weeks later Bill became a freeman of the city; the first had been Garibaldi and he, Bill, was only the fifth. As an honour he rated it highly, and his time with the Italian partisans was one he never forgot. The war was now over; he was forty-seven years old, a bachelor explorer and a war hero for the second time (collecting the DSO as a medal).

In his secret report to his superiors Bill wrote this of the campaign and of his partisan friends:

There is in my opinion no question that the Garibaldi formations were the most effective [They were all communist]. They were better led, better organised and attracted a more ardent more determined type of recruit than the so-called independent brigades or brigades formed by other political parties . . . Discipline was fairly good . . . I know of only two instances of Partisans being shot, one for drunkenness when out on patrol and one for the repeated taking of food by force from civilians for his own behoof . . . Spies of course were another matter and met with no mercy.

Militarily their faults were mainly due to lack of experience rather than the will to fight – experience either in any fighting at all, or, in the case of the leaders many of whom had been in the army, in Partisan warfare . . . Against all this it must be remembered that the risks they ran once having taken up arms were great. Capture almost invariably meant death, with the probability of torture and hanging. If badly wounded there was little hope of getting away, and even if they got away care and medical attention were bound to be inadequate. A successful action usually meant reprisals, friends or relatives might be shot or hanged, their homes or their villages burnt.

He concluded: 'It is with this in mind that the Partisans must be judged. That they held together during the long hard winter months, and were found able and willing to give of their best when the time came, is a measure of their determination, self-sacrifice, patriotism, and of their ardour to atone for the crimes of fascism.'

The war in Europe ended and Bill, briefly and unsuccessfully, tried to get himself out to the Far East where the war with Japan still raged on. Having failed to do this he returned home, his first visit since 1941.

For a few years Bill returned to climbing and exploring. The final expedition to Nepal had led to his meeting Betsy Cowles. Back in England he was clearly at a loose end, wondering what he should do with the rest of his life, perhaps thinking of seriously settling down. What followed was the only real interlude in his entire career.

INTERLUDE

In 1945 Bill's thoughts turned once more to his pre-war life as a mountaineer and explorer. As we have seen, though, the years between 1945 and 1950 did not bring him any particular success. Then came his last trek in Nepal in the company of the Houstons – and Betsy Cowles. Now fifty-two, he determined to give up mountaineering. He was still remarkably fit, despite his recurring back problems, and, as photographs of the time show, a very handsome man. But time was catching him up; if Bill may ever be said to have had a mid-life crisis, a faltering in direction, it was now.

After he returned from Nepal for the last time, in 1950, there came a period of three years when he was, in effect, treading water. Significantly, and for the only time in his life, he tried a career outside exploration and self-financed climbing. With an excellent set of references from two wars, he persuaded His Majesty's Government that he would make a good diplomat. And, as a result, for eighteen months he endured a miserable existence in upstate Burma as HMG consul at Maymyo. His letters home to Adeline are testament to his realisation – which came swiftly – that this life was not for him, or him for it.

Why Bill should have suddenly tried to make a go of such an odd (for him) post as full-time consul needs exploration. One obvious pointer is his own comment at the end of *Nepal Himalaya* when he explains he no longer feels able to climb those great but taxing mountains. Having eschewed the one arena in which he had operated for twenty years clearly gave him pause for thought. Then, and this has to remain surmise, there was Betsy Cowles. Could it have been that he was trying to find a career, this late in his life, in which a woman – a wife – could fit?

Bill might well have envied Eric Shipton's former life in Kashgar, too. Familiar as he was with it, he might have decided that there was a good life to be had in being a minor diplomat in a remote place. Bill's lack of imagination, a consistent aspect of his personality, would have helped.

One man who knew Bill – E. F. Given – who was in Burma when Bill was there, believed Bill was down on his luck. From the moment he arrived in Rangoon, he stuck out like a sore thumb. Given remembers one incident when Bill declined a lift in the embassy car back from a

171

dinner there to his digs, eight miles out. He walked back, to everyone's consternation. The paperwork involved in being even a minor diplomat drove him crazy and must have frequently reminded him of his time as second-in-command of his regiment.

As always, he wrote home to Adeline, many of the letters intricately involved with life at Bodowen, suggestive that he had little to do but worry about events there. It may be of significance that he wrote less frequently than when on many of his foreign jaunts: not that much to write home about.

On July 2nd, 1952, however, he had had some news. 'It was nice of John Morris to write about the RGS Founders Medal for little Willie. As he says it is about time but then I always took exploration a bit light-heartedly for the RGS pundits. I have not been told of it myself yet. Old R W Lloyd is the only one who has mentioned it and he did not say what medal it was.'

Apart from this, Bill was bothered by an incident to the old gateposts at Bodowen, a saga which was to occupy him a good deal in the coming months. 'By the time this arrives,' he wrote in the same letter, 'you may have seen for yourself what exactly has happened to the gateposts – not to mention the gate which I painted so carefully. Preston must put it right and I think he will. Ask him whether you are to have it repaired and the bill sent to him, or whether he wants his own men to do it. If he starts being difficult put Goldsmith onto him.'

Apart from this, he was trying to find a way to get Adeline out to Burma, a project in which he was eventually to fail.

About resuming your travels so soon. I agree that Mselle and Pugh [who looked after Bodowen for Adeline, living in the stables block flat] deserve a break and I will no doubt be tickled to death to have you about the place for a time. You might think about coming out early January and returning late April which would give you more than enough of Maymyo. It would be nice to return together and theoretically my tour is up next June . . . As I told you unless I got an offer of a more interesting job or place I shall drop out. At present apart from the routine consular stuff, I don't feel I am really helping HMG.

Of his time in Burma only fifteen letters are extant – but they seem to be the only ones he wrote. On June 24th, a week before he replied to Adeline and her news about the Founders Medal, he had written:

It is so long that I have had anything from you that I have forgotten when. I presume you are trundling across Europe but it begins to look as though you have got behind some Iron Curtain. [Adeline was travelling from Gibraltar to Germany with Pam and Derek Davis.]

I was away all last week on my railway journey to Mohnyin from Sagaing. It was 'hard' travel for even the so-called Upper Class carriages have wooden seats, and I had to spend five days and nights in one. The journey each way was only about 250 miles but the train accomplishes only about 100 miles in the course of the day and then lies up for the night. At Mohnyin there are about half a dozen BCMS missionaries but I was discourteous enough to spend there only three hours before catching the train back. I had to hurry because Smedley was due to leave on Thursday. The insurgents planted one of their mines on the line on our return. It was a home made job which only disturbed the ballast and charred two sleepers.

I shall have to stay put now until Smedley's relief arrives. I have not been told when this will be and meantime I have his work, the Consul's and my own job to attend to. The most horrid threat hanging over me now is the preparation of the Quarterly Account at the end of June – a most complex matter with vouchers in triplicate, schedules, votes 1,2,3 etc., and God knows what.

They [Rootes] threaten to ship the Humber on June 19th and I have had to pay for it. Rather more than I expected but as soon as I hear from Barclays how my account stands I will send you as much as I can for Bodowen. I cannot see that I shall have much use for the car here as I cycle about Maymyo and on tour the official station wagon is more useful.

The Humber Snipe he refers to was an indulgence which he was to regret. Apart from the car that eventually arrived, he also amused himself by planting a garden, to which, like the car and its travails, he constantly refers. 'It rains pretty well every day and night now,' he wrote in June 1952, 'but there is usually some sun during the day and it is by no means unpleasant; nor do boots and clothes grow moss and fungus like they do in Rangoon or Calcutta. There is a good show of Dahlias and Gladioli in the garden but not much else.'

At the end of July he wrote:

I got back yesterday from Rangoon and found here your letter from Bodowen of July 20th. It was good to have an eyewitness account of Taffy [the dog], Pugh, the garden, and the battlefield. Sorry to hear Taffy is getting fat, but he was always a little too fond of his food in which he took after his master. Pugh, no doubt, wants someone to direct his activities, such as they are, and cannot be expected to work flat out when left alone for six months. As we farmers say the master's eye is the best dung.

I think old man Preston will restore the wall and gateposts and I have written to him expressing hope and confidence that he will. He was right to take all the fir trees but there were one or two deciduous trees among them that should have been left. We must now wait and see whether the self sown ash have survived in sufficient numbers to make replanting unnecessary. You ought to have bags of firewood this winter. Has the water supply [Bodowen to this day has no mains water] been all right this year? I have sent you some money from which you can recoup yourself for Conservative dues and Club.

Rangoon was a change but not really a pleasant one. I never got to bed before midnight owing to the party habit they have and the house I stayed at was on a main road and noisy. It rained very hard and almost incessantly. I should have got back on Sunday in the Anson (small four-seater) but after flying for two hours in cloud we had to go back being unable to find Maymyo. We then ran out of petrol and the pilot was just about to put us down in a paddy field when he was told on the R/T of a strip at Pegu nearby on which we landed safely and gave thanks.

Petrol was sent up from Rangoon by road and we flew back that evening. I came back to Mandalay today by USA Dakota. I have to go there again today to meet a man, but will return tomorrow. We have not had much rain here and the lake gets lower and lower. I have written to Moss of Barclays for some fishing line to be sent by air. I have a rod and reel and will clinch the boat deal today in Mandalay. Could you send via the FO a small parcel of flower seed for autumn sowing. They should be in by September, larkspur, carnation, delphinium, clarkia, lupin, phlox, sweet peas, etc.

On August 11th he wrote again, worrying about the grounds back home:

We might get in touch with the Dolgelly Woodland Society in which we own £50 of shares and ask them what we should plant. The theory is to avoid having to fence it against rabbits. I don't think there are many but I believe ash was supposed to be immune to rabbit and it is a nicer tree than any of the firs.

Nothing much doing here. I got my sampan [the boat he referred to before] y'day. It arrived about 6.30 and at 7 pm I was up to my neck in the lake trying to moor it when I should have been at the Club where a film was being shown on our projector. However I was well out of it as the projector failed and everyone got very bored. We have one dicky projector; the American Information Service in Mandalay have 12 and 2 mobile cinema vans! But the Russians in Rangoon have gone one better by taking over a whole cinema where nothing but Russian films are shown.

I have also ordered a radiogram of all things with long-playing records. This is to help out the appalling cocktail parties with soft or loud music. I'm afraid my slackness in going to church (complete absence in fact) has soured our new padre Canon Tidy. When I was away in Rangoon he called here and left a book 'The Duties of a Churchman' with a note asking me to study it. Damn him.

He talked as well about a Dr Weekes, who had stayed with his family – very pleasant company, he said. Two weeks later, in another letter, he spent most of the page discussing the Bodowen garden. Homesickness – not an affliction one would normally associate with Bill – radiates from these letters. Never before or after would he devote so much space in letters to Adeline in talking about her, her family or the house and garden – or the servants.

At the end of September, however, he had his own – if minor – problems. The Humber was being vandalised. 'It looks so glossy and gorgeous that if I leave it anywhere urchins cannot refrain from scratching on it,' he wrote. The gateposts back home, though, were still an issue. On October 9th he wrote: 'Anyhow I feel a bit vindictive because it is affrontery to say that knocking over gateposts is unavoidable.'

His time in Burma, although not over, soon had a marker against it. Just before Christmas 1952, he wrote:

The important news is that the Anson was here y'day (with my radiogram but no records). Among others was a communication from FO in the usual cryptic way telling me that according to original contract my 2 years expires in March and I would not be required any longer. In other words sacked.

I am not really surprised as I felt all along that I was wasting my time and HMG's money in this job. A relief, about whom I shall hear in due course, will arrive about then and I shall proceed to UK as soon as possible after. So expect me about April. This solves one problem but opens many others. What does Willy do next? Go to sea I expect, or perhaps some new line. I should not blurt this out at once but begin dropping a few hints that my time expires in the spring and may come home then. I am rather pleased because the thought of sitting here for another year was a little daunting but I would rather the initiative had come from me than from them.

I hope your Irish stay is pleasant [Joan, Adeline's elder daughter, was married by now to John, an Irish wine merchant]. It was big of John to offer a car but I think you did right to refuse to be under any obligation there [Bill did not like John, Joan's husband], quite apart from the question of 'fiddling'. If it is easy to get a car I will

not bring the Humber back. It will be easier to sell it here. Let
me know what you think.

I saw Eric [Shipton] had become warden at Eskdale, a pleasant
enough job, I should think, if one likes dealing with youth in the
mass. The Ambassador (and his wife) are coming here about Jan
20th, God help me. I have to arrange a tour for them. If you want
to come out you will have to move smartly but perhaps it is not
worth it now, Best love . . .

In late February, with not long to go, he wrote about a possible sailing
trip on his return, an augur of the future.

I note what you say about Jimmy. I too am looking forward to an
extended cruise but I would look forward to it more if he wasn't
such a difficult chap to do anything with. I must try to get afloat
with a real sailor so that I can learn something. However, I must
not grumble at Jimmy. If he had not been down at Barmouth with
a boat I would not be able to do anything.

Bill had found out by March that the problems of buying a car back
home were easing; so he decided to sell his Burma car and to get
another when he returned. On March 11th, he wrote of this, among
other things, to Adeline.

I am off tomorrow for a short trip and shall not be back till about
the 18th. I am not sorry to get away as the work here gets less
and less. We have a Foreign Office Inspector visiting us next week
and I wonder what he will think of the set-up. He is supposed to be
adjusting cost of living allowances and we have all had to prepare
private budgets for his benefit.

I think I told you I had ordered a Humber on the strength of them
saying that delivery would be made in three weeks. Whether we
should do better to trade the old Humber in or sell it privately I
don't know, but I have told Miss Turnbull (some business female
in Rootes) to contact you for details of age and number. She said
that delivery of a *black* Humber might be less easy so I said let
it be any colour but black. Personally I am not particular but you
might want something to match your complexion.

I had a letter from the Sunday Express (of all London papers)
saying they understood I was going to India and would I write a
weekly commentary on the progress of the new Everest attempt.
Why they should think me being an advantage for commenting
cannot say but in any case I refused firmly. There is more than
enough published already about Everest and the Sunday Express is
the last place I should wish to appear in. Publicity of that sort would,

of course, please the Cambridge Press [his current publishers] but one can pay too dear for it.

Bill left Burma at the end of March and came straight home. His interlude, had he but known it at the time, was nearly over. For the rest of his life he would have a career – as a sailor.

PART FOUR

Ancient Mariner

CHAPTER 12

South

Bill Tilman's relationship with the sea began relatively late in his life but lasted to the end. Eventually, the sea was to kill him. He turned to sailing because he considered that he was no longer able to achieve what he called the 'stern standard' required in high-altitude climbing.

He kept up his writing, lectured, gave the odd talk for the BBC. Meanwhile, he was beginning to sail offshore; that is, apart from dinghy sailing which he had first done in earnest just after the war. He made at least two trips to Ireland in a friend's yacht, for instance, once he returned from Burma.

The sea had been preoccupying him and it is not unfair to say that, in his middle years, as restless as ever but in his own harsh terms too old to keep up with the burgeoning new class of mountaineers (1953, when he returned from Burma, was when Everest was first climbed), he discovered the true romance which had eluded him so far.

He wrote openly about it: 'The sea's most powerful spell is romance; that romance which, in the course of time, had gathered round the ships and men who from the beginning have sailed upon it – the strange coasts and their discoveries, the storms and the hardships, the fighting and trading, and all the strange things which have happened and do happen to those who venture upon it.'

Curiously, he added immediately after this that 'with the mountains there is no romance', and one might surmise that, finally, with the sea, Bill had found his ultimate vocation. The sea represents death, in the unconscious, and in its endless wastes Bill, finally, found peace. After quitting mountaineering, and having failed to find a career, Bill's embrace of the sea as a way of life became whole-hearted. It was his great good fortune to have discovered early on a partner in this great venture.

Bill's great love affair has been frequently remarked upon. By now a confirmed bachelor with an excellent home arrangement in the shape of his sister and his two grown nieces and their families, Bill's chosen partner was not of human form but a yacht. In fact, she was an old working boat, a Bristol pilot cutter, eight years younger than Bill, and when he first saw her, in a fairly sorry state in a boatyard in Palma, Majorca.

The discovery of *Mischief*, and the decision to buy her was hastened by Bill's urgent desire to undertake an expedition to southern Chile, to attempt a crossing of the Patagonian ice-cap. Bill had first mooted such a project immediately after the war, but had been defeated by currency regulations and the problems of finding a berth on any commercial ship in the aftermath of a global conflict.

Returned from Burma in 1953, this project took on an urgency that led, in the end, to the Mediterranean and *Mischief*. Bill had hoped to start his expedition that same year, but then he had not come across the vagaries of yachts, their builders, or the sea. No boat since Noah's Ark has ever been ready on time, Arthur Ransome wrote in one of his children's books, *Picts and Martyrs*. *Mischief* needed a good deal of work on her before she was fit to sail back to England, let alone embark on the trans-ocean voyage Bill had in mind, which involved her poking her wooden hull into the pack ice of the Patagonian channels.

He wrote to Adds, his sister, from Mallorca on April 3rd, 1954: 'The surveyor, backed up by Bobby [the noted sailor, Robert Somerset], thinks that there is nothing wrong with Mischief's hull. In fact, in spite of its 50 years, the wood seems as sound as ever. The trip is therefore on and the only remaining doubt now is whether the work that has to be done on her will be done on time.'

He added that he was now regretting the St Andrew's do (where he received an honorary D Litt in June, but which meant flying home and back again).

While *Mischief* was being refitted, Bill went sailing with Somerset and a party of others including Jan West of whom Bill wrote to Adds: 'I was rather alarmed to learn that the other hand for the Malta voyage is the woman Jan West who came round with us last Whit from Gosport to Plymouth.' From Bizerta in Tunisia, whence they fetched up on April 13th, 1954, he wrote:

It is all very interesting and amusing and I don't suppose Bradford [the previous owner of *Mischief*] will be ready to leave *Mischief* until after Easter. The more I see of Bobby in action the more I despair of ever being able to handle a boat. His energy and resource are extraordinary and he is never at a loss what to do or how it should be done. Jan West is good company and does most of the cooking. I do none at all; my queasiness when in the galley seems to be taken for granted. I did feel ill although not actually sick the first few days but am all right now.

Bristol pilot cutters like *Mischief* come in various sizes; they have very deep keels and were designed to be worked by a single man and a boy. *Mischief* was forty-five feet in length, thirteen feet in beam and drew seven foot six inches aft, weighing about fourteen tons. She had been converted into a yacht in 1927 and had had nine previous owners.

Although she was basically sound when Bill bought her, he was not the first yacht owner to discover that the word 'basically' when applied to boats or ships of any size could cover a multitude of detailed problems. Once slipped and examined in more detail – after Bill had paid for her – she was found to need an extensive refit. This included taking out a very large quantity of concrete ballast, putting in a number of new planks, recaulking, doubling of all fastenings and keel bolts, new rail caps, fitting stanchions and replacing all the running and standing rigging.

This was why Bill had left the yard in Mallorca to get on with the major work while he went for the yachting trip in *Iolaire*, Somerset's yacht. He had already had one longish trip in *Iolaire*, from Portsmouth to the Med. This time, he sailed to North African ports and to Malta.

When the trip was over he moved on to *Mischief* to oversee the refit. It was, by his own account, 'hard lying'. *Mischief* was still on the slip and although the ballast had been removed, there was no floor to the cabin. Spanish shipwrights took frequent siestas but Bill noted, on the positive side, that the work was costing about half what it would have done in a British yard.

After all the work that had been put in, by both the yard and by Bill, he was very satisfied, feeling, as an old whaling captain had remarked to Joshua Slocum about his *Spray*, that she was 'fit to shunt ice'. Bill was frequently to quote Slocum in the coming years; there is no doubt where his inspiration and admiration lay in this regard and he pointed out, with some pride, that whereas *Spray* faced worse weather in the Magellan Straits, she, unlike *Mischief*, never had to shunt ice.

Bill now had his yacht, suitably converted, but he had to get her back to England before he could start on the voyage south. He might have reflected, in the saga that ensued, that finding, buying and refitting a yacht was a mere trifle compared with finding, keeping and enjoying the company of a crew. Bill rarely solved the issue of how to find a good crew but then he was remarkably careless in his methods, as we shall on almost every occasion discover.

On the delivery voyage he had agreed that the previous owner would assist him as far as Gibraltar. This owner insisted that his wife come along too, and the experience – as Bill saw it – coloured him permanently against having women on board as crew.

On the passage, the relations between Grace Darling [his name for the wife] and myself had been strained although I had been self-effacing, as an owner should be, and as silent as usual. Perhaps one of the few remarks I had ventured had not been well chosen. We took it in turns to cook and the day after Grace Darling's turn, when one of the crew who knew how to cook was officiating, I thanked God aloud for having on board one whose presence ensured our having good meals on at least one day in five.

Bill never minded telling jokes against himself, indeed he revelled in them and, on occasion, saw that they were well spread around, as the numerous stories about him attest. No question, should such a place exist, that Bill is in heaven enjoying the retelling of these mishaps here on earth. But Bill never bothered how others took this extremely dry and often caustic humour.

The owner, along with 'Grace Darling', and the other two crew all left at Gibraltar and it was at this point that Bill realised, finally, that he was not going to get to Patagonia in 1954. He stayed stuck in Gibraltar until September when he was joined by David Drummond, a mountaineer who was to be one of the Patagonian ice-cap party. Drummond, who had been an Outward Bound instructor at the school where Eric Shipton had taught, had married Shipton's ex-wife, Diana. Bill said, in a rather bitter comment on his late crew, that Drummond 'knew nothing about the sea but being a mountaineer he would stand by me and not desert'.

To get *Mischief* back through the onslaught of equinoctial gales, Bill managed to obtain, by his own account, a weak crew, supplemented by two army recruits 'a likeable pair, and failed only in staying power'. Partly, this might be explained by Bill's subsequent aside that they, too, knew nothing about sailing. So here we have a man of some sailing experience, but not as a skipper, setting off on a 1200-mile voyage along a tricky coast with the Bay of Biscay ahead. For a man of Bill's fortitude and stamina not impossible, nor, strictly speaking, foolhardy, but certainly a hard stretch.

So it proved. For eighteen days, after rounding Cape St Vincent, they struggled against strong head winds; yachts of *Mischief*'s kind sailed very badly indeed into the wind and conditions on board would have been dreadful. Bill seems to have been taken by surprise by the attitude, if not of Drummond, then of his younger crew, who, he says, began to 'murmur loudly. Unwisely, perhaps, I had told them we were about the latitude of Oporto, whereupon the two NCOs declared that unless we put in and landed them they would no longer stand their watches. In fact mutiny on the high seas. The situation called for a bucko mate and a belaying pin.'

Although he had plenty of belaying pins, neither he nor Drummond had any stomach for a real fight. Knowing the entrance to Oporto, across the bar of the River Douro, was a nightmare place, none the less he struggled to get *Mischief* in – without any local tide tables. As they made this attempt a cannon was fired at them from the shore. In the confusion that followed Bill believed he was being warned off and anchored outside the river. The next morning, when they took a pilot on board to help them in, he was told that this had indeed been so: had they tried to come in the night before *Mischief* might well have been lost. At this point the two RASC men left, leaving Bill with three.

After more scratching around, an old yachting friend, Humphrey Barton, with a friend, flew out from England. Even so, the sail home was far from uneventful, although in writing about it Bill managed to squeeze one last drop of humour from the latter stages, when they were near to Ushant.

There, he says, one of his crew, a Scottish lad, made his one active contribution to the voyage: 'for which I forgive him all – [he] drew our attention to a pillar buoy on the port bow and breakers ahead. Having put *Mischief* about and brought the buoy on to the starboard hand we passed close enough to discover that it was the Ar Men buoy marking the reef of that suggestive name for which we had been confidently heading.'

Two days later they were in Lymington, which was to remain Bill's home port for over twenty years. 'I was left alone to clear up the mess and to lick my wounds,' he says. Apart from anything else, *Mischief* needed a new gaff, topmast and bowsprit; her deck, too, sagged when it was jumped upon and for a time Bill feared he would have to replank it. In the end Barton cured the problem by getting Bill to put supporting posts under the deck beams.

At this stage of his sailing career, lesser men might have spent the long winter months pondering the whole enterprise. Bill, however, was not a lesser man. He simply plunged on and although he wondered if the supply of 'rash, inconsiderate, fiery voluntaries' who knew either sailing or climbing had dried up, he was to find, eventually, one of the best crews he ever had, including the effective skipper for this first trip, W. A. Proctor.

Bill made three truly epic and successful explorations of the far south: the expedition to the Patagonian channels and ice-cap, in 1955 and 1956; then, the greatest of his sailing trips, to the Crozets and Kerguelen, in 1959 and 1960; and as the skipper of the yacht used for the Australian Heard Island expedition in 1964 and 1965.

These were offset by two major failures: Bill had tried for the Crozets in 1957 and 1958 and had failed, eventually circumnavigating Africa. Then, between 1966 and 1967, no doubt fortified by his recent experiences with the Australians on Heard Island, he tried for Smith Island, and Mount Foster upon it, and failed – the voyage which would lead, eleven years later, to his demise.

The voyages south have a quite different flavour to the series he made to the north – usually to Greenland. As with his climbing, he gave them up as a bi-annual programme because it meant sailing for so long before any worthwhile objective could be reached. Travelling north, as the first Greenland trip proved, was quicker and it meant voyages could be made in one season, from May to October. The final voyage south by Tilman – in *Mischief* – was an aberrant one, as I say, the result of his success the year before on the Heard Island expedition.

In some respects Bill made or broke his voyages absolutely; notwithstanding the crew 'problems', certainly in the later northern voyages, there are times when one feels he has decided, almost from the start, that this one will be bad, this one all right. The northern voyages were to become Sisyphean in their great labour for little or no purpose, especially after the loss of *Mischief*. Bill seemed unable to unhook himself from an annual voyage north; by then he had little else to do. They were to cost him more than a second yacht lost; his reputation as a curmudgeon arose during the last voyages north.

The first voyage south was always set fair. 'When I got in touch with Bill Proctor . . . I found him eager to make a long voyage and not a whit perturbed either by the cruising ground or the prospect of a year's absence. Nor did he waver, as several others did, from his first decision.' But Bill was shocked when he found out, on visiting Proctor's home 'that he had a wife and three children'. He felt like a wrecker of homes, he remarked.

He found out that Mrs Proctor was happy to let her husband go, a 'sensible view' he thought, merely requesting that Bill brought him back at the end. With Bill Proctor firmly on board as the sailing master, Bill Tilman set about seeking out the rest of his expedition. He put advertisements in the yachting press (later, famously, he was to use *The Times*). Of the replies, none proved viable. He had several from undergraduates 'some . . . were accepted, only to withdraw later, deterred either by the advice of illiberal tutors or nervous parents.' Among the rest 'there were several girls and one married couple (an application which made me wince)'.

While all this was going on, Bill set about getting *Mischief* fully commissioned, an activity which he admitted so overtook his interests as to leave the goal almost unseen. Bill had been intrigued by Patagonia for nigh on a decade. Immediately after the end of the Second World War, he had been casting around for some adventurous caper and the ice-cap had for a while seemed ideal. It covered between 400 and 500 square miles, varying in width from 20 to 50 miles and in height from 6000 to 10,000 feet. Remarkably, the glaciers flowing out of this region penetrated to the sea and thus, as Bill said, 'a mountaineer can step from his boat and begin his climb at sea level.'

It was the glaciers which really drew him on. Bill had scorned his most recent mountain home during the war, the Dolomites of northern

Italy, until he found out that one at least, Marmolada, had a permanent glacier on it.

But Patagonia attracted him for other reasons. It was then, and remains, an incredibly remote region of the globe, and many of the stories told about it bordered on the fabulous. Bill relates with relish some of them: that trees grew on the glaciers, and humming birds and parrots mixed with penguins. He mentions with glee the pampas on the Argentinian side of the ice-cap with its gauchos and their bolas. He ponders on the natives whose heads were supposed to steam if they ate marmalade. The very best part, though, was that the available maps had the Spanish word *inesplorado* in two places and although, by 1954, the ice-cap had been climbed from the Argentinian side, it had not been traversed from the Chilean channels, tucked in behind the Andes.

'The adventure of crossing an ocean, the seeing of new lands and little known coasts, and the setting foot on hitherto unvisited glaciers were for me sufficient reasons for travelling so far afield,' he wrote. However, in 1955 there were still currency restrictions on British travellers and Tilman, ever the reluctant supporter of science and all its works, agreed to provide the expedition with a scientific rationale – collecting plants and, he had hoped, surveying the glaciers. In the event, they only collected plants.

By May 1955, shortly before *Mischief* was due to set out, he had still only Bill Proctor as a firm crew. His luck then turned and he rapidly acquired Michael Grove, a young artillery officer who took a year's leave of absence, and Charles Marriott, another gunner. The presence on board of two scions of the RA, apart from himself, no doubt hugely improved Bill's belief in their eventual success.

The final member of the crew was found through Bill Proctor. John van Tromp (upon whose illustrious name Tilman was moved to comment as a favourable augur) was a farmer. Bill was much taken, on first meeting him, by both his deerstalker hat and his offer to do all the cooking. 'I am not alone in liking good food and plenty of it,' he said.

With just van Tromp and Proctor on board, along with a woman friend of van Tromp's, Tilman set out from Lymington on June 27th, sailing along the coast to Falmouth, their departure a little delayed by a common error among ocean sailors. 'The engine did not start immediately,' Bill wrote, 'but it did as soon as we had turned on the petrol.'

Along the English coast, all had worked out well, except that Tony (the female friend) was 'deathly' sick. Off Falmouth they tried out the twin foresail arrangement, known to thousands of ocean sailors as the best means of running down the trades in a yacht. Van Tromp's girlfriend, Bill remarked, was once more heavily ill in the blustery weather.

Then Grove and Marriott arrived: 'at last I descried a bearded figure in a white yachting cap who, viewed from far enough off to conceal the slightly motheaten blazer and flannel trousers, had something of the air of King Edward waiting to join the royal cutter *Britannia*. It was Charles Marriott whom we gladly took off, for his appearance did *Mischief* credit.'

Bill ends this chapter from *Mischief in Patagonia* by saying: 'At 10 am we got out our anchor and sailed out,' adding a quote from Sir Francis Drake to Sir Francis Walsingham about 'the true glory'. It is stirring stuff, traditional heroic mode expeditionary rhetoric.

Bill Tilman, however, is too good a story teller to allow himself the luxury of heroics. He begins his next chapter thus: 'Although it smacks of seamanlike efficiency, to say that we got our anchor and sailed out is not strictly accurate. It leaves much unsaid. In fact we had two anchors down and their cables were so lovingly entwined that for some time the foredeck was the scene of a fearful struggle and resounded with unseamanlike oaths.' Eventually they made it out of the harbour only to find the wind had died.

The voyage was under way, though, and, with few mishaps, they sailed to Las Palmas in the Canary Islands. One thing Bill was learning about on this trip, and learning fast, was how to navigate at sea where no landfall can provide an aid. Like many sailors before and since, he did not find this easy. He cheerfully admits their many mistakes. After a bad landfall on the north coast of Spain he remarked:

The navigator can always attribute his errors – unless, of course, they are fatal – to abnormal tide sets or the perverse behaviour of currents, whereas a man who leads his party into the wrong valley or onto the wrong ridge has no such scapegoat and is written down an ass. We should have to do better after taking down our departure for the Canaries, for it would not do to miss *them*.

All, except van Tromp, took turns at working up the sights. Their 'expert' was Marriott but he, said Bill, had refused to move with the times, preferring 'time-honoured methods employing logarithms, haversines, cosecants, and God knows what, and these seemed not only to take longer than ours but gave more scope for human fallibility. The scope was, in fact, so wide that an error of a degree or so in working became known to us as a "Charles".' When they got a good result they called it a 'Henry' after the great Portuguese navigator.

By these means, heading south all the time, they improved. Sixteen days after leaving Falmouth, a time that *Mischief* was never to vary from on this run, they knew they were close to the Canaries. Even so, their faith in their navigation was not quite so strong that they had felt able to turn west when they should have done. Sailing on, and then heaving to in murky weather, Marriott finally spotted Grand

Canary after they had sailed past it, the resulting beat back taking nearly a day.

From the Canaries they made their departure for the great trek south, expecting their next landfall to be off the coast of Brazil, their next port Montevideo well inside the River Plate. By now their navigation was improving; they crossed the equator on August 29th in longitude 28°W, 'about the right place', Bill remarked. They made their landfall on the South American coast at Capo Polonio after two months at sea. Soon after they were sailing up the River Plate, dropping anchor in Montevideo harbour at 1.00 p.m. on October 1st, sixty-four days out from Las Palmas.

Marriott temporarily left *Mischief* in Montevideo, suffering from a bad shoulder, but agreeing to rejoin the ship in Punta Arenas. Bill took a German, Gird Breuer, as the makeshift crew and they sailed south on what was to be their slowest passage, the 1200 miles to Punta Arenas reeling off at only an average of fifty-six miles a day. They reached the entrance to the Magellan Straits, Cabo de Virgenes, on November 5th, Punta Arenas on the 9th. They arrived in flamboyant style: 'we were sailing fast, a little too fast for accurate navigation, and presently a jar and a shudder warned us that *Mischief* had indeed reached Patagonia . . . we lost no time in handing the sail and dropping anchor a cable's length from the jetty.'

Punta Arenas was, in 1955, a far-flung outpost of Chile, very unlike today when it is the bustling and rapidly expanding part of a development region, seen very much as the gateway to the riches of Antarctica. They spent three weeks there, gathering their strength for the voyage into the unknown, just around the corner, so to speak, but well outside the hopes and fears of civilisation. They had already experienced the fierce winds and currents of the region and *Mischief*, even tied up in harbour, had had some narrow escapes.

Marriott, after various adventures of his own, now rejoined the ship, along with a young Chilean climber, Jorge Quinteros, who Bill took sight unseen but of whom he wrote: 'I don't think Jorge ever regretted having joined us and our only regret was when he left.' As an example of Bill's idiosyncratic methods of picking people, however, the episode of Quinteros is hard to beat. 'I took him,' said Bill, 'because, like Hillary, he was a beekeeper and this seemed to me to be good enough.'

On November 26th, in the southern hemisphere spring, they left. It was a Saturday.

By then a large crowd of friends, admirers, and no doubt some critics, had assembled to see us start . . . we hoisted the jib so that her head would sheer away from the jetty, and cast off the remaining warps. For some as yet unexplained reason the jib promptly fell into the sea and the next minute saw us stuck hard and fast by the stern less than a ship's length away from the waving crowd.

Worse was to come and Tilman milks it for all it is worth.

Having recovered the jib and unavailingly tried the engine which we had hitherto been too proud to use, we sent a warp ashore to the accompaniment of much friendly advice from the experts with the idea of pulling her off the mud. *Mischief*, who had so eagerly taken the ground on her arrival, seemed to have a liking for the place and would not budge. In the roads two Chilean cruisers lay at anchor and at this moment of crisis one of their picket boats was approaching the jetty at the good round pace common to picket boats, a sailor with a boathook standing rigidly to attention in the bow.
    Either by seamanlike intuition or at the instance of the loud instructions from the crowd, her helmsman grasped the idea that we wanted pulling off. Perhaps he thought we wanted shoving off, for putting her helm hard over, with little diminution of speed, he rammed us fair and square, projecting the still rigid, well-disciplined bowman half-way up our shrouds. It was a Saturday afternoon and one could almost hear the happy sigh of the crowd as they realised how wise they had been to spend it on the jetty.

The same picket boat managed to pull them off and, Bill wrote, 'with all speed we hoisted sail' and, thankfully, left. This whole episode is in his diary as: 'All on board 3pm, Large crowd on quay, Photos. Cast off, jib fell in sea, went aground. Sent warp ashore but finally pulled off and then rammed by picket boat from cruiser. Good sail as far as Santa Anna.'
    Soon, after leaving the straits, they entered the 'channels', a maze of waterways with appallingly treacherous shores and winds, seeking Peel Inlet and the Calvo Glacier, the departure for the climbing party.

It was fascinating sailing: rounding miniature capes, peeping into hidden coves, tacking between rocky wooded shores, backed by sombre fells of yellow heath and grey slabs, and over all the low driving clouds. Desolate and forsaken as the scene was, it had the powerful appeal of an untrodden land and the bracing challenge of unsparing harshness.

It was hard work: on December 2nd he wrote in his diary:

A horrible day of cold rain. Made good about 7 miles and had to use the engine for an hour at either end. Got into rocky inlet about 5 pm and anchored in kelp in 7 fms about 30 yards offshore. Everything on deck sodden and no chance of doing any work on the sails or sheets. However it is nice to get down below after such a day to the cabin where the stove soon makes it warm.

Later, Bill remarks on the unfailing accuracy of their charts, mostly prepared a hundred or more years before by men of ships such as HMS *Beagle* of Charles Darwin fame. 'We were humbled by the thoughts of those men who had spent so many years in these tempestuous waters, hemmed in among islets and hidden rocks riding out gales, drenched by constant rain, and who in open boats sought out and sounded all the various channels and anchorages.'

Bill wrote too, of the extraordinary lives of the relatively recently extinct Patagonian Indians who, naked, lived in these harsh waters largely on a diet of mussels. 'They had nothing to fear. Nothing to fear, that is, until the coming of their so-called betters; the sailors, sealers, and traders who traded drink for skins; and the missionaries who killed by misguided zeal and ill-directed kindness. As Mark Twain said: "Soap and education are not as sudden as a massacre, but they are more deadly in the long run."'

Finally they reached Peel Inlet, picking their way through myriad small icebergs or 'bergy bits', many of which were giving *Mischief*'s skipper heart attacks as they ground into his yacht's hull.

After some six miles of threading our way through patches of ice and occasional stretches of clear water we at last turned into a small bay to reconnoitre the approach to the next 'sea-level' glacier. Waterfall Bay, as we called it, was magnificent if nothing else. Quite near and high on our left a great white stream of ice swept round the foot of a black ridge to break into myriads of cracks, seracs, and crevasses, many of them scintillating with a vivid blue, as they plunged steeply to the ice-strewn water. On one side was bare rock; on the other, almost as steep, evergreen forest.

It was from this setting that the ice-cap party, Bill, Charles Marriott and Jorge Quinteros, set out. Grove, Proctor and van Tromp were to stay with *Mischief*, finding a safe anchorage away from the ice. Tilman and his party left on December 17th. Each Sunday, until February 12th, the yacht was to return to the glacier. If nothing was seen of the shore party one week after that date, she was to return to Punta Arenas. Tilman and his companions had fifty days' food with them.

The successful crossing of the ice-cap – Bill had a bathe in the waters of Lake Argentino on the far side to celebrate – was completed with one or two near disasters, best told by Tilman in *Mischief in Patagonia*. It was a great triumph of willpower on all their parts. Charles Marriott was now suffering from an infected foot; Bill fell into a crevasse and on the way back they nearly missed finding a crucial food dump in a blizzard.

Bill's diary, for Monday, January 23rd, records this:

Still blowing hard but sun shining. Visibility about 1/2 mile 10 am. Started out to look for dump . . . Gave up partly because I think the snow is so deep we would not find anything . . . C complaining of cold. Decided to start noon. Job of packing tents. J said we ought to try to go back to Argentina. C agreed. Vetoed. Started 12.50 in high wind and plodded up to crevasse which marked the dump (Bearings compass left in glove in dump). When abreast dumped loads and went searching – J very reluctant to leave loads scared of getting lost. No good very thick went on with J leading v slow. When past crevasse C suggested another look. Off again on slope, finally unroped and C and J scattered. J again staying. C spotted a black thing 200 yards. Sure enough. Cheers. Saved my photos and possibly our lives. I doubted if I could have got these two over the pass to Camp VII. Was really getting very worried. Have been since the storm began on 20th.

Their problems were by no means over but they got back to the shore. When they made contact with *Mischief* they discovered how lucky they had been. In a decision Bill found hard to understand, Bill Proctor had, as Bill put it, 'swanned about', as a result of which he had tried to go into a narrow entrance at the extreme end of Peel Inlet. There, *Mischief* went aground. Ice floes were banging into her with alarming speeds in the current. As the tide fell, Proctor and his crew rigged the topmast, carried on deck – and nearly left behind in Montevideo as being too much of a nuisance – as a stabilising leg. At low tide only two feet of water showed around the yacht, which drew nearly eight.

The three on board now began a frantic effort to lift out what turned out to be three and a half tons of ballast, mostly pig iron. By this time the ice had scraped large parts of the hull bare, planking had been scarred and the propellor had an entire blade chewed to pieces. Finally, they managed to float her off. But getting the ballast back on board proved as hazardous as lifting it off. Right at the last moment, with all the ballast back, *Mischief*'s engine failed and they began to drift back towards the reef from which they had rescued themselves. Water, meanwhile, was pouring in around the stern tube. With more luck than judgment, they escaped.

Bill's diary for this story simply reads: 'Clot Proctor went up N to the narrows, ran hard aground, bent prop shaft chipped propellor.'

His anger at Proctor's stupidity was in part directed at himself for failing to give much more explicit instructions about *Mischief*'s disposition during their absence. It would have been hard living, though, for the three on board to have anchored for the five weeks the shore party had been gone and Bill's ire was tempered by the account Proctor gave of their epic struggle to save *Mischief*. That Bill held no grudge is seen by his delight that Proctor was able to come with him on the long voyage to the Crozets, two years later.

Meanwhile, he had to get *Mischief* to a harbour where she could be slipped and the extent of the damage checked. For a while he considered returning to Punta Arenas but in the event he made for Valparaiso in the north, sailing well out into the Pacific and then, because the ship's chronometer had not been recently calibrated, using the sixteenth-century sailing master trick of 'plane sailing'. This involved finding a latitude (in this case of Valparaiso) and then sailing along it, no accurate time-piece being needed.

Bill relied a good deal on what remains the greatest bible of navigation aids for the practical mariner and one which repays close study for all ocean yachtsmen and women: Captain Lecky's *Wrinkles in Practical Navigation*. As on many other occasions, it was to provide him with the answers he urgently needed. Charles Marriott was one good reason for heading towards civilisation as soon as possible. He spent this leg of the voyage in his bunk, his feet now seriously infected.

They reached Valparaiso where Charles left with Jorge; Bill took back to England another Chilean, this one a sailor, George de Giorgio. *Mischief*, to Bill's relief, was found to be much less damaged than many other yachts of her age might have been, a discovery which confirmed to him that he had chosen well in this kind of old-fashioned heavy working boat for what he wished to accomplish.

He left Valparaiso in March, sailing back through the Panama Canal – where Michael Grove left as his year was nearly up – and on, through the Caribbean and Bermuda. A year and a day from the time they had left Falmouth, they passed St Anthony's Head; three days later, on July 9th, 1956, *Mischief* sailed into her home port, Lymington.

I will not pretend [Bill wrote] that at all times throughout this 20,000 mile voyage we were a band of brothers. Patient Grizelda herself and a company of angels would sometimes find their tempers strained to breaking point when cooped up in a small ship for months together . . . But we were old enough or sensible enough to bear and forbear, and to put the ship and the enterprise in hand before our own feelings. It . . . enabled us to bring a worth-while undertaking to a successful end.

In 1957, a year after this triumphant return, Bill tried to get to the Crozet Islands, one of the remotest group of islands in the seething heart of the Southern Ocean. He was defeated by a mixture of circumstances, including his own illness at a critical moment in the Southern Ocean.

After his triumphant return from Patagonia Bill believed he had found the way to marry sailing and climbing. He set about looking for his next objective. His attention was on the southern wildernesses and three sprang to mind. The first was Heard Island in the sub-Antarctic, really just one big mountain of 9000 feet, draped in ice and snow from sea to summit and thus very appealing. As there was no secure anchorage a party would have to be dropped and left, the yacht returning to safer waters – probably Kerguelen. Bill, thinking no doubt of what had nearly happened to *Mischief* in Patagonia, did not like the idea of this at all.

He turned next to Kerguelen itself, a large island with many good anchorages. Kerguelen had been used extensively by sealers and whalers in the nineteenth century but of late – it was a French possession – it had been permanently reinhabited by a French research establishment and, for that reason alone, Bill dismissed it as an objective. As he puts it: 'There was no denying that the presence of other human beings did to a large extent detract from the glamour. The word "uninhabited" on a map casts a spell almost as powerful as the word "unexplored", and the lure of a remote, uninhabited island is hardly to be withstood.'

It was for this reason that Bill substituted the uninhabited Possession Island, one of the Crozet group, as the destination in 1957. In the matter of his crew Bill was as casual as ever. He found Michael Clay at the end of a lecture he gave at Cambridge University. Jim Lovegrove found out about it on the 'jungle drums'. Gerry Levick, an engineer, and two others, Howard Davies and Pat Green, all turned up, the latter two both South Africans looking for a passage home – even if it went via the Crozets.

They left on June 30th, 1957 and arrived in Las Palmas on July 17th. Bill noted in his diary 'back-ache, cramp, headache', which might have been a warning. Of more concern to him though was the behaviour of the crew who took to spending their nights ashore in drunken revelry. *Mischief* left the Canaries in mid-July and sailed to Brazil, and thence on to Cape Town, which she reached on October 23rd, forty-four days out from Bahia in Brazil.

A month in Cape Town – a week more than Bill had wanted due to Pat Green abruptly leaving – meant they did not depart until November 21st. Five days later they ran into a gale which, after two days, worsened. By now, as well, Bill was seriously ill, lying in his bunk and more or less comatose.

Early in the morning of November 29th, Mike Clay, who had been on watch, allowed *Mischief* to broach. A big heavy working yacht like *Mischief* would be the very devil to bring round from such a condition where she had turned her beam to both waves and wind. So it proved. A large sea breaking on her deck demolished the remains of the dodger, flattened all its stanchions, and started inboard the cockpit coaming which in turn wrenched up the adjacent deck plank. Water spurted through every seam of the skylight while the fenders and two heavy blocks lashed abaft the skylight went for six.

The square spars lashed on deck came adrift but luckily remained on board. On its way forward the wave swept the dinghy overboard, bending at right angles the life-line stanchions as it went. With the dinghy we lost a bag of anthracite, two small water tanks, the working jib folded and lashed, and several coils of rope. So much for the deck; except of course, for the unlucky Mike who had been thrown violently to the cockpit floor, half drowned and half dazed.

Down below similar chaos reigned for a while.

Bill's diary relates among the incidents on deck and below: 'Dinghy swept away. Big crash below got me up. Water through skylight.' His writing is almost impossible to decipher, though – worse than usual even for material he was noting while on a passage. Most significant, although he writes an entry for the 30th, there is nothing then for ten days, a unique gap in Bill's accounts down the years.

His published account suggests he had a large hand in the clearing-up operation and in the subsequent decision to return to South Africa. In fact, neither is true. The loss of the dinghy meant that no landing could sensibly be tried on Possession Island but it was the condition of *Mischief*'s skipper which was giving the crew more concern; that and the thought that they had only just begun to penetrate the terrible waters of the Southern Ocean. They persuaded Bill, still sick, that common sense dictated they return.

Bill writes thus:

I wondered weakly how many more such batterings we would receive in the course of those 2,000 miles away in Lat 49° S, whereas a man of more robust mind would have argued that the weather had done its worst, that we had come through in tolerably good shape, and that since the summer was advancing we were unlikely to meet with any more such breezes lasting for three days. Another worrying thought was that besides myself only two of the crew could be relied upon to steer safely in bad weather, and the prospect of that long haul under those conditions so daunted me that prudence decided me to give up and sail back to Durban.

This defeat rankled so much he was unable to write about it for ten years, eventually adding the account of this failure alongside the much bigger failures of the Smith Island expedition of 1966–67. He ruefully began his account of the abortive Crozet Islands voyage by saying, 'a man's experiences are said to be the name he gives to his mistakes.'

Had Bill not succeeded two years later in getting to the Crozets, we would never have had even this account of what happened. Bill could never accept that he was not in command and here we have it starkly. The coded parts of his message are in the words 'weakly' and 'more robust mind' both of which ideas have two meanings. Bill, one can be sure, would never commit the sin of falsehood. To those four others who knew, this was Bill describing his actual condition. To his readers, they meant he was, as usual, playing up his faults as a leader, not discussing a real medical condition.

So they returned and from Durban Bill took *Mischief* up the east coast of Africa, through the Red Sea, the Suez Canal, the Mediterranean and home. They had been gone thirteen months.

He wrote to Adds from Gibraltar: 'What mugs we were to come by the east coast [of Africa]. I am feeling better and can work on deck. But walking ashore I still feel very queer in the head – physically, not mentally, for I have been queer that way for a long time.' The last cryptic remark is a typical Bill joke but the illness he refers to is one reason why he never made it to the Crozets. Probably it was Meunière's Disease, a crippling affliction of the ear which creates nausea and dizziness and which is slowly self-remitting.

His published account says that on his return to England in 1958 he had not felt strong enough to write about this attempt on the Crozets. The illness which had affected him had also caused some memory loss; Jim Lovegrove who was on this voyage with him says he never remembered being ill at the critical moment at all.

Bill Tilman was more determined than ever in 1959, when he made his second attempt at Possession Island, that he would succeed. This was to turn out to be what many judge the greatest of his sailing successes, matched in part by the Patagonian trip and by the later Heard Island expedition. Neither of those two expeditions match the overall achievement of 1959, nor the fact that this was the most taxing voyage ever made by Tilman as skipper of a yacht.

It was this voyage which first produced his famous advertisement in *The Times*: 'Hand (man) wanted for long voyage in small boat. No pay, no prospects, not much pleasure.' Bill only inserted it a month before he planned to set out. He really wanted five hands, although four would do. 'All must be of cheerful equable temper, long-suffering, patient in adversity, tolerant of the whims and uncouth manners or habits of others, neat and cleanly, adaptable, unselfish, loyal – in fact, possessed of most of the qualities in which the majority of men, including myself, are notably deficient,' he wrote, tongue firmly in cheek.

For once he was lucky. Bill Proctor agreed to come again. 'As he is a married man with three children, his wife's consent to his going showed admirable complaisance on the part of a wife towards her husband's whims,' he thought, possibly comparing Mrs Proctor favourably with his own sister Adeline, who indulged him so much. Roger Tufft was an Antarctic survey man and, to Bill's amazement, had hardly got off the ship from that distant continent than he joined *Mischief* to head on back – and under notably worse conditions.

As usual, and despite his advertisement's minatory tone, he had many offers from women. 'Although girls are often more enterprising and some of them more capable than men, I did not care to run the risk of being talked or ogled into an act of folly. For I had already had experience of the truth of the Chinese sage's remark that discord is not sent down from heaven but is brought about by women.'

Part of his reasoning was touching. It was that if he did not find a woman congenial, the chances might be that the rest of the crew would, thus ganging up on him. It never seemed to occur to him that it would be the other way round. But his judgment, overall, cannot be faulted. Finally, he picked another Dutchman, Jan Garnier, and a schoolteacher, John Lyons.

Bill's general naïvety with people at large and crew in particular is shown up well by the John Lyons story. In his published account Bill says, wonderingly, 'Lyons had crossed the Atlantic fifty-one times in the *Queen Mary*, playing the double-bass in the ship's orchestra. When he produced a Sailor's Discharge Book, one realised how numerous are the various callings with little or no flavour of the sea comprehended by the significant word "Sailor".'

Indeed. This was another rich, if densely presented, joke against himself. When Lyons had first approached Bill, the significant part of his application for Bill had been the word 'sailor' and his trans-Atlantic crossings. Only after did he find out Lyons was a musician, but he kept this joke going for a long time. Lyons turned out to be an admirable choice as cook so all was well. In fact he was older than Bill which meant on this voyage there were three elderly men on board.

The last crew member was Jim Osborne and Bill liked him because he did not say much. 'Silence, the Chinese say, is worth buying,' Bill said. 'That it is particularly valuable at sea is shown by the words addressed to his new mate by the skipper of a coasting schooner: "What I want from you, Mr Mate, is silence, and not too much of that."'

It was this happy band who set out on July 30th, 1959. *Mischief* had caused her owner much grief before this departure as, on her return from her circumnavigation of Africa, Teredo worm had been found in a large part of her hull. It was Bill's fault as he admitted: he had skimped on the anti-fouling he had applied and the worms had found a way in. The expense was appalling and, with the cost of replacing parts of the deck and strengthening it, he had had to sell his car.

The usual multitude of small jobs had also to be done but *Mischief*, when she left, was in a good condition for what she would face in the months ahead.

From Las Palmas he wrote to Adds: 'We got in here yesterday . . . Old Double-bass does well in the galley . . . Besides cook, he is the life and soul of the party, full of quips and quotations, very well read and knowledgeable. The trouble is his knowledge does not seem to extend to Primus stoves . . .'

This time they sailed directly to Cape Town after they left Las Palmas, the days of sailing south being spent in watching the endless displays of dolphins around their bow, in undertaking the many small jobs of maintenance on a small yacht on a long sea voyage, and in reading. 'There was an ample collection of books on board – I will not call it a library – from the *Odyssey* in the original Greek (Proctor) to geological tomes. Space travel, Westerns, and the *Scragged in her Silk Stockings* type. They catered for all tastes, and they might have come off the sixpenny barrow.'

They played chess, Bill noting that, for Bill Proctor, it was not a silent game, as he commented on every move. He also noted, with approval, that Proctor's appetite had abated. Later in his voyages, Bill was to gain a reputation for appalling food and meanness in their portions. On this voyage, food was not a problem, in any sense.

For lunch we rang the changes on cheese, sardines, herrings, bully beef or 'Spam', with dates, Marmite or peanut butter as 'afters'. The cheeses were whole ten-pound Cheddars . . . For tea we had biscuits and jam, sweet biscuits and occasionally cake, pancakes or soda bread . . .

But the evening meal we regarded as our main hope and stay, like so many gross rustics 'whose principal enjoyment is their dinner, and who see the sun rise with no other hope than that they shall fill their belly before it sets'. It consisted of whatever dish the skill and ingenuity of the cook might concoct from ingredients limited to bully beef, sausages, Spam, rice, beans, lentils, peas, macaroni, spaghetti, potatoes and onions, helped out with dried vegetables and soups for flavouring. This would be followed by stewed prunes, raisins or apples, or a massive steamed pudding.

Thus regaled they reached Cape Town on November 1st, after seventy-one days at sea and even for Bill this was a little on the long side for an ocean cruise. There Bill had numerous friends to greet and many social activities in which to indulge. Bill was often happier in these colonial settings than he was at home and he seemed to like South Africans as much as he later liked the company and comradeship of Australians. Essentially a loner, he liked the right sort of congenial company and the rather brasher, less class-conscious stuffiness of these southern countries appealed to him, much as he liked the 'wild west' elements still to be found in parts of South America. Bill, the explorer, liked least the formality of England in the 1950s, still stuck in its out-moded class-ridden ways.

Mischief, meanwhile, was hauled out for anti-fouling, whereupon her stern block was found to be rotten. The replacement of this massive piece of timber delayed them again and it was not until early December that *Mischief* sailed out of Cape Bay for her second attempt at the Crozets.

This time there were no serious gales to trouble them and on December 20th they sighted their first sub-Antarctic island, Marion Island, to the west of the Crozets but on course. 'I don't know what we expected to see, but from the disparaging remarks that passed I gathered that the crew were not pleased with the view,' he wrote. 'Certainly Marion looked grim and sombre enough in the fading light.'

They sailed on, through Christmas Day when 'we had a lot of mulled wine and . . . were not in an over serious mood' to December 27th when, at last, they found their objective. Bill was more relieved than his crew might have guessed. The Crozets are a difficult enough target but Possession Island is guarded by a group of deadly reefs and smaller islands, any one of which could have spelled grief to their little ship.

Perhaps the earlier sighting of Penguin Island had taken a little off the edge of this landfall but not much. For here was the long-looked-for prize at the end of a 10,000 mile voyage, a prize with a true romantic flavour – a lonely island set in a stormy sea, and *Mischief* borne towards it on the crest of great following seas, with albatross wheeling in her wake.'

To Adeline he wrote from the yacht:

28 Dec – Isle Possession, Isles Crozet. Am writing this more for the sake of the envelope than anything else. The crew are busy sending off their stamped envelopes with the idea that in a few years' time collectors will give £5 for them. What a hope. We got in here y'day after a pretty strenuous voyage. At least half a dozen gales or near gales, and y'day when we were near the island was one of the worst. The wind off the land was so strong that it was all the engine could do to push her into the anchorage, the water being whipped off the surface into the air like the willie-waws of Patagonia.

It is a strange place. An easy sandy beach to land on swarming with King Penguins which don't bother to get out of one's way.

Also great slug-like Sea Elephants weighing a ton or so which just open their eyes and grunt. Roger and I went for a walk today. Clouds covered what looked like the peak and it will be frightful with about a week of load carrying even to get to do a ridge of the 'main' mountain.

Saw and photographed albatross on a nest. They too don't move. Crew all well. Self very tired. Will take a day off tomorrow,

Best Love,

Bill

Though they found the mountains marked on Possession Island were lower than they had thought, Roger Tufft and Bill climbed them both successfully. They were all amazed by the wildlife – penguins and elephant seals aplenty, for instance. He wrote to Adds when he got back to Cape Town that, on Possession Island:

Roger Tufft and I cleared up what peaks there were. They were disappointing. We were led to believe in 5,000 foot snow-covered mountains . . . in fact the height was only 3,200 feet and the little snow only temporary. There were two others of 3,100 and 2,700 but there was no climbing. The wild life compensated for this. There was a penguin rookery (king penguins) of several thousand on the beach, one had to brush them off with one's feet to get anywhere. On the beach, too, were hundreds of elephant seals, great creatures like slugs, hardly bothering to open their mouths and bellow unless one kicked them. On the grass slopes above albatross and giant petrels were nesting. Roger ringed over 200 of them. Their eggs and penguin eggs make good omelettes, and we also knocked off the odd penguin to eat. The meat is not bad. The vegetation is very scant, but we collected what there was.

From Possession Island they sailed on to Kerguelen and, eventually, to the French research station. Much wining and dining followed and it was a very merry skipper and crew who finally left for Cape Town on February 2nd, 1960.

On February 20th, on their way back to Cape Town, Bill wrote again to Adeline:

I'm thankful to say we pulled it off this time visiting not only the Crozet but Kerguelen as well. We had the dirty weather one expects in the forties. Cold, wet, gales, but no prolonged storms with the seas building up to dangerous heights like they did in '57. Altogether it was much easier than I expected once we got used to the conditions.

The crew and self are all well though naturally getting a bit bored with each other. Proctor and Double Bass are not on speaking terms and I have had to interfere on several occasions. I think it's largely Proctor's fault as he is seldom content with what's given him.

They made it to Cape Town, however, and from there they sailed for home, via St Helena in the south Atlantic, reaching Lymington on June 30th, 1960, sixty-five days out from St Helena. Bill quoted Conrad at the end of this voyage: 'The ship we serve is the moral symbol of our life,' and, as before, he emphasised the bond they had found together, not he insisted in himself but in their goal.

CHAPTER 13

Triumph and Tribulation

After the triumph of the great expedition to the Crozets and Kerguelen Bill turned his attention to northern waters for a number of reasons. Among the more significant of those, however, was his disappointment that the peaks they had found on the Crozets were only 3000 instead of the expected 5000 feet high. 'To misquote Prince Hal,' he wrote, 'this had seemed to me an intolerable deal of sea to one half-pennyworth of mountains.' As a result, between 1961 and 1964 Bill made four summer trips north to Greenland, both east and west coasts, in their way, all successful.

In the winter of 1963–64 Bill was contacted by a former army major, Warwick Deacock, then living in Australia, and asked if he would like to act as the navigator on a sixty-three-foot steel-hulled schooner, *Patanela*, which Deacock had chartered for an expedition to Heard Island. Once there, the plan was to climb a 9000-foot mountain, Big Ben. Bill had known about Big Ben for some while; indeed in 1957 Heard Island and its mountain had been among his choices for the voyage which eventually turned into the Crozets trip. The problem had been that there was no safe anchorage for *Mischief*.

Deacock told Bill that in their case *Patanela* would land the climbing party and then backtrack to Kerguelen, returning after the climbers had completed their work. Bill knew, from the start, that he would not be among those climbers and that, effectively, he was being asked to skipper *Patanela* while the climb was under way. To this he agreed after checking out the *bona fides* of Deacock and his friends. What undoubtedly tempted him was first the thought that one of his early sailing and climbing objectives would now be met; that he was being asked as a sailor to navigate and, as it turned out, also to skipper a much larger yacht than *Mischief*; and, finally, that he would again visit Kerguelen and enjoy the hospitality he had been so taken with in 1960.

Deacock knew Bill from a lecture he had given at Sandhurst Military

College at the end of which, famously, asked by a student how to get on an expedition Bill had barked 'put on your boots and go'. 'Later,' wrote Deacock to me, 'I spoke to him at length at a Climbers Club dinner in Wales when he dissuaded me from trying for a climb of Gosainthan (Xixapangma).'

Suitably reassured by what he already knew and what he found out, Bill arrived in Sydney on October 20th, 1964, to find *Patanela* in a chaotic state, undergoing, as she was, a major refit. She had been used for cray-fishing in the Bass Strait which meant that she had a huge hold amidships to hold the crustaceans. When Bill saw where the ten of them were supposed to bunk, he objected: 'Being a bit of a cissy, I thought some other arrangement desirable,' he wrote. He suggested that they reduce the amount of diesel fuel they were to carry from 2000 gallons to 1000 and to provide accommodation for four of the crew in the lightless but stable hold. Altogether, though, *Patanela* was a very cramped ship. All washing, for example, had to be done on deck; there was no lavatory at all.

With tongue in cheek Bill, now in his sixty-fifth year, suggested these arrangements, far from putting him off, might affect the rest.

Our crew of young, eager, resourceful Australians and New Zealanders, whose morale, I feared, might have been affected by this too ungracious living, took it all in their stride, making light of deficiencies and of their gloomy quarters. The steel door of the foc'sle soon bore the legend 'Saloon and Bar'. Over the cray-tank door they painted 'All hope abandon etc.,' and below, in lighter vein, 'Knock twice and ask for Maisie'.

Bill approved of the food they took, amazed by its variety and its quantity. We lived like princes, he wrote, although much later, when offered an entire barrel of wine by the French on Kerguelen, he declined, suggesting they provided only two jerry cans instead as a barrel was too generous. In this he was being doubly prudent, no doubt, for drinking at sea can be literally fatal and, expecting his climbing team to triumph, he would have not wanted to spoil the celebrations at sea, and in those waters, with drunkenness.

He was also impressed by Deacock's decision to act as the cook: 'In Warwick we had a man born to grapple with these ingredients [their stores] on a scale of the necessary grandeur. Thrice daily throughout the voyage he satisfied ten voracious appetites, his only relief coming on Sundays when the crew took it in turns.' He notes, too, that each day they had a can of beer, with spirits for high days and holidays. Of Bill, Deacock says: 'Several things came together to make the Heard trip a success not least of these being the presence of Tilman not just as a skipper and navigator but I suspect for several of us the knowledge that we were privileged to share all this with such a personality.'

Once in Sydney, Bill moved aboard *Patanela* with Douglas Hunt – who did not make the voyage – to help with the fitting out.

In the various stages of this long process Doug Hunt and I lived like nomads, moving our bedding from the saloon to the foc'sle and back again two or three times. Cooking was out of the question. For breakfast we walked up to King's Cross, a sort of Australian Leicester Square, where an eating place remained open all night; we lunched on board off meat pies and beer, and after work went ashore for a meal at night.

Gradually, the rest of the crew joined: among them, Ed Reid, the radio operator; Phil Temple, writer and entomologist; John Crick, a New Zealand climber; Tony Hill, the mate, 'of great help to me, competent, reliable, and able to jolly the crew along'.

Patanela sailed for Heard Island on November 5th, 1964. They had first to sail 1800 miles along the south side of Australia before they could take their departure off Cape Leeuwin for the further 2200 miles to Heard Island. In a typical Bill fashion, he wrote of their departure thus: 'For my part I believed and hoped that the most worrying part of the expedition was behind us; for the next few months our only contentions would be with the elements.' *Patanela* had to put into the small port of Albany, in Western Australia, to pick up the remaining three crew. Bill was candid about his navigation, as they approached this port.

When land appears at a distance the navigator is tempted to begin at once to identify various features. This is a mistake. The first surmises he makes are as often as not false and once made they are only grudgingly abandoned. On this occasion the nearer we drew the less I could reconcile my first ideas with the chart, and I had worked up quite a stew before we satisfactorily identified the lighthouse on Breaksea Island, when at once everything fell into place.

Much later in the voyage, when they first sighted Kerguelen, where they had to sail in order both to test their gear and to position themselves for the run south to Heard Island, Bill wryly wrote: 'The surprise shown by the crew at this precise landfall was, I thought, a little uncalled for.'

In his diary he had noted, only three days out from Sydney 'Badly out in pos'n, about 20 m. Not very clever navigation so far.'

They arrived at Kerguelen on New Year's Day, 1965. Midnight had seen them all on deck singing and ringing bells to see the New Year in. 'The middle watch sang and had a drink,' Bill noted. He had been in contact with the French authorities in Paris, who controlled the research station on the island, to ask their permission for *Patanela* to stay at Port aux Français while the climbers were on Heard Island, a request readily granted.

But, on their way out, they had merely wished to use a quiet bay on the island for testing the rubber Zodiac, their only means of getting the climbers ashore on Heard Island, while getting all the climbing and other gear into shape. But they were surprised by a helicopter from a small out-station and, as a result of this encounter, ended up having lunch with the inhabitants who had paddled out to meet them 'on a crazy raft of oil drums'. Ashore they toured the base: 'two huts, two tents, two helicopters, and three wine barrels'. Needless to say they had a splendid meal, at the end of which 'we sang the *Marseillaise*, Grahame playing the accompaniment on his recorder while lying under the table, then arm in arm we went down to the beach, a swaying picture of international fellowship.' In his diary Bill noted that the singing was mostly 'dirty' songs.

They left Kerguelen on January 4th. Three days later, while still sixty miles away from Heard Island, they spotted Big Ben. 'There was no mistaking the characteristic lenticular cloud sitting over the summit and below it the glint of white snow slopes.' At midnight they hove to, while about ten miles clear of Winston Cove, where the climbers intended to land. At this first attempt no landing could be made, the wind rising quickly to gale force. It was two days later that they finally got the shore party away, two days in which they had drifted forty miles to the south of the island. Astonishingly, Bill managed to get *Patanela* anchored in what were still gale-force winds.

His diary for January 12th reads:

Heavy breakers on lagoon bar. Decided to land on beach to W[est]. 11.00am First soft load off capsized on beach. 3 underneath lost nothing but Budd's camera. Radio contact after some delay. Reported surf too bad for launch. Said will wait till night. 2pm launched again. 4pm ready to go. Met strong wind off C Lambeth . . . increased to gale foce with rain. Went on motoring W[est] (true) till 00.30 and then hove to under bare poles.

The first raft had been loaded by 11.00 and Deacock, Grahame Budd, John Crick, Philip Temple and Colin Putt went ashore. It was a perilous operation throughout, although each of these men was wearing a wet-suit against the cold and the sea. An hour had passed after the first trip before the yacht party knew the climbers were safely ashore.

Then it was a question of running the raft back and forth until they had their month's supply of food on the island. 'By 4.00pm the shore party were safely established . . . and we had squared up on board and were ready to go,' wrote Bill. '11th February was the day appointed for our return.'

Bill now set about clawing them back to the relative safety of Kerguelen, 300 miles to the north-west, that is to say, to windward. To Bill's surprise, it was an easy passage and three days after they left Heard Island they resighted Presqu'île Monarch at the south-east end of the island. Reaching Port aux Français they found they had timed their arrival to perfection. When the 'Chef de Mission' came aboard it was to say that lunch was being served and, once again, the French did not disappoint Bill. 'Amidst a great welcoming uproar of cheers and banging on the table we took our seats. We had an undeniably excellent meal, a meal such as only Frenchmen could produce on what is a desert island. I noticed my companions going at it hammer and tongs.'

In the course of these celebrations Bill was told that at the Baie de Navire on Possession Island, where he had spent a fortnight five years before, a base had now been established. A *téléférique* now passed above the penguin rookery through which he and the others had struggled so often, 'a piece of news that decided me to write off Baie de Navire as a place to be revisited'.

Bill was invited to stay the entire fortnight at the base but he felt this would be too much of an imposition and *Patanela* moved on, agreeing to take six of the French along the coast to Ile Longue. The barrel of wine having been swopped for two jerry cans, they set out. Back at Port aux Français from this interlude, Bill had a considerable fright when *Patanela*, anchored in winds reaching gale force ten, had dragged and then banged heavily into rocks. Russ Pardoe, using an aqualung, was able to inspect the hull and to report no damage but it was a relieved Bill who ordered the sail back to Heard Island on February 6th. They reached the island on February 10th and 'we were relieved to see the tents there and at length a moving figure, though it seemed to us that they took our arrival very calmly. In fact it created so little stir that we began to wonder if they were all there or even all alive. After a tense hour Warwick came on the air and we listened in awe-struck silence to a remarkable bulletin.'

The gist of this was that all five had made it to the top of Big Ben. Even so, getting them off the island cost each man all his personal gear and all the other climbing equipment. Heard Island retained to the last its reputation for being a highly dangerous place. Bill's regret was that, having arrived a day early, the shore party were tempted to return to the yacht when conditions were so bad. Thus had the gear been lost.

Nevertheless, the shore team were in fine fettle. Now *Patanela* showed her paces, making 1000 miles in the week after they left the island. 'On 14 February the crew obstinately refused to let me stand my watches [it was the skipper's birthday], and to have all night in at sea is about as nice a present as a man could wish.' Eighteen days out from Heard Island, they picked up the Eclipse Island light and early the next morning they were tied up in Albany.

Bill's final description of this expedition should be quoted in full.

In his famous description of a prize fight Hazlitt summed it up as 'a complete thing'. In my opinion, devoted as I am to both sea and mountains, to sailing and climbing, this expedition deserves to be so described. A long voyage, much of it in unfrequented waters, and at the end of it a remote, uninhabited island crowned with an unclimbed mountain. It was an enterprise that needed to be undertaken, one that I myself had shrunk from attempting, and that now, thanks to Warwick Deacock's initiative and drive, had at last been accomplished. From first to last we had been a happy party, each man pulling his full weight. I may have regretted not to have set foot on Heard Island, much less on Big Ben, but that was implicit in the job I undertook. Besides enjoying every minute of it, I considered it a great privilege to be skipper of so fine a vessel and to sail with so eager, lively and resolute a crew.

Never again was Bill to express such fulsome praise for any of the people he voyaged with. At sixty-seven, this single voyage may have provided him both with a benchmark for what could be done, given the right mix of people, and, more sadly, as a dream never to be realised again in his own life. After he returned home it is no surprise that Bill, looking at the age of both *Mischief* and himself, decided to make one last voyage to the far south from England.

After another successful summer voyage in 1965 to, among other places, the recently arisen volcanic island of Surtsey off Iceland later that same year, Bill set about planning a trip to that other goal he had long had in mind: Mount Foster on Smith Island, almost due south from Cape Horn.

In *Mischief Goes South* he feels an urge to explain this in some detail to his readers, by then accustomed to his voyages north. 'Fired by the divine spark of discontent or out of cussedness, after five voyages to Greenland waters I felt in need of change,' and as I have suggested, this was brought about by the Heard Island expedition.

Smith Island, part of the South Shetlands, on which Mount Foster stood, was a difficult target, as far as Bill knew, untrodden by any man. Moreover, on this expedition he would get to climb the mountain: 'Smith Island offered a supreme challenge to the sea-going mountaineer, an even sterner challenge than that accepted recently by Warwick Deacock and his party of Australians and New Zealanders . . . For at Smith

Island a party would be starting from scratch, without foreknowledge of a possible landing place.'

Bill was approaching seventy now but his old competitive spirit, manifested laterally rather than directly, was still strong. He quotes Beowulf again – Bill had a fund of quotes but frequently used a favourite half-dozen – that same quote he had used to justify giving up the Himalaya. This time he uses it to argue *for* making the voyage to Smith Island. He was inspired, too, by the thought that no ship of *Mischief*'s size had sailed in these waters before, apart from that epic voyage made by Shackleton from the South Shetlands (Elephant Island) to South Georgia.

Having decided to go, Bill faced once more the problem of who to take – or, more accurately, who to find who would or could be willing to lose twelve months to such an undertaking. 'There must be plenty of men of the right stamp who would come forward if they knew what was afoot or if one could make contact with them.' This was written after the events that follow but Bill never gave up the idea that the right people were around; it was just that he had great trouble in identifying them.

Yet he could write: 'The crew's ability to get on with each other and to work together is more important than what seamanly qualities they may have,' following this with the thought that the Heard Island expedition 'were picked men, known to each other or to mutual friends, men with like interests and with expedition experience'. In this quite accurate assessment Bill seems curiously detached from his own methods. Not least is the way he leaves himself out as if he did not count at all. Therein lay some of his future woes.

On this voyage Bill had some of the worst experiences he ever had at sea and his long justification for his methods of picking his crew take up an inordinate space in his narrative. He writes:

My system, if system it could be called, had worked well enough so far. Even if it could be arranged, a short preliminary voyage to try out the crew would have little value. They would be on their best behaviour, zealous and willing to an embarrassing degree, and if one did take a dislike to one of them, a replacement would still have to be found at short notice. Always on past voyages the crews had shaped up to their jobs . . .

Leaving aside the fact that the last statement is flatly contradicted by his own accounts of the problems he had already had, Bill's fault lay simply in his indifference.

Picking a yacht crew is tedious, long-winded and does create all kinds of tensions. But it pays dividends, as he himself had seen, when the crew do all get along. Bill's method was no method at all. He had taken Jorge on as a climber in Punta Arenas, sight unseen, simply because Jorge had kept bees – like Edmund Hillary. So, Bill reasoned, he must be all right. In correspondence elsewhere, he was to remark that he had always been prejudiced against young men with beards. He always believed what people told him and he was, in the words of his good friend Sandy Lee, prey to boasters and con-men.

Forced by his age to accept younger crews from the mid-1960s on, he simply did not see that many of those who volunteered were likely, to put it mildly, to be unreliable. The consequent mixing of the genuine adventurer with the eccentric or merely disaffected, occasionally the sad and mad, led to all kinds of misery. Bill's attitude, as the years wore on, was to retreat to his bunk and let the crew sort it out among themselves, cursing under his breath that young men were not like they used to be.

Bill's own judgment about crew seems to have been stuck on two false premises: first that a sailing trip was much like a climbing trip; second that the youngsters he had to rely on in the 1960s and 1970s were just the same as the ones he had fought with in the First World War, or climbed with in the 1930s. But sailing on long hard cold voyages in cramped conditions does not mirror trekking into the mountains, where men can vent their feelings merely by walking away from conflicts, by breathing in cool mountain air.

At base Bill's attitude was stubborn: if a man has chosen to come with me, knowing the circumstances (and, one supposes, having read the books about previous trips) then he should stick with it, he says in effect time and again. It seemed never to have occurred to him to explore in any way the motives of those who offered to come, other than at face value. He never much bothered that crew had any expedition experience, let alone could handle an ancient heavy 'classic' yacht, her eccentric sailing, or her maintenance and repair.

In this regard he might be thought to be a hero of a different kind: providing many young people, without the benefit of experience, with the chance of a lifetime. Many of course took it; but Bill, who on his last voyage was to express surprise at the coherence of Simon Richardson's crew, once they all met, could not shake off his impressions, as the years passed, that he had been ill-served. It has left a sour taste to this day, and many believe they 'know' Bill Tilman for a cantankerous and ill-tempered old man, sailing a leaky old tub.

Perhaps worst of all, his simple honesty led him to accept as the truth whatever people told him. If a man said he was a brilliant sailor with a vast experience, Bill believed it. And, having lived a life of iron frugality when on expeditions, he could not understand the needs and desires of his crews for the fleshpots of the world, or for the more prosaic comforts of home. To Bill Tilman, expeditions were between a rock and a hard place – and so they should be, or else why bother?

This flaw in Bill runs so deep it needs to be investigated. Part of the trouble lay in the times in which he had grown up – the Edwardian world before the First World War. The 1914–18 war changed everything in Europe: the culture of pre-war Britain was transformed by the experiences of the slaughter. Bill was a late Victorian in attitude. He believed, in a way we have simply forgotten, in honour, in integrity, in the literal sense that a man's word is his bond.

He further thought that he was offering the crew he took on his voyages the chance of a lifetime and that, if they were not grateful for what he provided, then at least they should be glad. In this way he espoused a Victorian patrimony, harsh in its judgments. With many of his earlier crew he felt equal: they were either from the army or of a not dissimilar age. Not having children of his own, as his crew grew younger, so he grew more judgmental.

From their point of view, they were doing *him* a favour but he never saw it like that. They – the crew – ate his food, sailed on his yacht, and the fact that, rather than take them sightseeing in the Med, he chose to give them expeditionary marvels, meant, from his point of view, that their recalcitrance at times of adversity was pure ingratitude.

Early in 1966 Bill got his first crew – Roger Robinson – a young sailor who could take a year off. John Ireland brought along David Shaw; Ireland was a climber, Shaw a merchant sailor 'just the man I always hope to have with me and so seldom get. I took to him at once; red-haired, sturdy, quiet, and self-reliant.' This was to be the man Bill planned to leave in charge of *Mischief* when they went ashore at Smith Island. Added to this list, when they sailed, were Mike Edwards and Tom O'Shaughnessy. It was Edwards who occasioned Bill's remark about beards. 'Stupid prejudice though it no doubt is, I feel totally opposed to young men with beards.' He took Edwards, though, because he had served in the navy as a photographer and Bill had had an idea that they should make a film of the voyage. Typically, this was all last minute and, once he had given Mike the job of cameraman there was barely a week in which the camera equipment could be bought.

They left on July 14th, 1966, sailing as usual through the Canary Islands. From there they headed on the old route to Montevideo. The voyage, so far, had been going well. Bill was impressed by David Shaw's navigation, suggesting he was a much quicker and much more accurate navigator than himself. Bill, from his own account, was more an instinctive than a precise navigator, as shown by his extensive use of Lecky's *Wrinkles*. Closer to the earlier sailing explorers than to the modern high-tech merchants of position-fixing, he says, 'my sextant, made by Bassnett of Liverpool, a firm long defunct, must be pretty vulnerable. Old shoes, old coats, old friends, are best, but, perhaps, not old sextants . . . However, since the Polynesians navigated successfully with a coconut, price 1/-, one grudges spending £50 or so on a new sextant.'

In the Canaries, Bill noted, his crew were models of decorum, unlike

211

the crew he took on the first attempt on the Crozets. At the same time, for Roger Robinson, Bill's efforts at getting them out of Las Palmas harbour led to his first real doubts about the man who he had thought of as a very great seaman indeed. Bill had tried to sail off *Mischief*'s moorings without apparently understanding which way the yacht would 'pay off' once the sails were hoisted. As a result they ended by sailing further into the harbour. *Mischief* was a very heavy boat which turned badly. What Bill did was to hoist the staysail, not the jib, and then to sheet in the mainsail hard.

Roger Robinson, on the foredeck, was horrified. He noted in his own diary:

We saw wire hawsers stretched taut between the jetty and an off-lying buoy. We couldn't avoid that but now there was a little bow wave. We hit the wire about three feet up the bobstay. It tightened and stretched until twang it shot down the bobstay hissed along each side and appeared astern in a flash. But by then the the boom was only feet away from the jetty and about to crash into it and snap clean in half. Two of us rushed aft and hauled in the mainsheet; at the same time a puff of wind just lifted it clear of the jetty by a couple of inches. As we swung round the end of the jetty a gap about ten feet wide appeared in the middle of a cluster of boats but by now everything was possible and we swept through them all, our last defiant gesture. How she missed everything I shall never know but I hope we never have another chance to test the skipper's devilish luck again.

They left for Uruguay on August 6th. David Shaw had begun experimenting with *Mischief*'s helm, to see if he could get her to steer herself in these downwind conditions, with just twin headsails up. Three weeks after they left Las Palmas, on August 27th, Bill came on deck to find the helm lashed, the ship on course, but no sign of David Shaw. It was, Bill said, hard to believe but a quick check of the deck, and then below, showed that Shaw must have gone over the side some time in the night.

The ship log entry reads: 'Skipper came on deck 07.40 to find helm lashed, ship steady on course (WSW compass) and no sign of David Shaw who had the 06.00–08.00hrs watch. Called all hands and gybed ship 07.50 and started sailing back on reciprocal course, ENE.'

To his diary he confessed, 'Can't understand how this could happen. No reason to leave cockpit and in any case although she was heeled over she was fairly steady. Crew seem to want to go on. It will be an even tougher trip than I expected.'

Having called out the rest of the crew, Bill turned *Mischief* round in what they all knew was a vain attempt to retrack to find him. As they did, they noticed that the patent log – the towed device which gave their speed through the water – had stopped working.

> On hauling in the line we found that this had broken about two-thirds of its length from the counter. It is by no means unusual to lose a rotator; on the present voyage we lost two. Either it is bitten off by a shark or a porpoise, or the line frays at the point where it is attached to the rotator. But the line is less likely to break or be bitten through at any other point, accordingly we assumed that it had broken when David grabbed at it, or even later on when his weight on it had combined with a sudden lift and snatch of the counter to put too much strain on the line.

Examining the logbook and comparing it with the log-counter, they found that it had stopped at 1831, only a mile after the watch had been relieved. That meant he had been in the water for at least one and three-quarter hours. It was at this point that Bill knew they had had a fatality. Even so they searched all day.

> At 6.30 pm, the sun about to set, I decided that no more could be done. Setting main and staysail, we hoisted a riding light and hove-to for the night, unwilling to leave the scene of the tragedy and uncertain of what course to steer. Were we to continue to South America or turn for home? It seemed best to sleep on it. In the morning I could ask the crew what they wanted to do. Apart from all its other sad aspects, the loss of David Shaw was a well nigh fatal blow to my hopes and expectations. As mate, as a competent navigator, a reliable, likeable man with whom I could get on, a man whose training imbued him with a sense of loyalty to the ship in which he served, his loss was irreparable.

It was not only Bill who was hit hard by this accident. The crew, too, took it badly but they insisted that *Mischief* sail on, somewhat to Bill's surprise. He agreed that they should, suggesting that if they could not land on Smith Island and climb the mountain, at least they could explore the South Shetlands. As a result of this decision, *Mischief* arrived in Montevideo on October 6th, sixty days out from Las Palmas.

Bill now made a stupid mistake, born of his anxiety about what had happened and his lifelong distrust of authority and, in particular, of foreign bureaucracy. He removed David Shaw's name from the crew list, arguing that the real reason was that the port police would tell the press and thus the news would reach David's parents before he could tell them. Bill went to the British consul in Montevideo to file the details of David Shaw's death; the British press of course got the story anyway which then rebounded back to Montevideo; thus did the local authorities find out. They were not pleased.

Sorting this out took some time and had Bill managed to keep hold of his crew, and leave fairly smartly, all might have been well. As it was, he had a mutiny, begun by John Ireland who complained that, notwithstanding David's death, *Mischief* was unfit for the voyage. He singled out the lack of distress signals and a life-raft and as this point has been used to condemn many of Bill's later trips, as well as this one, some comment should be made.

Bill defended himself thus:

In my view every herring should hang by its own tail. Anyone venturing into unfrequented and possibly dangerous waters does so with his eyes open, should be willing to depend on his own exertions, and should neither expect nor ask for help. Nor would equipment of this sort be much help in Drake Passage where the chances of being picked up are so slim as to be hardly worth considering. A yacht is supposed to carry distress signals but is not over-reliance placed upon them by owners of small craft?

Some of this is fair enough, some specious nonsense. In fact crew from abandoned yachts in the remotest places, using a life-raft, have survived; psychologically, having one on board is invaluable. Similarly, distress signals might, for example, have been needed on this present trip to signal to the yacht that the shore party were in trouble. A radio was the most obvious missing item on board *Mischief*. Bill was parsimonious in the extreme: these items of equipment need regular servicing and checking, if not replacement. The truth was that he was justifying the unjustifiable – and he knew it.

On the other hand, his crew had known the yacht before they sailed and they had had a second chance to get off in the Canaries. David Shaw's loss had rattled them and now they and Bill were to pay the penalty. John Ireland left, along with Mike Edwards.

Robinson, in his diary and in letters home variously wrote:

We took no precautions against the expected Pampero which blew up mid-morning, we dragged hitting two yachts and a wreck before Tom and I could get the chain up enough for her to go ahead under engine. Then we eventually made fast alongside some fishing boats. This mismanagement has decided me to leave. John and Mike were going to go to Falklands but there wasn't room. Now all three of us will go to BA . . .

All the same feel very low. So many problems with gear and money . . . Ship leaves 22nd. Oh God if only it hadn't come to this . . .

In a letter home of the same time, he wrote:

I shall look forward to getting home – actually you'd be surprised at how much. The cruise has fallen through. Losing the best man overboard didn't help matters but from then on the crew situation has become steadily worse. It leaves a very stubborn skipper whose reputation as a skipper is grossly over-rated and a very thick surly yob from Liverpool who is now the skipper's slave who won't now let anyone suggest anything let alone criticise. The ship leaves much to be desired. There is no life-saving equipment apart from one cork lifebuoy, hardly any medical stores and none of the winches work properly – much of the gear is nearly worn out. The mast is rather dicey and the engine has no spares.

It is heartbreaking to see such a fine ship rotting away . . . today the weather has broken, it pours with rain and I'm in the dumps . . .

Bill was now stuck in South America with just Tom O'Shaughnessy. Desperate, he eventually trawled the local Salvation Army sailors' home from which he made, now perhaps inevitably, a dreadful choice. The man was called Carreo Javiel – black, probably Brazilian and an itinerant who pressed his suit heavily on Bill and Tom. 'Mixed crews in small boats, like mixed marriages, need thinking about,' Bill wrote. 'We are all as God made us, some of us much worse, and no one can help his colour. Racial integration is a subject much to the fore and I felt sure that Tom, who hailed from Birmingham, would assimilate or stomach a black crew as easily as I could. Besides we could not afford to be choosy and this man Carreo had one skill which we needed. He was a marine engineer . . .' The other man Bill took was a German, trying to get back to Europe, Herbert Bittner, a one-time racing cyclist but, as Bill discovered, no sailor. They sailed south on October 28th, after Bill had had a hard time from the port police about both David Shaw and the ship's papers. At the last minute Mike Edwards rejoined them.

What followed was a nightmare. They went first to Punta Arenas where Bill gained one more crew member – Louis. They sailed directly for Smith Island, reaching it on Christmas Day, 1966. Bill notes in his logbook 'My worst?' as his crew were by now becoming more and more bloody-minded. They did not attempt a landing, sailing on instead to Deception Island where they made contact with the British Antarctic Survey and the *Shackleton*. Their reception was very frosty, Bill attributing it to the behaviour of his crew who used up hot water ashore and, he thought, were spreading tales about his abilities on the *Shackleton*.

Whatever it was – and it must be said that many Antarctic bases are very unfriendly indeed to the 'drop-in' visitor – they moved to the nearby Chilean base where they received a much warmer welcome; Bill compared his treatment by the British unfavourably with that of both the Chileans here, and the French on Kerguelen.

Bill had intended to sail direct to Cape Town from Deception Island but he now diverted them via South Georgia. 'By calling at South Georgia we had the slight possibility of finding there a ship and no chance, however slight, of relieving ourselves of Carreo, our black incubus, should be missed.' Bill noted that they had taken just slightly less time than Shackleton, in 1915, but of course Shackleton, as Bill freely acknowledged, had made the voyage in an open boat and in some desperation. He is buried on South Georgia and Bill later visited his grave. (He had, as a schoolboy, heard him lecture.)

The welcome *Mischief* received from the tiny community on South Georgia more than made up for what had gone before: 'the warmest and kindest that *Mischief* has anywhere enjoyed', he thought, although this has to be tempered with what had recently occurred. He was welcomed into the manager's house and asked what they could do to help.

> From the sublime to the sordid and the ridiculous. Upon returning to *Mischief* I found Louis drunk and Carreo incapably drunk, kneeling on deck crooning quietly to himself . . . the locker containing what remained of the ship's liquor store bashed open with a hammer. On the table were two empty gin bottles and a half-empty bottle of cherry brandy.

Worse followed. Carreo, when he sobered up a little, was found wandering about the base with a knife, threatening to kill Bill. To the north, Port Stanley refused to accept Carreo who now refused to go to Cape Town; the rest of the crew were unhappy at the thought of him awake, on watch, while they slept below. Bill decided, reluctantly, that he had to return to Montevideo to put him ashore there and this decision drove Herbert to despair. It took them four weeks and 2000 miles as they had first to clear the westerlies which lay across their course. All the while Carreo was convinced they were heading for Cape Town, despite the marks on the chart. Even so, when they sighted the skyscrapers of Montevideo, Bill could not resist telling Carreo that, in fact, he was looking at Cape Town. After they arrived, all left, except Herbert.

It might have been, as Bill would have said, a trifling sum to add to the foot of the account of his misery, but he now discovered most of his traveller's cheques were missing. Suspicion fell on Carreo although nothing could be proved. Bill was forced to borrow money from the local (British) shipping agents. The final blow came when Herbert disappeared with most of this money too. Back Bill went to the agent, Mr Maclean, prudently lowering his request for more money from £100 to £40.

In the end Mike Edwards stayed, and Bill found three others, Roberto, Robin and Sergio, and sailed for Lymington, via the Azores. They arrived on July 15th, a year and a day after Bill had set out. 'My relief at having arrived was more heartfelt than it normally is,' he notes with some irony.

As the reader may have gathered, this 21,000 mile voyage had not furnished the enjoyment that is desirable and is expected on such voyages. Nor had it resulted in any achievement. We had nothing to show for it except the fact that the Antarctic, or the least hostile part of it, can readily be reached in a small boat. A voyage like this naturally entails the endurance of small privations and wearisome duties, and obviously all were not up to it. A man, however, must do his work with the tools provided, and if he himself provides the tools and finds them unsuitable, then so much the worse for him. On the other hand when we sail the seas we expect to be confronted with difficulties – that is the reason for doing it – so perhaps with a crew of thorough seamen and agreeable staunch companions everything would have been too easy. But to have four misfits in a crew of five is too many.

CHAPTER 14

Northern Lights

Bill Tilman first turned his face away from the south because he felt
the enormous effort of sailing thousands of miles before reaching the
chosen mountains was becoming too much. Even so, he regretted the
losses it entailed. He had, by 1960, made three long voyages south.
They had each entailed a year away from England but, on the up side,
had provided skipper and crew with three summers in a row.

> Starved of sun as we are in England this is no small thing and no
> doubt accounts for the fact that almost every yachtsman contem-
> plating a long cruise confines his choice to the Mediterranean, the
> West Indies, or the South Sea Islands, places of sun and warmth,
> blue seas and skies, palm trees and hula-hula girls.
> And since these voyages are supposed to be pleasure cruises,
> the fact that one can drink wine almost throughout the voyage is
> not to be overlooked. One may stock up in the first place at the
> Canaries or the Azores, and replenish in Brazil or Chile if bound
> west, or at Cape Town if bound eastwards. True, the wine will be
> cheap and will not much benefit by keeping or by being well shaken
> up every day. But, as they say in Spain, cursed bad wine is better
> than holy water.

His rejection of northern climes, until 1960, was in part due to his
belief that getting there would be very hard – harder than a crew would
contemplate.

> A voyage to northern waters, unlike one southwards, has little
> to offer in the way of pleasure to a yachtsman beyond a bracing
> climate and spectacular scenery. Instead of the crew delighting in
> the freedom of shorts and a shirt, or complete nudity, they may
> be pent up in winter woollies. As for basking on deck, only the

helmsman will spend any time there and he will be wrapped up in sweaters and oilskins.

However, he began to think that a summer voyage to the north would have certain advantages. Some of these mixed well with his own philosophy of expeditions and exploration:

A man need not be an ascetic, devoted to hair shirts, to relish a voyage under the moderately adverse conditions that prevail in the North Atlantic, or even in the Arctic, in *summer*. Men who go to sea or climb mountains for fun derive some of their satisfaction – a lot of it retrospective – in facing and overcoming rough weather and rough terrain, cold fatigue, and occasionally fright.

Further, Bill thought there was a vicarious pleasure among his readers for what he and his crew undertook. 'A favourite moral reflection of Mr Pecksniff was that if everyone were warm and well fed we should lose the satisfaction of admiring the fortitude with which others bear hunger and cold.'

Bill's problem was that he still craved remoteness and inaccessibility and he had believed, until he studied the globe more closely, that these desirable characteristics were only to be found in the near or sub-Antarctic. Looking north, he first thought that perhaps Spitzbergen would provide the answer but he was immediately put off by Roger Tufft (of the Crozets expedition) who told him that a large number of expeditions were now operating there.

So he turned to Greenland, an ice-bound hostile environment he was to return to again and again. Between 1961 and 1976 he visited these parts no fewer than thirteen times, coming in the end to identify with that earlier great northern navigator, John Davis. Bill was attracted to Greenland because he was sure few people had heard of it, let alone been there. It is the largest island in the world, so large that if it were to be placed over Europe it would extend from Scotland to the Sahara and from the Bay of Biscay to the Po Valley. The island is covered by an ice-cap, thousands of feet thick, the remnant of the last great ice age. It has few inhabitants (about 30,000 in 1960), mainly in small settlements on the west coast, and belongs to Denmark.

So, late in 1960, he made his decision: it was to be a summer cruise north in 1961. For once, Bill had early luck with his crew, getting the first two via a *Down Your Way* radio programme on Barmouth, one of whom, David Hodge, had a first mate's ticket. The other of this pair, Terence Ward, was an electrician but with experience of Norfolk wherries (and therefore, Bill reasoned, of heavy gear on boats). He then persuaded Charles Marriott to join, his stout companion from the Patagonian trip.

Finally he recruited Michael Taylor-Jones, a young physicist in the making and John Wayman, a keen yachtsman. On this occasion Bill also recruited a medic, Dr Joyce, who left them in Belfast feeling insufficiently fit to undertake the voyage. Ironically, Terence Ward later suffered an appendicitis and had to be evacuated from Greenland, a condition that would have been much alleviated had the doctor stayed aboard.

One major task before they left was the replacement of *Mischief*'s engine. This was an old petrol-driven device, supplemented by a charging engine for the batteries. Bill never placed much store by the engines of his yachts. Apart from that, the propellor which the engine drove was offset on the port side of the rudder. This meant the old yacht was difficult to steer under power and could almost never be persuaded to go astern.

On the long return from the circumnavigation of Africa, *Mischief*'s charging engine had finally expired; as a result the batteries went flat and, as a result of that, the engine, unused, had rusted itself to oblivion.

'The removal alone of the old engine was something of a feat. To the casual eye it appeared that it must either have been installed piece by piece or the boat must have been built around it,' wrote Bill. They got it out, eventually, and then some months passed before the new engine – a Perkins marine diesel – was delivered. Bill's relief at getting this job done was increased by the knowledge that he no longer had to carry up to seventy gallons of petrol aboard, a fire hazard he admitted that had not been helped by the number of 'engineers' he had employed down the years who seemed addicted to smoking while tending their charge.

While the engine replacement was under way Bill was busy, as he was every year, dealing with the standing and running rigging, the guard rails, blocks and purchases on the yacht. This involved taking it all back to Bodowen for cleaning and overhaul, an arduous task but one which stood them all well when, at sea, in a rising wind, skipper and crew at least could have faith in their ship. Bill further decided that, for Greenland, he would not take his topmast.

Some critics have remarked that in their opinion *Mischief*'s mast, in the words of Mr Chucks the bos'un, is 'precarious and not at all permanent'; and although it is staunchly stayed with shrouds of two and a half inch wire there have been times when I agreed with them. The extra strain of a heavy topmast aloft – 20ft of it above the cap – as well as the windage of it and its five supporting wire stays, is hardly offset by the small advantage of being able to set a topsail. The more so on a North Atlantic voyage where we might expect some rough weather.

Came the day, May 14th, 1961, when *Mischief* set sail from Lymington.

The first voyage to Greenland [wrote Bill] seemed to me a less momentous undertaking than the three voyages southwards. The time involved did not amount to more than a long summer cruise, nor did so many ominous question-marks hang over the enterprise as they had, for example, over the voyage to the Crozet Islands. On the other hand I was not happy about the Atlantic crossing and the expected head winds to which I was unaccustomed. In Davis Strait, too, we might expect trouble with fog and icebergs. Unknown perils loom the larger. I had never seen an iceberg; my experience of ice was limited to the small floes we had encountered in the Patagonian fjords.

Their departure was not an unalloyed pleasure – and in some senses set the tone for so many of the northern voyages to come. Bill's first diary entry for this voyage reads: 'Sun, 14th May. Cast off 10am. Hoisted outside Jack in the Basket [a well-known fixed mark at the entrance to the Lymington River]. Wind fair NNE. Wind freshened and headed us. Tear developed near throat of mainsail. Ran into Swanage Bay and anchored in 6fms 5pm. Repaired sail. Got anchor 9pm.'

Bill has gained a reputation for great skill in navigation but this needs to be put in a precise context. His methods were often slipshod in the extreme but in his own writing he generally admits this to be the case. He was worst in the English and Irish Channels, where the mean streak in him refused, year after year, to have his charts updated. He was best in the unknown, mountain or sea, where his acute observation and natural antenna in general ensured that even where he was uncertain of a landfall, he was able to pilot his yacht to a place where identification was possible. He used all the signs in the ocean: birds and their flight, sea temperature, cloud formations, any telltale which gave a hint of where he was. In this he was, indeed, a great navigator – a modern John Davis.

On the first voyage to Greenland, both sides of the navigator showed. Thus:

sailing westwards towards the Tuskar we presently spotted a red flashing light where, according to both uncorrected chart and the Pilot book, there should have been only the white flashing light of the Barrels buoy. A feverish search through the list of lights in the current *Brown's Nautical Almanac* revealed that a light-vessel with a red flashing light had replaced the Barrels buoy. That my chart and the Pilot book had not been kept up to date shocked our professional sailor [David Hodge]. He disliked such slipshod methods, though he admitted that while poking around at four knots in a 30-tonner one had more time to correct these little mistakes than when proceeding at 18 knots in a 20,000 ton ship.

Bill went on to say that he only changed his charts when they were so stained they could no longer be read and that a well-bound Pilot book ought to last a lifetime.

Later, off Greenland, a different order of navigation entered the lists.

On 29 June – a red-letter day for us – fog prevailed almost throughout the day. Although the sun shone brightly overhead we could get no sights, our horizon extending to no more than 200 yards. The clammy fog made it perishing cold despite the sun and despite the cabin stove which we had long since been lighting daily. As we sailed on through the mist it became obvious that we were in a situation that the prudent mariner does his best to avoid.

We had little idea how near we were to some unknown part of a rock-bound and probably ice-bound coast towards which we were sailing in fog, surrounded by scattered icebergs. If we went about, as caution advised, we could steer only south. So we carried on and at four o'clock that afternoon our boldness or rashness had its unmerited reward. A vast berg looming up ahead obliged us to alter course to clear it and at that moment the fog rolled away. After a month at sea the dullest coast looks exciting, but a more dramatic landfall than the one we now made, both as to its suddenness and its striking appearance, could scarcely be imagined. Two or three miles ahead, stretching away on either hand, lay a rocky coast thickly fringed with stranded icebergs and backed by high, barren mountains. Beyond the mountains and over-topping them was the faintly glistening band of the Greenland icecap. To identify any particular part of this strange, wild coast was hardly possible, but we guessed that a bold cape a few miles westwards might be Cape Desolation at the western end of the Julianehaab Bight.

Their evening sights confirmed this to be so. A month at sea had led Bill and his crew aboard an old working boat to the right coast of Greenland and within five days of their intended first destination. This was navigation of a very high order indeed, and one for which Bill's crews down the years had reason to be grateful. The problem was that many of these crews, as the years wore on and they got younger and he became more indifferent, identified him with those English coastal mistakes and judged him harshly, fearing for what would follow.

In Godthaab, their first port of call in Greenland, all was informality.

At five o'clock, when we were still apparently of no interest to anyone, I rowed ashore to find the harbour-master. As befits a harbour-master he was a big cheerful man, and spoke fairly fluent

American. He said he had seen us arrive and since where we were lying was in nobody's way we might stay there as long as we liked. What about coming ashore, I asked. Why not? Having come so far it would be a pity not to land, and provided none of the crew had venereal disease there could be no possible objection. And there the formalities ended. No bother, no police, no Customs, no Immigration, and no health officials to harry us. Would it were everywhere thus!

A rare but heartfelt exclamation mark placed by Bill is telling. He had found his new hunting ground and only three times more in seventeen years would he ever turn his face south.

The 1961 voyage was a success. Everything was new and exciting to them. The icebergs, for instance:

We never tired of looking at bergs. At first we counted and logged all those in sight but north of Disko Island they became too numerous to count. If some particularly vasty or grotesquely-shaped monster hove in sight we sometimes went out of our way to have a closer look at him. According to the light their colour varied from an opaque dazzling white to the loveliest blues and greens. Some had caves or even a hole clean through them in which the blue colour was intense and translucent.

Their intended objectives were fairly gained, Bill and Charles Marriott coming within 200 feet of the summit of a 6500-foot peak, before successfully climbing a 6370-foot peak on Upernivik Island. It has to be remembered that these peaks were climbed from sea level and thus, compared with land-locked mountains, like the Alps, might favourably be set against much higher mountains – 12,000-footers, for instance. It was a considerable feat for Bill, now sixty-three.

Apart from the incident with Terry Ward, who had to be landed at Godthaab with suspected appendicitis, a cracked rib for Bill, who slipped on deck, and a bad case of infected foot for Marriott (again), the voyage confirmed to Bill that he had found his happy hunting ground.

Writing about it, in *Mischief in Greenland*, he was in skittish mood.

Having undertaken to collect plants for the Natural History Museum I spent most of my time botanizing around the settlement where flowers might be found growing up to the 500 foot level. I now had lumbago – 'a trifling sum new added to the foot of my account' – so that I had to be careful when bending to dig out a plant for fear of not being able to straighten up. Really, I thought, I should be far better employed exploring the Brighton front or Cheltenham from a bath-chair rather than Greenland; to be joined there no doubt, in the very near future, by Charles, provided that vehicles of that kind were procurable on easy terms.

But Charles was on the mend. Our second-hand accounts of life's busy scene in Igdlorssuit would no longer serve. He must see for himself. So rising from his bed of pain he announced his intention of going ashore, and in order to save him a long walk we rowed the dinghy to a landing place just below the store. The populace, scenting something unusual afoot, had gathered in strength and they were well rewarded for their pains. In yachting cap and gumboots, his beard a sable silver, monocle in eye and supported by an ice-axe, Charles stepped ashore like a slimmer edition of King Edward VII landing at Cowes from the Royal Yacht. The crowd were speechless with delight. At last, they thought, the captain of *Mischief* had condescended to visit them.

It was at Igdlorssuit, too, that Bill had been tempted to buy some sealskins. 'My thoughts were running on sealskin trousers and the figure I should cut in them at home. This novel idea never came to fruition though it seemed to me to be a more proper use for sealskins than the elegant coat for my sister that, as I should have anticipated, they eventually made.'

Mischief arrived back in Lymington on September 26th, 7000 miles on her log. 'The crew went their several ways. It was sad to see them go, for we were unlikely to sail again together, or even to meet again, and I owed them much.'

Having found Greenland, Bill now began to think about just how far he could push himself, a future crew and his beloved *Mischief*. In 1962 he decided to try to get to Baffin Island, on the Canadian side of Davis Strait. In part this was dictated by Bill's dislike of any form of 'civilisation' when he was exploring.

Taken by and large, the west coast of Greenland can hardly be called remote and desolate, and it is far from being uninhabited. Letters from Europe reach Godthaab in three days; few of the fjords are without either a small town or a settlement, or that at any rate are not frequently visited by Greenlanders for fishing or hunting; and off the coast the sea is thick with vessels of some kind – trawlers, schooners, coasters, or local fishing boats. On the other hand on the Canadian side of the Straits the Cumberland Peninsula is as desolate as a man could wish, more or less uninhabited, and besides that mountainous.

He set off, with a crew of five, on May 23rd, this time sailing past the south of Ireland and straight for their destination, arriving off Greenland on June 15th, a much quicker passage than the year before. On the coast of Greenland Bill, with Roger Tufft, once more on board, climbed Agssaussat, at just under 7000 feet and later Amausuaq at 4620 feet, along with another peak. They sailed then to Baffin Island but found the ice too thick, returning to Greenland to await better conditions. Eventually they closed the Baffin Island coast, anchoring in Exeter Sound where Bill and Roger Tufft climbed Mount Raleigh and another mountain, 'false' Mount Raleigh which Bill had found wrongly named on his chart. The second 'false' peak was eventually officially renamed Mount Mischief. They were back in Lymington on September 28th.

In 1963 Bill voyaged to Bylot Island, much further north (in latitude 73°). 'As the Texan oil-man put it: "When you strike oil, stop boring,"' Bill began his account of this voyage. He felt he had found a cruising ground that more than lived up to expectations. To reach Bylot Island they would almost certainly have to negotiate pack ice and that, with its attendant dangers, was a challenge Bill found he could not duck. His encounters with pack ice would eventually lead to his losing *Mischief* but that was still five years away. His crew of five were to prove another very solid lot. They sailed on May 23rd, reaching Cape Farewell, the southernmost point of Greenland, in twenty-three days, the same time it had taken the year before.

Bill cheerfully admitted his crew were probably the least experienced he had taken. Only one, Ed Mikeska, a Pole, was a sailor.

> Ed doubled the role of mate and engineer. As a matter of routine he spent an hour each day wrestling with the charging engine, the session ending invariably in failure and abuse both in English and Polish. Having found an old sparking plug that looked as if it should have long since been thrown overboard I gave it to Ed to try. Whereupon the engine started without a murmur. This much relieved Ed who, for the next few days, until we were out of range, could listen to the weather forecasts to which he was much addicted. Though we may all like to have our fortunes told few of us are weak-minded enough to believe what we are told. Similarly I think it a mistake to rely for one's peace of mind upon forecasts of fair weather or to become unduly worried by forecasts of foul weather. When far from land the weather must be taken as it comes and fortunately bad weather seldom springs upon one without warning, leaving no time to shorten sail. If it behaved like that one would want not forecasts but a running commentary.

The objective of the voyage was a crossing of Bylot Island. To reach this they had to get past what is known as the Middle Pack, a band of sea ice which extends down Davis Strait in a pear shape. In order to avoid this Bill had to head north to an area of open water, a 'polynia', around which he could sail west to Bylot Island.

At midnight we came up with the ice that earlier had been betrayed to us by the 'blink', a yellowish-white appearance of the sky produced by the reflection of pack-ice on the clouds. It proved to be another projecting cape which we presently rounded and resumed our westerly course. Throughout that next day we met scattered floes, so widely scattered that for the most part we could maintain our course. Seals were fairly plentiful, sticking their heads out of the water or basking peacefully on the floes, and since we were under sail the latter took little notice of our passing. The crew seemed anxious to have one shot and equally in favour of casting me in the role of murderer. I must have been talking too much of my misspent youth in East Africa, of elephants and rhino, for they evidently took me for Buffalo Bill.

Bill got his seal, though, and with one shot.

His obsession with pack ice – and getting through it – could lead to grave difficulties. Bill had a rash – or indifferent – attitude to what others perceived as grave danger. In 1962 on the Baffin Island voyage one of his crew, Mick Rhodes, wrote of one of their encounters with pack ice thus:

Eventually the cry 'below' went up and cursing the skipper's idiocy in trying to beat the pack ice at the darkest time of the night – and very angry – I climbed up, to find heavy pack ice all around us and everybody rather grim-faced. One way and another we eventually – about two hours later – emerged under engine having run down wind.

At this stage a big tabular berg was cutting a swathe thro' the smaller floes and leaving an open lead behind him and travelling faster than his small companions and faster than us until eventually only one floe separated us. At other stages one was jumping onto floes and pushing *Mischief* away from them. All rather frightening, very cold and extremely exhausting – and one felt unnecessary. It seemed that what had happened was that Roger Brown the stupid great bastard had suddenly woken to the fact that there was ice around him. He called the skipper who admits that he took several minutes to get up and arrived on deck roughly as we started hitting ice. Roger claims that it just got thicker all round him – a kind of polar spontaneous generation – and he lacked the nous to turn away from it. Once in, it probably took the skipper some time to sort directions.

The significance of this incident is twofold. First, that in his published account Bill dismisses this whole sequence as a 'tap on *Mischief*'s hull' leaving the crew 'with a sense of insecurity'. In short, as in so many of

Bill's mistakes at sea he either turns it into an amusing incident, suggests the hand of fate, or largely ignores it. Second, and a consistent point made by his crews down the years, he gave little or no instruction to them as to what to do in terms of sailing the yacht, or what to expect in the way of conditions. In this case he expresses surprise that they found ice so far south. Yet they were going to find it sooner or later and he had given no lessons in what to do when they did.

As it happened, the crew of 1963 reached Bylot Island without mishap and Bill set about crossing it with Bruce Reid – a first crossing. Although only fifty-three miles in extent, it proved hard going, not least because the snow was so soft. It involved fifteen camps and fifteen days, as well as crossing a col at 5700 feet.

On July 26th Bill's diary reads:

A very disappointing day. Reached glacier in an hour (9.30 start) with high hopes but soon found going deplorable. 18″ snow and water underneath. Tried the middle – no better. Tried the side – worse. Struggled on till 2pm and camped by a flat boulder. Started down 3pm avoiding the glacier and back with the loads by 6pm. Much better going. Outlook not very promising. Can't see ahead as there is a shoulder in the way. Much seems to depend on avoiding snow. Doubt it will be hard even at 2,000 feet. Bruce did very little stamping. Afraid he is not very powerful. Carries no more than me either.

The crossing remained hard going: July 28 – 'Another hard grind; August 3rd – 'What I have been fearing nearly happened. Nearing camp slipped on loose boulder and blotched my left arm. Useless at present but hope only bruised'; August 7th – 2 hrs of hellish snow till we got to dry ice on left bank'. On August 8th they made it to the coast. Bill wrote in his diary: 'The hardest 50 miles I have ever done.'

But the most dramatic part of this trek came in the next few days. *Mischief* had been sailed back to the settlement in Pond Inlet, on the north side of Baffin Island, by Ed. He was tasked with watching from this settlement, ten miles from Bylot Island, for smoke. If he had seen nothing a week after August 12th, when they expected to have traversed the island, he was to sail over and make a search. Bill noted, but with not much concern, that on the north side of Bylot Island there was little in the way of kindling. He surmised that, at worst, they would have to burn their tent – in which case Bruce and he would have been shelterless, of course.

They had made the crossing to a point opposite Pond Inlet. 'We need not have hurried. The whole Baffin Island coast lay covered in cloud.' They had brought food for eighteen days; fifteen of these had now passed. If *Mischief* had failed to reach Pond Inlet, no one knew where they were. For the next four days they made smoke signals at the agreed times and for this they were grateful for clumps of heather they found growing. But their signals were not seen.

Help came in the form of Inuit hunters who had been curious about the smoke they had seen from Bill and Bruce's signal fires. One, Kudloo, had a smattering of English. 'In no time at all we had packed up, carried the loads to the beach, and dumped them on the big canoe, generously bestowing our remaining biscuits on Kudloo's companion, a young lad.' Bill was disappointed to find the canoes were not traditional Inuit build and that they were propelled by outboards.

Two hours after being rescued, they were alongside *Mischief*. Bill was not pleased by what he found. *Mischief* had been the first boat into the settlement that season and the crew had enjoyed liberal doses of local hospitality, one result of which was that *Mischief* sailed for home with more food on board than when she arrived. Bill eventually conceded that it might have been hard to see their smoke signals against the dark background of the island but 'we remained secretly convinced that their combined vision, even assisted by binoculars, must be singularly myopic.' His diary, laconically, reads: 'Still don't understand why our fires were never seen.'

None the less, Bill had good reason to feel the voyage had been a triumph. They were home on September 26th. 'We had made our voyage, as the saying goes, had achieved what we set out to do. I felt we had been lucky. There is no water anywhere that is fool-proof, and northern waters are less so than average.' There is a footnote to this voyage. Some years later Bruce Reid, an RAF navigator, was involved in an air-crash in which he was permanently disabled. Bill stayed in touch with Bruce, as he did with many of his crew, counting them as friends as well as colleagues. Bruce's accident was one of many occasions on which Bill showed great concern and kindness.

His luck ran out the next year when, with Charles Marriott again as part of his crew, they attempted to reach Skjoldungen, a mountainous peninsula on the inhospitable east coast of Greenland. *Mischief* had caused Bill great anxiety in the winter before they set out, so much so that he decided to sell her and look for another yacht. He had found that many of the oak frames were soft – that is, rotten. A full survey, initiated after this discovery, found the problem to be extensive. But Bill simply could not bear the thought of abandoning his boat. Eventually he found the advice he really wanted. *Mischief* was hauled out and her rotten frames were doubled – an expensive job but, as Bill wrote, less expensive than buying another boat.

They sailed first to the Faeroe Islands, thence via the newly formed volcanic island of Surtsey to Reykjavik. From here they took their departure for the east coast of Greenland, and the settlement on Angmagssalik. Ice is much more prevalent throughout the summer on the east coast of Greenland, frequently blocking that coast for miles out to sea. So it proved in this case. Bill found there was too much of it, and too thick, for them to try to get in.

'There now occurred another of those chance meetings that so often decide the course of events for good or ill. In this case the chance meeting, though it resulted in our reaching Angmagssalik, brought about nothing but ill.' They sighted a ship heading for the port and, talking to her, found she was awaiting a local vessel to escort her in through the ice. Bill was invited to join this little convoy and he agreed.

The lead ship was able to smash her way into the ice, creating a path for the second and, in theory the third – *Mischief*. But these others were big steel-hulled vessels. As they thrust their way through the ice, and *Mischief* followed, the ice leaped back behind the stern of the ship ahead. *Mischief* would have been safe had she been able to follow close behind this ship but as she steered so badly under power, she had to fall further and further behind to avoid being tossed on to the ice by the wash. So she became boxed in, eventually grounding on an underwater ice projection. Stuck fast, another floe now crushed against her, pushing in the port-side bulwarks. The old wooden ship was leaking badly and they were lucky to reach Angmagssalik.

Here emergency repairs were made and although *Mischief* still leaked, she was seaworthy enough to get back home. The primary objective, Skjoldungen, was abandoned. They were, in any case, trapped by the ice pack, an event which enabled Bill to climb a local peak, Poljemsfjeld, at just under 4000 feet.

They sailed back, intending to stop at Bill's home town of Barmouth, with its little harbour on the Welsh coast, but even this proved a bit of a disaster, and they sailed past in the night. Once again Bill was proving a poor home coast sailor. Rather sheepishly, they motored in the next day, to find they had missed what amounted to a civic reception, put on for them the previous afternoon, when they had been expected.

The town, including the mayor, had waited from 3.00 p.m. until dusk. It was not a happy homecoming. Bill's general gloom must have been complete when he nearly steered them all into the Warden Buoy in the Needles Channel. 'Safely anchored off Lymington river to wait for daylight I had leisure to reflect on the varied perils that beset our coasts, while only the gentle clang of the pump reminded me of those we had escaped in Greenland waters.'

In the winter of that year, perhaps mindful of the need for a success, Bill had flown to Sydney and the eventual triumph of the Heard Island expedition already discussed, but in 1965 he set sail for Greenland and his second attempt at reaching Skjoldungen. 'Defeat rankles,' he wrote. This time they were successful. Sailing once more via Surtsey and Reykjavik, they reached Angmagssalik on August 3rd and Skjoldungen on August 10th. Bill and Brian Holloway, a New

Zealand climber, attempted a 5000-foot peak and climbed a smaller one. Later, they moved to Sehesteds Fjord where another peak was successfully climbed. They had a fast passage back, reaching Lymington on September 19th.

Bill now freely acknowledged that he was getting old. The climb of the 5000-foot peak in Greenland had been made in stages; even so, Bill had declined to try the last snow-covered ridge to the summit. He quotes Dr Johnson: 'Prudence quenches that ardour of enterprise, by which everything is done that can claim praise of admiration, and represses that generous temerity which often fails and often succeeds.'

He had no intention of giving up, however. As we have seen, the Heard Island success led him directly to his long voyage south in 1966 and 1967. Rebuffed by his experiences there, he turned again to Greenland in 1968. *Mischief* had now sailed 115,000 miles with her master. Bill had been immensely frustrated by the failure of the Smith Island voyage, and angry with himself. He looked now for a challenge in the Arctic and he found it in Scoresby Sound, the biggest fjord in the world, far up the east side of Greenland. Around 300 miles north of Angmagssalik, the sound also contained two big mountainous unexplored islands, Milneland and Redland. He was to attempt this passage no fewer than four times, a measure of its difficulty as well as the hold it had on him.

A Danish friend had written to him suggesting Scoresby Sound as the kind of objective Bill would relish; further, he believed that in a normal ice year it would be possible to get a small yacht into the sound by August. Bill began to lay his plans.

By leaving at the end of June and going direct one should arrive off the Sound at about the right time early in August. It would be a pity, however, to lose the whole of June, a pleasant month to be at sea, when the crew might enjoy some real yachting weather, the sort of weather that would do little to inure them to the rigours ahead but would at least afford some compensation. Moreover, with time in hand, we could call at the Faeroes, Iceland and Jan Mayen.

This plan was to be the undoing of *Mischief*.

Bill's crew was assembled relatively easily. Charles Marriott elected to make his fourth voyage with Bill and in *Mischief*, a record which would remain unchallenged. Two Yorkshiremen 'blew in' one night at Bodowen and Bill had engaged them on the spot. A fourth, Ian Duckworth, was eventually found, appealing to Bill because he was a climber.

For Bill, trouble began early – before they had started – when Simon Beckett, one of the Yorkshiremen, asked Bill if he intended taking a life-raft. Bill realised that this was an argument he was not going to win but his principal remaining objection – the cost – was removed when

Simon pointed out he had a brother in the marine business who would lend them one. 'The life-raft duly arrived and a home was found for it by the cockpit. Strangely enough, at the sight of this white blister installed on *Mischief*'s deck my mind was filled with foreboding.'

They sailed first to the Faeroes where Bill met his Danish friend Captain Toft who, with his survey vessel *Ole Roemer*, was also heading for Scoresby Sound. From the Faeroes Bill headed for the east coast of Iceland, to Akureyri. There Bill, Charles and the three younger crew variously walked and climbed. Bill went off on his own to climb a relatively low peak (under 5000 feet), which he did successfully although he noted rather ruefully that it was fatiguing.

One of his reasons for going on to Jan Mayen Island was that there was on it an extinct volcano, the Beerenberg. After his Icelandic excursion he thought that, perhaps, with the aid of a halfway camp, he would be able to reach the top of this 7677-foot peak. Bill by now was seventy.

On the morning of July 18th they sighted the southern edge of Jan Mayen Island. What follows now is Bill's own account, from an extraordinary obituary he had privately printed after *Mischief* had been lost. It is published here, more or less complete, for the first time and it gives a clear insight into Bill's true feelings. Ian Duckworth, whom he blamed for the first of what were to prove fatal errors, never recovered from Bill's outpouring of anger. (Tragically, he died in a motorcycle accident some years ago.)

On July 18th, six days out from Akureyri, in fog, we made our landfall off the South Cape of Jan Mayen, and next day anchored off the old Norwegian weather station on the west side of the island. There was no ice in the vicinity but pack ice could be seen some three miles to the north extending westwards. I walked across to the east coast, made contact with some vehicles, and got a lift in a truck five miles to the present Norwegian base, a large installation with some fifty men. The Commandant, who was surprised to see me, showed me a small bay close to the base which they used for landing stores and suggested that we move there. We were, so to speak, uninvited guests, so I deemed it best to comply, though the bay was more than half covered with ice floes. This was the mistake from which all our troubles stemmed. The Commandant told me that a Norwegian naval vessel had recently been turned back by ice.

We started round on Saturday, July 20th, a brilliant morning on which we enjoyed a view of the ice slopes of Beerenberg, the mountain we had hoped to climb. The brilliance soon faded and we rounded South Cape in thick fog having to tack twice to weather it. The wind died at night and having steered east for two miles to get clear of the land we handed sails and let her drift, waiting for the fog to clear. The coast runs NE–SW so that by steering east we had not gained much offing, and although we had no way on it was a mistake to assume that we were not moving. I had the midnight to 2 am watch and on the assumption that we were not moving sat below, going on deck about every 15 minutes. It was, of course, fully light, but the fog was cold and wet, visibility less than a quarter mile. I told my relief, Ian, that he need not remain on deck all the time provided he went up at frequent intervals. He interpreted this liberally and must have remained below most of his watch.

At about 3.50 am a terrible crash roused me, to be presently informed unnecessarily by Ian that we were aground. We were almost alongside a lone rock pinnacle some 20 foot high lying about half a mile off the coast. I could have touched it with a boathook. The slight swell bumped us heavily on its plinth. The consequence of his neglect seemed to have unnerved Ian who had already pulled the cord of the liferaft without troubling to launch it, so that a huge yellow balloon now occupied most of the starboard deck. He had also cut the dinghy lashings. The engine started quickly and she slid off easily but not before having struck hard at least six times. She proved to be leaking a lot but the Whale pump and deck pump together kept it under control. To hit this rock we must have drifted in the course of the night some three miles to the north at a rate of about a half knot.

Owing to the fog and a lot of ice inshore we had trouble in finding the bay. At about 7 am we anchored outside it while I went ashore to tell the Norwegians what had happened. They said, and I agreed, that the only thing to do was to beach her to get at the leaks. So we brought her in through the ice until she grounded on a beach of black sand. In order to float her further up we started taking out all the ballast (some five tons of pig iron), drained the water tanks, and put the anchor and cable ashore. The rise and fall of the tide was only three feet (*Mischief* draws seven feet six inches aft) and the beach shelved quickly towards her stern, so that we could not get at the garboard strake or anywhere below except at the forefoot. On examining what we could of the port side at low water we saw no sign of sprung or started planks; in places the caulking had spewed out and aft about ten feet of the lower part of the keel had broken away.

With the help of the Norwegians, who supplied anything needed, we covered the likeliest leak sources with tar, felt, and copper. Then we hauled her round and hove her down again with a bulldozer so that the starboard side showed. Here, too, there were no obvious signs of damage. The leaks had been reduced though we still had a spell of pumping every two hours. I thought

233

that we would easily sail her back to Iceland or further. Ian thought otherwise and made arrangement for a passage to Norway in *Brandal*, a sealing vessel on charter bringing stores, due about August 2nd. Charles I knew would come with me, while the two younger crew, Simon and Ken, though apprehensive, were willing to try.

Meantime the ice, which a day after our arrival almost filled the bay (thus helping us by damping any swell) had begun to move out. Preparatory to refloating her we put back the ballast all but a ton; no doubt, another mistake. By Saturday, July 27th, there remained only an unbroken line of big floes inshore, most of them probably aground. The Norwegian who had helped me realised better than I did that *Mischief* was now in peril. By means of a wire led from the stern to a block slung from an adjacent rock and thence to a bulldozer we tried to haul her off. She moved a bit but anyway there was no forcing a passage between the floes and no means of hauling them away.

Next day Sunday, July 28th, the Commandant came down and managed to break up with dynamite a floe threateningly close to our rudder. The floe lying a yard or so from our port side was too big and underwater explosions close aboard might have damaged the ship. That morning it began blowing hard from the south causing the ice to surge forward and *Mischief* to bump heavily on the sand. I rallied the crew for a last effort to get her off by means of a warp to the anchor winch and the engine. She would not budge. With a couple of bulldozers we might have succeeded, but when I ran to the base for help there was no one about. By the time I got back the ice had battered a hole in the hull and started several planks. That evening, in despair, I wrote her off. She was one third full of water so we took ashore all the gear below deck. Charles, who had not been well, now collapsed and retired to a bed in the base sickroom. After first beaching *Mischief* we had all lived in a small hut fifty yards up from the beach.

Next day a red bearded Norwegian whom I called The Viking, who was as anxious as myself to save the boat, suggested that she should be hauled right out and that in the winter he would repair her. I doubted the feasibility because it meant hauling her some fifty yards in very soft sand sloping at about fifteen degrees. However, clutching at straws, I agreed. Once more we took out all the ballast and that evening a bulldozer moved her about two yards. She still lay right among the breakers. The wind continued to blow and the swell rolling in lifted and dropped her heavily on the sand.

A big float with an outboard engine used for bringing ashore stores, on which we had deposited the ballast, lay hard by on the beach; and the next night *Mischief*, driven ever higher by the seas, had her bowsprit broken by the float, in spite of our having reefed it. The idea of hauling her right out seemed to be tacitly abandoned. Instead, on July 30th, we put a big patch over the hole, having arranged with *Brandal*, then about to leave Norway, to tow us to Bodo. She was also to bring out a small petrol driven pump to cope with the leaks which by now were well beyond our two hand pumps. With a gale on August 1st the breakers tore off *Mischief*'s rudder, but *Brandal*, with whom the base spoke by radio telephone, reckoned they could still tow. *Brandal* arrived on August 2nd, fetching up well north of the island in spite of radio beacons, radar, and Loran; and that morning the big patch we had put on was torn off by the seas. Upon this The Viking and I reverted to the idea of leaving her there for the winter hauled right out, but the Commandant to whom we appealed poured cold water on this and said she must be towed. So on August 3rd The Viking and I put on another patch, a wet job since waves were sweeping the stages we had slung overside to work from. That evening I went on board *Brandal*. To make all safe they agreed to lend us a small electric pump to reinforce the petrol pump they had brought which we had already installed in our cockpit. I had to sign a guarantee against the loss of this pump. The Commandant had also arranged for a Walkie-talkie and a field telephone to keep *Brandal* and *Mischief* in touch.

Overnight we rove a three inch wire through a big block slung on the adjacent rocks and hung a length of six inch nylon rope twice round *Mischief*'s hull. At 7 am on Sunday, August 4th, exactly a fortnight after we first limped in, the Norwegians rallied in force to get us off. Now we had no ballast on board. Either the sand had piled up on *Mischief*'s starboard side or she had dug a hole for herself, so the biggest bulldozer dropped its scoop into the sand and using this as a cushion advanced on *Mischief* and pushed her bodily sideways. The two bulldozers in tandem then coupled on to the wire, a big dory with an engine pulled from seawards, and *Mischief* slid slowly into deep water. Simon and I were on board with the motor pump going. We needed to be for she leaked like a basket.

Having secured astern of *Brandal* lying half a mile out we remained there tossed in a rough sea until late afternoon. Meantime the float made two or three trips out to *Brandal*, the last with seven Norwegian passengers and the remaining three of our crew. Charles was to travel in her while the other two helped in *Mischief*. (As we were to be closely attended Ian consented to come.) Our only contact with *Brandal* was by the float and in the evening it came alongside with three of *Brandal*'s crew to arrange the tow, the electric pump, field telephone, Walkie-talkie set, and a life-raft. Our own had no gas cylinder, that having been expended when Ian had pulled the string a fortnight before. Ken and Ian, too, joined us. For the tow they used a nylon rope shackled to 10 fms of our anchor chain on which they slung three big tyres to act as a spring. The remaining 35 fms of our chain with the 1cwt anchor attached we led to *Mischief*'s stern to drop over when the tow started. This served in place of a rudder and kept her from yawing. The heavy cable to supply current from *Brandal* to the electric pump they merely drooped loose into the sea. Its own weight imposed a heavy strain, no current ever passed, and soon after the tow began *Brandal* informed us that it had broken. It should have been hitched to the tow-line or to another warp in which case *Mischief* might have survived. It meant that the little petrol pump must function for three days without fail. I did not think it would. Since early morning Simon and I had been running it for five minutes in every ten to keep the water at bay.

At about 8 pm in a rough sea the tow began. At 9 pm, Simon and I lay down leaving Ken and Ian to carry on until 1 am. With the water sloshing about inside sleep was hardly possible and for food we made do with hard tack and a cup of tea. Just before midnight I heard that the pump had given up; the engine was running but it was not pumping. Three of us were certainly ready enough to quit and I confess that the skipper and owner, who had so much more at stake, had no longer the will to persevere, a fortnight of toil, trouble, and anxiety having worn me down. *Brandal* had already been told. She lay to about a cable away and told us to bring off only our personal gear. So we collected our gear, launched the life-raft and abandoned *Mischief*. She had then about three feet of water inside her. Paddling over to *Brandal* we went on board while three crew returned in the raft to salvage the two pumps and telephone. The electric pump, which was very heavy, we had already hoisted on deck through the skylight. The pumps met with scant ceremony, being thrown overboard on the end of a line to be hauled through the sea to *Brandal*. While *Brandal* got underway I remained on deck watching *Mischief*, still floating defiantly, until she was out of sight. We were then about 30 miles east of Jan Mayen.

For me it was the loss of much more than a yacht. I felt as one who had deserted a stricken friend, a friend with whom for the past fourteen years I had probably spent more time at sea than on land, and who when not at sea had never been far from my mind. Moreover I could not help feeling that by my mistakes and by the failure of one of those who were there to see her to safety we had broken faith; that the disaster or sequence of disasters need not have happened; and that more might have been done to save her.

In his last book in which she stars, *In Mischief's Wake*, Bill added to the paragraph above these heart-rending words: 'I shall never forget her. "The world was all before her, where to choose Her place of rest, and Providence her guide."'

In spite of everything, though, Bill could not give up the idea of sailing. Within a few days of getting back to Bodowen he was scouring the yachting magazines and bought what turned out to be a pig in a poke – *Sea Breeze*. Bill's own judgment might now be seen to be in decline. The next eight voyages were, with only three exceptions, either disasters or nearly so.

CHAPTER 15

Ships Are All Right; It's the Men in Them

After the loss of *Mischief* Bill, like so many sailors before and after, wanted, not to give up, but to get back to sea. His prayers were answered swiftly. *Mischief*'s loss had been reported in parts of the British press, but not widely. However, within a month of his repatriation from northern Norway he had a telegram from Sir Atholl Oakley, a tinned ham manufacturer, offering Bill his Bristol pilot cutter, *Sea Breeze*. Bill was to write of this encounter and what followed from it: 'No wonder Barnum believed that a sucker is born every minute.'

Part of Bill's subsequent troubles came from his own incorrigible romanticism. When he went to look at *Sea Breeze*, lying close to Lymington, in the Hamble River, he was struck by her authentic rigging; most of all he was taken with her tiller. 'This diminutive cockpit lay under the shadow almost of a great wooden tiller, the sort of thing John Davis might have had on *Mooneshine*, decorated with spirals running the entire length and culminating in a cunningly carved Turk's Head. I could see myself grasping this massive masterpiece, smiling with content.'

Bill was an impulse buyer in the sense that he was much affected by details of this kind, rather than the big questions. Subject to survey, he agreed to buy her.

As before with *Mischief*, Bill's surveyor John Tew roundly condemned her. This time Bill decided not to fly in the face of what Tew told him which was, in effect, not to buy *Sea Breeze*. Bill had argued to himself that Tew's advice about *Mischief* had proved wrong (insofar as she had kept on going); 'On this occasion a repetition of such obstinacy would be going to cost a lot more and I finally decided to take his advice.' But Sir Atholl, who disingenuously expressed great surprise that Bill's surveyor should have found so much wrong, was smart enough to know he had his trout hooked, as Bill might have written. He promptly reduced his price.

'With some misgivings I agreed and *Sea Breeze* had changed hands. It would be tedious to list all that had to be done,' Bill continued, and it is fair to say that *Sea Breeze* now underwent a major refit. Bill was particularly disturbed by the ballasting arrangements which meant that in this boat his crew would not be able to lighten ship by throwing any of it overboard should she run aground.

But he had his vessel and, knowing she would be ready for the 1969 season, Bill began to look for a target. 'A return match with Jan Mayen had its attraction, but apart from thus tempting Providence rather blatantly I doubted whether we should be altogether welcome having so recently made a nuisance of ourselves.' Bill settled, once again, for an attempt on Scoresby Sound, then turned his attention to getting a crew. 'Living, while at home, in a remote part like a hermit, albeit in a pretty comfortable cell and not underfed, I have no large circle of friends and acquaintances through which to put out feelers; while diffidence, or idleness, makes me unwilling to write and canvass possible sources such as universities, youth organisations, or even yacht clubs.' In short, even his experiences of the year before, which had in some respects cost him his ship, were not going to change him. But Bill was realist enough to know that: 'The critical might well say that the man gets the crews he deserves.'

In fact, as often happened, Bill got lucky in one respect; one of the crew for this second attempt on Scoresby Sound was Brian Potter, a retired bank manager, who came as the cook. Bill liked him on sight, not so much because he inspired confidence 'as all bank managers should' but because he looked as if 'in no circumstances would he let a man down'.

As usual Bill arrived in Lymington early and began the pre-voyage overhaul with help from some of his crew and from his good friend Sandy Lee, who fashioned a new companion ladder. Lee had first met Bill by accident some years earlier and they had grown close.

In 1965 I had cycled down to the quay and there was an elderly man coming up and when I was close enough he accosted me and inquired was there anywhere in Lymington where he could get a pressure cooker repaired. I remember saying, 'I should think not on a Saturday' and I asked if it was urgent. He said it was as they were sailing the next morning so I offered to have a look at it. I could see what the problem was and I said, 'I think I might be able to manage it for you.' I took it back and when I got to the yacht, who should be on board but H. W. Tilman whom I had heard of but never met.

The upshot was that he was grateful and he invited me on board to have a look around. I thought that he was a gentleman, no bombast, no false airs or graces, but great quality. We made it our business to see them off. Eventually he used to stay here; he would come in February or March to take the tarpaulins off the boat, and generally he would clear up any mess, prior to coming down in April or May. We were getting letters, of course, and we would get to know when he was due back and go down for his arrival.

'It all developed very slowly; I never felt we were in his closest circle,' Lee now believes, although his wife, Mary, is not so sure. 'He was always very much at home here,' she says. But he was painfully shy, she adds. Lee and Mary were to remain friends until the last voyage, when Lee helped on *En Avant*. Mary remembers Bill always kissing her goodbye when he left. The Lees were invariably among the small crowd of well-wishers who saw him off each year. 'He was a lovely man,' says Mary Lee.

In 1969 they left on June 19th, and as usual Bill had the Berthon yard boatman, Ted Mapes, lead them down the river to warn yachts of Bill's unsteady passage down this very narrow winding and shallow course. The Royal Lymington Yacht Club gave him the usual starting gun, too. Uniquely in his sailing career, Bill had decided on what was almost a shakedown cruise with his unknown yacht (the first time he had sailed it) and crew. They were to sail about the Solent and to anchor for the night in Yarmouth, immediately opposite Lymington on the Isle of Wight and thus sufficiently foreign. However, before they could raise any sails Bill noticed water coming in by the galley, high up and when he removed some of the lining 'we enjoyed a view of the Isle of Wight between two of the waterline planks where a foot or two of caulking had spewed out.' They went across to Yarmouth and put into the harbour, Bill having his usual trouble in manoeuvring *Sea Breeze* into a berth without wreaking havoc on the small and densely packed harbour. 'The ornate gangway of a large Royal Yacht Squadron power boat narrowly escaped destruction at our hands, and the crew of the yacht ahead of our mooring must have thought their time had come.'

Bill was desperately depressed by this incident. Worse was to follow; after the Berthon yard men had come over and recaulked the seams, they took *Sea Breeze* for her trials. She sailed well but was still leaking badly. 'I felt something akin to despair,' Bill wrote. That night, after *Sea Breeze* was back in Yarmouth harbour, he took the ferry back to Lymington, turning up late at the Lees', unannounced, asking for a bed for the night. Both Sandy and Mary remember him looking utterly defeated, like a tired dog. 'After all the time and money that had been spent the boat was obviously in no condition to take to sea.'

Sea Breeze, on the hastily summoned John Tew's advice, was brought back to Lymington to be completely recaulked at huge expense. The crew were told to regroup a week later. No doubt this unfortunate start ensured that what happened later was inevitable. The incident throws further light on Bill's own slapdash approach to things. A man who intends to set sail to Arctic waters in a newly bought but very old and tired yacht, and for these purposes, untried, might be thought to be verging on the insane not to have extensive sea trials well before the departure date. Not Bill; in all the years he went off on his voyages only this once did he make an effort to trial his yacht or his crew. Disappointment, in this case, was bound to follow.

Bill's attitude to his crews, as we have seen, time and again, bordered on the totally indifferent. It seems not to have occurred to him that their morale, on this occasion, might have been shaken. As with the life-raft question, Bill hardly ever looked at the reasons behind his crews' concern. Although he often displayed great kindness to them, he equally often displayed a towering arrogance. As he said in *Mischief Goes South* why should they complain when I am giving them a free holiday?

Despite their misgivings, his crew reassembled and they set off on June 30th. Off the Cornish coast things began to go badly wrong. *Sea Breeze* parted company with both her topmast and her bowsprit and they had to put into Appledore for repairs. There, two of his crew, Mike Brocklebank and Ralph Furness, decided they had had enough. Bill must have cursed the ship for forcing him to put into a home port, thus enabling this desertion. Exactly like a Victorian shipmaster in this respect he favourably – and often – quoted the old saying 'ports rot ships and men'. He invariably believed all his life that if you stuck a thing out for long enough it would at least become tolerable. As the years went by his contempt for feckless youth grew all the greater. In the end he never expected his crew would amount to much, hence his overblown praise when any one of them came close to his standard.

He managed to find two replacements, one of whom he said would always 'figure as Cassandra Ken'. The other, Colin Kavenan, 'wore a beard, but at this crisis in our affairs I would not have minded had he worn beads and had hair down to his waist'. They finally sailed for Iceland on July 15th and made a fast passage. Already, though, there were further rumblings from among the crew about turning back. In Iceland, Bill and Brian Potter climbed Strandertinder at 3310 feet.

The voyage on to Greenland saw them beset by mist and ice. They crossed the Arctic Circle and Bill was disappointed that there were no skylarks, no ceremonies, no visit from 'Le Père Arctique'. Off the coast of Greenland, finally, the mutiny broke. On August 7th the fog thinned and they could see what Bill described as an astonishing coastline, wild, mountainous, with two big glaciers – always a pull for him – also in sight. They were in fact off Cape Brewster, at the southern entrance to Scoresby Sound.

Between *Sea Breeze* and her goal, though, was pack ice and, almost immediately, the refusal of the crew to go on. That night Bill hove to on the wrong tack, bringing them closer to the ice than he intended.

Now in a short but sharp gale, Bill cursed that they were being driven south. In the evening of the 8th, when he proposed heading back to the sound, the crew, with the exception of Brian Potter, said no.

> Brian, John [Murray] and I argued, standing for some odd reason round the foot of the mast below. I knew it would be no use. I am not eloquent and it would have needed the fiery eloquence of a Drake or a Garibaldi to stiffen John's spine . . . To give up when so near, in an able boat with ample supplies, was hard enough to stomach, but with an unwilling crew there was nothing to be done.

Bill's misery was later completed by the same John, who executed what Bill called 'an imperial Chinese gybe' bringing down the gaff spar. Bill now compounded this when they were nearly home, and in the Irish Sea, by taking *Sea Breeze* through a 'short-cut' through Calf Sound, between the Calf of Man, Chicken Rock and the main island. He was lucky to get away with it, as even he admitted later. Sailing down the Irish Sea, he took *Sea Breeze* into Barmouth before sailing her back to Lymington, arriving there on September 9th. He wrote: 'We had landed nowhere and achieved nothing. From that point of view the voyage could hardly be reckoned a success. On the other hand, if regarded as a trial run in a boat new to me, a shake-down cruise, it had won several prizes by the shaking down of no less than three spars.' He was less complimentary about the crew.

He had now had, by his own admission, three bad years of sailing, achieving far less than he had hoped and, each time, returning home disillusioned. He was, in the winter of 1969–70 about to celebrate his seventy-second birthday, too, and all these factors may have pushed him to a far easier target in 1970. This year he had some luck with crew as well, getting Colin Putt, of the *Patanela*, Heard Island, trip to come with him. Putt brought along a climber, Iain Dillon, and Bill was ready to accept him on Colin's recommendation.

Bob Comlay and Andrew Harwich made up the rest of his crew. An insight to Bill's attitude to his younger crew is given by his remarks about Bob Comlay. 'He was extremely keen, put the boat first and foremost, did not forget his obligations to me, always asking for more work, and was generally first on deck and last to leave. In short the type of lad that one has the right to expect from those who offer to go on voyages of this kind.'

He had advertised for crew on this occasion and, as usual, half the replies came from women. Bill rather disingenuously says elsewhere that he had 'forgot' to stipulate only men should apply. In the case of one woman, 'Georgina', 'she sounded the right sort . . . I was sorely tempted to take Georgina at her word until I considered what effect the springing of such an unlikely and possibly unwelcome surprise might have had on Colin and Iain.'

Bill set sail on June 5th. Off the west coast of Greenland in early July they became marooned in pack ice but they made the port of Faeringehavn on July 14th. They faced increasing problems with the ice when they left this port, but they finally entered Tasermuit Fjord where Putt and Dillon got in three days' climbing; this was later followed by another four-day climbing trip.

It was a happy time and Bill's own account of it in *In Mischief's Wake* shows a skittishness missing from most of the later voyages. On food, for instance, he insists: 'Food plays an important part at sea – all ills are good when attended by food – and I hope these frequent references to it may dispel a myth, current since Himalayan days, that to climb with the writer spells slow starvation.' As a footnote to this, Roger Robinson, of the 1966–67 trip, remembers that the food was adequate, sometimes good.

Bill in 1970 was in his element. Ice, like a giant floating ocean-borne glacier, followed them wherever they went. It was difficult sailing and hazardous in the extreme. Bill's description of the ice pack, and the icebergs which lurked within it, are lyrical. His confidence was enormously boosted by his crew. They arrived back in Lymington on September 27th and he wrote: 'For my part it has been a good voyage, if not the most successful then certainly the happiest which is almost as important.'

We now enter a succession of voyages, all north, and involving two Bristol pilot cutters, *Sea Breeze* and then *Baroque*. Bill said this of the three voyages in 1971, 1972 and 1973: 'the first comparatively humdrum, the second totally disastrous, the third exceedingly troublesome'. In 1971 and 1972 Bill made his last attempts to reach Scoresby Sound. With a good crew (including Bob Comlay), they sailed first in 1971 for the Faeroes and thence to Iceland. Here *Sea Breeze* lost a propellor. After this delay they sailed for Greenland and they were sixty miles off Scoresby Sound when they met bad pack ice.

After several attempts to get through it, Bill sailed south to Angmagssalik; thwarted as well in an attempt to get some climbing in, they sailed back for Lymington, arriving, as in the year before, on September 27th. Bill, though, would not give up.

So, in 1972, he set off once more to try for Scoresby Sound. One of his crew was Brian Potter, the former bank manager, who wrote to his wife on June 4th:

The crew seem to be settling down quite well. The Australian, Brian McClanaghan and the New Zealander, Mike Clare, seem to improve as I get to know them. Although Richard Capstick is quite pleasant, I am less sure of him. He has more sailing experience than the others, and has been a little pompous, but the lads from the Antipodes do not stand for that and I do not think he will have any pomp left if he lasts the whole voyage.

Incidentally, the rations of protein are substantially better than they were three years ago. Perhaps Colin Putt's enormous appetite raised this standard two years ago.

On the way north they suffered a cracked boom and, instead of heading directly for Greenland, once again they made for Reykjavik, which took them thirty-six days from Lymington, mainly due to bad weather. Here one of his crew, Richard Capstick, left. Potter had been unhappy with him, as had Bill. 'Skipper referred to him as a fat slob and I described him as a lazy flabby lump of fat. Eavesdropping, he heard both assessments of himself which will not do him any harm.' Bill was again forced to look locally. He found an American, John Lapin, and they sailed on July 10th for Greenland. But Lapin turned out to be badly seasick so Bill was forced to put into the Icelandic port of Isafjord where he managed to recruit, from England, a sixteen-year-old, Dougal Forsyth, who proved to be a sturdy addition to the crew, although Potter described him to his wife as 'an insolent little brat'.

Bill now sailed *Sea Breeze* to Jan Mayen Island, where *Mischief* had been lost. At one point they lay becalmed just a mile from the rock which *Mischief* had struck. They went ashore to greet the research station personnel and Bill was greeted, on the beach, with the words, 'Mr Tilman, I presume?'

They sailed, finally, for Scoresby Sound. Bill had been delighted to note that even as far north as Jan Mayen, there had been no ice of any kind. On August 3rd they met their first floes, just ten miles out from the sound and, thereafter, the ice pack thickened. After spending several frustrating days close to, but not in, the sound, Bill found that *Sea Breeze*'s engine had packed up. It would have been impossible for him to manoeuvre in the ice without an engine so, reluctantly, he sailed south towards Angmagssalik where he thought he would be 'giving the crew the slight satisfaction of having set foot in Greenland'.

They were still meeting a lot of ice but they were closing Angmags-salik. 'The wind was light and what little there was unfavourable and I had half made my mind up to spend the night at sea. However, when an opening appeared in the thin line of floes ahead I decided to sail through and try to find an anchorage for the night in Sermilik fjord which lay temptingly wide and open to the south-west. This was an error of judgement.'

It seems extraordinary that Bill should have now sailed *Sea Breeze* into a fjord with a large glacier at its head, calving great chunks of ice, and where a sailor of his experience might have thought about katabatic winds.

The more unexpected . . . was the fierce onset of wind that came in suddenly from the north just as darkness fell, the herald of a dirty night. The first blast laid her over until the lee deck was half under water. The boat shot ahead, rapidly closing the dimly seen shore. She had way enough on, I reckoned, to take her in, and the rate we were going and the fear that we might hit something induced me to get the sails off in a hurry [all the sails, note]. I had misjudged the distance and we could get no bottom with the lead.

By this time the wind or the tide had brought quantities of ice down the fjord. Increasing numbers of floes were spinning by, so many that the thought of rehoisting and trying to sail among them in the dark with that strength of wind was too daunting. In fact all hands had their work cut out fending off the floes.

They drifted in this way for two or three hours and then, as they saw rocks to the leeward and tried to hoist a staysail to get clear, the yacht was caught by a floe under her bow.

'Her heel caught on a ledge and she spun round to be pinned by wind and wave against the rock . . . She was hard and fast and taking a terrible hammering as she rose and fell on the ledge. Fearing she would soon break up or slip off the ledge into deep water I told the crew to take what gear they could and to abandon ship by jumping for the rock.' There followed a chaotic scene that burned itself into Bill's memory as the crew more or less scrambled for the shore with little regard for their own safety let alone that of their mates. Bill went last. He was left on board with the weighted end of the lead line to tie around himself. 'Thinking rather stupidly that 7lbs of lead round the waist might be a hindrance if it came to swimming I had to go below for a knife to cut the lead off. Normally I wear a knife on my belt and to be without one then was unseamanlike, as indeed was much of our behaviour that night.'

Bill was further ashamed to admit that he did not think to take his diary, logbook, films, money or sextant ashore with him. They spent an uncomfortable night on their rock. In the morning they saw that only the top of the mast of *Sea Breeze* was showing above water; Bill had lost his second ship, utterly. They were in potentially serious trouble, wet and without much food, although they found their rock – more a tiny islet – had plenty of rainwater in pools, and they had salvaged a tent.

But, at around 3.00 p.m. the next day they were spotted by a local boat and taken off – a most seamanlike rescue, Bill noted later, somewhat ruefully. Later, in Angmagssalik they were kept in the hospital overnight. They were penniless, passportless: real destitute seamen and the Danish authorities took no time in getting them away. In the event they were lent the money to charter a light aircraft from Iceland so they left in some style. In Iceland they got a laissez-passer, bedded down in the old airport control tower, and were flown home, courtesy of Her Majesty's Consul in Reykjavik.

'At the moment there are few if any amateur sailors likely to profit by it, but for me the lesson of this sad story is not to mess about in Greenland fjords without an engine, especially when they are full of ice,' Bill wrote. He was now seventy-four and, victim of two sinkings, he still wanted to find another yacht. He had never insured his yachts outside home waters, and his income, fixed as it was on stocks and shares, the income from the family trust and the vagaries of the book-buying public, was going to suffer for the second time in four years.

To Victor Gozzer he wrote that Christmas, 'Lost *Sea Breeze* last summer off Greenland and everything in her except the crew. Am looking for a new boat but so far no luck. Never give up.'

Bill quotes Winston Churchill in this regard: 'never look back, look to the future'. He toyed with a boat that he went to see, but her owner withdrew her from sale. He thought he might try to get *Sea Breeze* raised but she was comprehensively sunk, as even he had to admit, eventually. Then, at the end of 1972 he found *Baroque*, his third and last Bristol pilot cutter and 'needless to say, I bought her.'

If Bill wanted to identify with John Davis by the frequency of his voyages to Greenland, then, by 1972, the connection had been more than made; Davis made only three voyages to Greenland, Bill had made nine. Davis's southern voyage to Patagonia had ended a disaster; Bill's had been a great success, among his finest sailing achievements in terms of objectives reached and the morale of his crew. In truth, by 1972, the sailor with whom one would most identify Bill Tilman was the Flying Dutchman, condemning himself to sail endlessly northward. Or, as he put it: 'A cruise to northern waters every summer had become almost as essential as breathing, so strong is habit.'

Really, there was nothing left for him to do. As his friends and acquaintances died around him, one can sense this growing inertia, the ennui of each year trying to find a good crew, with the same slapdash methods, the same almost inevitable result. He grew more parsimonious, too, and *Baroque* suffered as a result. His indifference to the conditions in which he lived and sailed infected his crews; with no exception, morale was now to be poor. Only one of his crew did he now rate, an emotional decision that would lead indirectly to his death.

Bill made five voyages north in *Baroque*; only one could be counted in any way a success, the last of *Baroque*'s voyages in any case being the sorrowful return from Reykjavik in 1976 when he had decided to sell her. Even the successful voyage, to Spitzbergen, was marred by the death of his beloved sister, Adeline, and by his running his ship heavily aground.

These voyages were yielding less and less in another sense: in his first account of a northern voyage, *Mischief in Greenland*, Bill's published account was around 112 pages; the last five *Baroque* voyages cover 170 pages, an average of thirty-four pages a voyage, two-thirds down; what, really, was there left to say?

Baroque, by Bill's own admission, was never up to either *Mischief* or even *Sea Breeze*. She had a doghouse on deck which drew her new owner's instant dislike but this was mere cosmetics compared with the troubles awaiting him below.

Baroque had just had a major overhaul and Bill, unwisely, believed this meant that she would be unlikely to need much work. Phrases like 'no fool like an old fool', one feels, hang just under the surface of Bill's own assessment of his behaviour. But he could not stop for a very good reason: 'since in the natural course of things there could not be many more I did not want to leave 1973 blank.' This growing sense of urgency explains two crucial things about these last voyages: the growing carelessness Bill showed about both boat and crew.

To Victor Gozzer he wrote thus, in February 1973, about the boat and, more generally, how he saw the state of the world:

> I have at last found another boat *Baroque* a 1902 pilot cutter now lying at Falmouth. She needs a lot doing to her inside . . . From what we read of Italy one might conclude that it was already mob rule but I expect you have the same impression of life in England . . . I can sympathise with your wish to have done with it. Any teaching job or anything to do with the young must be hell. If the staff are not on strike, the pupils are. I attribute most of our ills to TV but I don't see how you can abolish that any more than motor cars.

Sandy Lee remembers the beginning of *Baroque*'s first cruise with Bill, largely for the perennial problem of who to take with him.

> On May 7th I drove down from Lymington to lend a hand and, on my arrival, found him alone there. After showing me the boat and the work he would like me to do next day, he referred to a letter from a Charles Wrigley which was the source of his immediate concern. As I remember it, the substance of the letter was an impressive summary of the writer's accomplishments. The one small cloud on the horizon was that the day had come for his arrival with no sign of him.

Lee suggested they phone.

This course had presented itself to Tilman but what with his slight deafness and deep dislike of the telephone, he had preferred to wait. With dusk falling we found a telephone box in which he closeted himself. Eventually he emerged muttering something about a 'stupid woman'. When I looked at the letter I found it signed 'Charles Wright', so perhaps the 'stupid' woman had a mite of reason on her side when she was unable to produce Charles Wrigley.

The 1973 cruise was to west Greenland again; Bill's crew now contained Simon Richardson, as well as Ilan Rosengarten (who proved to be a good cook, always important for Bill), Brian McClanaghan, John Harradine (to Cork), John Barrett (from Cork). They left Falmouth, where *Baroque* had been bought and refitted, but were almost immediately plagued by problems, which in the first instance necessitated their putting into Cork.

For Richardson all this was a lark; one of the reasons why Bill took to him was his apparent disinterest in anything other than the immediate issue of problem-solving. Bill wrote: 'I . . . later found that I had picked a winner in one, Simon Richardson, active, energetic, knowledgeable about boats and engines, and a thorough seaman so far as an amateur can attain to that honourable title.'

Bill by now was freely acknowledging in general that he was a hopeless judge of character: 'I have long since given up trying to assess a man's character by his appearance or his behaviour at a brief interview, and in consequence of numerous errors of judgement have often lamented, like the hapless Duncan, that: "There's no art to find the mind's construction in the face."'

Richardson wrote later: 'Tilman hates the bother of doing something like this' (picking a good crew). He added: 'He enjoys himself when talking to one person, but with a crowd he retreats into his shell a little.' On deck Richardson sometimes heard Bill singing: 'You can always tell when he's on watch, his deep croaky voice and his stamping foot – never together – it's an excellent method of keeping the feet warm and passing the time.' In his bunk, he noted, 'The Old Man sleeps totally encompassed by his sleeping bag in a foetal position, occasionally his head sticks out and he looks even more foetal – large head on small body, hand near top mouth as if sucking thumb.'

In Greenland, which they finally reached after numerous difficulties with the yacht, Richardson saw *Mischief's* name written up on the cliff-face at Godthaab, 'which made the skipper sad. "I almost wept when I saw it." Not surprisingly, he talks of her as a lost friend which she was, a home for fifteen years or so. He does not want to come out tonight but tells us to piss off, where to I can't imagine.'

But the trip was a trying one, for all that Bill eventually got to solo a peak and Richardson and David Meldrum climbed another (Mount Change). Richardson records in detail the state of *Baroque*. The chain plates on the port side gave way early, which was why they ended up in Bantry Bay. Later, in the Atlantic, they found *Baroque*, like her predecessors, leaked like a basket. 'The skipper has the best method of attacking at source: he makes drainpipes that run along beneath the beam, but he still gets wet all the time, but it does not seem to worry him. He wears the same clothes day in, day out, and does not have any others.'

And, 'the cheap sails are not wearing very well,' Richardson added. 'The bulwark up forward has disintegrated, new wood as well, just one section between staunchions . . .' and, 'I hope we can get on the starboard tack to bung up the hole that has been giving all the trouble near the skipper's bunk.' They were pumping *Baroque* continuously.

Richardson, watching Bill over this long period late in his life, was interested to know what made him tick. Rigorous self-discipline, he decided. He considered Bill's attitude to the voyage in this leaking boat to be the right one – no worse than the attitude of Elizabethan sailors, in fact, that this is how boats behaved and that in this environment, one simply had to get on and make do and mend.

'No doubt in about a year's time the Old Man will have found them all [the leaks], and it will be safe to heel her right over and thrash to windward, for which purpose she was designed back in '02.' (In this he was wrong – working boats rarely went well to windward, the trick was to sail a course that did not need such 'thrashing'.)

On Bill's navigation and seamanship skills Richardson, like Roger Robinson and Jim Lovegrove before him, was puzzled:

We tack again at ten and then at 4 pm when we have closed the land. The Old Man is very strange about this – presumably he likes to keep well away from land. He always somehow manages to get a good sight in per day even if there is no meridian. We have closed the shores about four times since leaving Godthaab. He gets very worried when he can't identify the coast, assumes it to be so and so from his sometimes dicky sight – very odd for someone of his sort to close the land if he is uncertain of our position when we still have 300 miles to go.

The troubles remained with them all through the voyage back to England, where they arrived off Lymington on October 6th. 'It was a Sunday,' wrote Bill, 'and there were many yachts out even in October. The first yacht we hailed said he was bound for Poole and he seemed a little shaken when in reply to his query, "Where from?" we answered "Greenland".'

It had been 'troublesome' as Bill put it, but he had enjoyed himself. Buoyed up by this thought, he turned his attention to Spitzbergen. 'Years ago some American climbing friends took it into their heads to label me Himal Bill, a title that no doubt owed more to length of association with the Himalaya than to entire success. I might now qualify for the title of Greenland Bill, or perhaps Eskimo Bill, not to be confused with Eskimo Nell, the heroine of a long sexual saga.' He now broke, for one year, from his regular long haul to the north-west. The voyage was Bill's last great sailing success.

They sailed on June 1st, 1974: the crew were David White, Paul Reinsch, Alan Stockdale and Andrew Craig-Bennett. Passing for the first time in his life through the Straits of Dover, Bill made a major error of navigation in the North Sea, although one that caused embarrassment rather than danger. David White had had enough of this, however, and asked to be put ashore; 'request not granted' Bill noted laconically.

Bill sailed first to Bear Island, south of Spitzbergen, and then on to his main objective, arriving on July 7th. They headed north, did some climbing and they then made for the extremely hazardous Hinlopen Strait, through which they passed on July 31st. With pack ice to the east they worked their way down the east coast but they ran aground in Freemansund.

The breeze having died we were again under engine when at 4 am I took over the watch from Alan. What followed is not easy to explain and still less easy to excuse. Perhaps, having spent the last three days mostly on deck and enjoyed only disturbed nights, I was not as bright as I should have been. Zeiloyane, the two islets mentioned above, were in sight ahead and with the west-going ebb under us we were rapidly approaching them. We had already discovered that west of C Heuglin along the north coast of Edge Is the water was shoal and we intended passing north of the Zeiloyane islets. I had my eyes fixed on one but the northernmost looked to me like a spit of land projecting from the coast of Barents Is. What with the engine and the tide which, as we neared the islets seemed to gather speed for its rush through the channel, we must have been making 7 or 8 knots over the ground. Before I had really hoisted in what was happening we were heading between the two islets which are a mile or so apart. To attempt to pass between unknown islets however wide apart they may be is always a hazardous proceeding. A shoal extended the whole way between the two and the rate we were going ensured our being carried right up on the back of it before we ground to a halt.

They were, as in 1968 and 1972, in deep trouble. Once again their first moves failed to get *Baroque* off. After trying to kedge off, they began to throw out the ballast. Fortunately, for the days they were stuck, the sea remained calm and the boat motionless. Even so they were under dire threat from ice floes driving past under a strong westerly wind. 'Twice the rudder sustained a savage blow,' Bill wrote later.

After the ballast they lightened ship in any way they could – an old flax mainsail being one victim. Finally, using their main anchor they managed to pull themselves off, losing that anchor, however, as they did so, along with another anchor they had to use when *Baroque* hit the very edge of the shoal on her way off. They collected water and ballast (stones) before they set sail for home. On the way the engine more or less packed up; Bill could only marvel that this had not happened while they were using it to get off their shoal.

It was a very sad homecoming. Bill's beloved sister, the 'sheet anchor' of his life, since their parents deaths, had died on September 7th. He had that day telephoned from Stornoway in the Shetlands to say they were safely back in British waters. It was a Sunday. Adeline had dressed for church and then sat down. A true Tilman, she had died in her chair with no fuss and, as far as was known, peacefully, knowing her dearest Billy was safe once more.

Bill did not arrive off Lymington until September 24th. Frantic efforts had been made by Pam his niece and her husband Derek to get a message to him but Bill still carried no ship-to-shore radio. In the end it was Sandy Lee, coming aboard *Baroque* as she entered the Lymington River, who had to break the news. 'He said very little,' Sandy says, 'but he ran aground twice in the river on the way in.'

Bill mentions this in his last book, *Triumph and Tribulation*, as he does the death of Adeline; he blamed the low tide and the weekend yachts. Yet, he concluded, it had been a happy voyage.

By the autumn of 1974 circumstances had changed for the worse. I had now to face life entirely alone like a Himalayan ascetic in his mountain cave – a spacious cave, I admit, far too spacious for one man. Instead of making it easier, this made it harder to get away either for long or short periods, what with the dogs who shared master's cave and other considerations.

One of these was his health. Bill had been going deaf for some time, and seems to have had arthritis; he also suffered increasingly from debilitating bouts of flu when he would retreat reluctantly to bed, like the proverbial bear with a sore head. Thus Pam found him more than once. Bill was not a good patient. In fact, even Bill was thinking perhaps he should ring down the curtain after the Spitzbergen voyage. But, as he put it, 'strenuousness is the immortal path, sloth is the way of death.'

Bill sailed again and among his crew was the son of Eric Shipton. 'Like father, he loved talking and arguments, but had such volubility, and such a rush of words to the mouth, that when I was concerned I had to have everything repeated in slow time.' They managed to reach a point north of Godthaab, although the problems of *Baroque* were again multiplying, but then the boom split in two and it was all over. They were home by mid-September.

Bill's target in 1975 had been Ellesmere Island, an ambitious and audacious plan indeed. Having failed to achieve it, naturally it was his target for 1976. It was the last voyage north for Bill and it was a disaster. *Baroque* was in poor condition, as was her skipper, his crew, David Burrows, Richard O'Connor, Jim Gaitens forming the nucleus, eventually forcing him to turn back. They, in this case, made the right choices.

The truth was that finally, in his seventy-ninth year, Bill was in the process himself of recognising emotionally that he had become an old man. He had, from the 1970s on, frequently described himself as growing old and feeble but in all of this one detects defiance. Since his sister's death, in 1974, he had deteriorated, unable to get off the treadmill of annual northerly sailings, perhaps perceiving there was little future in it.

His mental toughness held him together, but even in this regard he was becoming weaker, manifest even in his published words. For Bill the truly awful part lay in his own knowledge that it could not go on for much longer, this endless and largely fruitless quest to the north. Like the pack ice in whose grips he frequently languished, Bill was freezing up.

One of his crew on this voyage believed at the time that Bill actually wanted to die on that trip. What worried him and other crew members was that they feared Bill was not too bothered if he took them with him. The state of *Baroque*, even allowing for some exaggeration by them to justify their action, hardly helped morale on board. The final straw, in what was a very unhappy trip altogether, came when Bill ran her aground in Angmagssalik harbour; subsequently, she listed and was swamped. At this point the younger crew members effectively threw in the towel.

What drove Bill to despair, though, was not this disaster but their attitude, after *Baroque* had been salvaged and some of them had managed to sail her back to Reykjavik. At that point David Burrows, the older man Bill felt had been his greatest support throughout, suggested the voyage back from Iceland was going to prove too much for both skipper and yacht.

Bill wrote:

On the Monday, therefore, we unbent the sails, unshipped the bowsprit, and unrove the running rigging, stripping her to a gantline as the saying goes. In the absence of anyone else able or willing the skipper, despite his recently alleged failing health, spent an hour or so aloft unshackling and sending down all the wire ropes, blocks and strops. When the gear had been labelled

Jon took it to his store. Nicholas and John were still on board to give us a hand, and apart from my own feelings over this mournful affair I felt that they had been badly let down. In due course, I hope *Baroque* will sail back to England and that will probably be my last voyage in her. As my birthday is in February it would have been difficult to celebrate my eightieth north of the Arctic Circle, though I should have liked to have made a voyage in her in 1978 if only as a gesture of defiance. However, steeply rising costs and waning strength had already inclined me to call a halt, and now with the boat lying at Reykjavik, together with the frightening possibility that one might again be stuck with a similar crew, the decision is no longer in doubt.

Bill did find a final crew to sail *Baroque* back to England in the late spring of 1977 but by then he had found his 'gesture of defiance'. Simon Richardson, the arrogant, self-willed and self-styled adventurer who had sailed with Bill to Greenland in 1973, had invited Bill on a trip to Antarctica, to climb Mount Foster.

CHAPTER 16

The Sailor Home on the Sea

Bill Tilman's grave will never be marked. The evidence, such as it is, suggests that somewhere off the coast of South America, between Rio and the Falkland Islands, the converted tug on which he was sailing foundered. There were no messages, there has never been a hint of wreckage. One suggestion was that *En Avant* was wrecked on the Sea Lion Islands, to the south of East Falklands. On the night in question, the wardens reported a wreck but were unable to reach it; winds were gusting between fifty and sixty knots. The next morning nothing could be seen. Whether it was *En Avant* remains speculation.

The dates between which we know that Bill's end came are definitively marked at one end only – he died between November 1st, 1977, when *En Avant* left Rio, and some time in December, when she was due in Port Stanley, Falkland Islands, to pick up two New Zealand climbers.

The motives which must have led Bill to accept Simon Richardson's offer, in which he would take little more than a supernumerary part, were not just about seizing what he must have known would be the last chance ever to go on an expedition. In part, no doubt, the idea of spending his eightieth birthday in Antarctica was even more appealing than being in the Arctic. Second, and no less significant, Richardson's avowed objective was to climb an unconquered peak on Smith Island, the goal which had defeated Bill twenty years earlier.

It went further than that: Bill had actively discussed the Smith Island voyage with Richardson when they had sailed to Greenland in 1973. During these conversations, Bill would have told Richardson that it was on this voyage that he lost a man overboard – the only time in his career as a sailor. The voyage was one of the worst Bill ever made and the temptation to redo it with an eager and ambitious young crew must have proved irresistible. Bill also liked Simon Richardson. In the lexicon of failed or unhappy voyages of the past years, the 1973 trip clearly stood out in Bill's mind.

Simon Richardson espoused some of Bill's philosophy; one can surmise too, that in his own slipshod arrogance, he appealed to Bill: the devil take the hindmost belief in his own ability to get the Smith Island expedition together and to make it. But what also appealed to Bill was Richardson's belief in himself and his ability to achieve – against great odds – an impossible goal. Dorothy Richardson, Simon's mother, may be forgiven for wishing to compare her son directly with Tilman but it may not be so fanciful. The evidence is that Bill might well have seen something of himself in Simon's attitudes, if not directly his character.

As the project ended in disaster, and as it ended the life of a great explorer, it is worth looking in some detail at the way it was conceived and how Bill came, finally, to take part. In this we are fortunate that Simon's mother wrote an account of the expedition, such as it was, and has included parts of Simon's earlier journal of his voyage north with Bill. We have, therefore, a picture of Bill written by the man who was to make the final voyage with him; we have as well an insight into Richardson's attitudes and character.

Simon's judgment of Bill is in its own right interesting: at the time he wrote, a twenty-year-old assessing a seventy-five-year-old as they sailed on what was proving to be a rather rickety yacht. To some extent Richardson viewed the relationship between the crew and Tilman as one in which Tilman set them problems they then had to solve. His respect was tempered by what he saw as the need by the 'Old Man' for them. 'The Old Man hangs off us like magnet,' he wrote.

At the same time Richardson admired the way Bill handled the yacht and her tribulations, which were many. He saw, too, how Bill navigated: 'getting his sights off in his efficient manner with amazing alacrity and precision.'

Later, he says:

I have been talking to the skipper a lot lately during his watches . . . We were talking of his expeditions to Antarctica and how he would like to have another go at Smith Island – somewhere south of the [South] Shetlands. The only thing that seems to stop him is the lack of reliable crew, and the difficulty of finding people who would be prepared to go down there for a year and spend 83 days at sea. He was also telling me of an expedition just before the war to the Himalaya that cost them £300 each . . . It's a pity that people of today have to mount a vast expedition raising thousands of pounds as opposed to quietly sailing off and not telling anyone, like the Old Man . . .

I must say it would be fantastic to set off in a boat down there. I reckon I could dig up a crew who would really be prepared to go and like it.

No doubt, then, where the seeds for the 1977 expedition Richardson put together came from. Who can say that Bill, in those long night watches, was not hoping to plant them? It might also be that, influenced by Bill as he unquestionably was, Richardson believed that the 'shoestring' approach was the right one. In this he was mistaken – perhaps when he said it even Bill believed it true. Bill did no service when he suggested exploration could be planned on the back of an envelope.

For all their difference in age, Bill liked Richardson and, in particular, his ability to do the tasks he was set on board. Of him Bill wrote later: 'I was thankful to have Simon, active and competent, backed up by the others who were equally active, if less competent.'

From this time, Richardson identified strongly with Tilman, imagining himself some kind of heir to the old man's ambitions, if not his achievements. It was that combination which was to prove so fatal to them both. Richardson's own last comments in his journal say a great deal: 'There was no doubt about it, I thought it was going to be tough. Small wizened old man, tough wiry, disciplinarian, but no, sad old man, let down so he thinks by countless people – his own fault – and sometimes I feel worthless. I will always value this trip, and set other things against it.'

Bill had asked Simon to go on his trip to circumnavigate Spitzbergen and Richardson had agreed when his father was taken ill, and then died. He wrote to Bill explaining why he had decided not to go; instead he took a job in Scotland, working on a new harbour, eventually being appointed, in April 1975, as the assistant marine controller. In this post he suffered a serious accident – a shattered lower left leg. It was while he was recovering from this at home in Hampshire that, so his mother believes, he began seriously planning the Smith Island expedition.

In November 1975 he had received a letter from Bill, explaining that the year's trip north had not been an unqualified success – *Baroque*'s main boom had snapped. He told Simon that he hoped to go north in the following year adding, 'probably (almost certainly) the last time'.

Partly as a result of this letter, and no doubt because of the comment in it, Richardson persuaded Bill to come and stay, much to the incredulity of both his mother and, according to her, of Bill's niece, Pam Davis. It was at this meeting in the Richardson family home in Stockbridge that Simon discussed the Smith Island project although it is not known whether Bill was asked to join, or what his response was. We may surmise that, whatever Richardson asked him, Bill would have kept his counsel. After all, there was not even a boat at that stage.

Richardson was moving ahead, however, eventually buying a semi-wrecked tug hull from a Dutch yard in February 1976; his intention was to convert this hulk into a gaff-rigged cutter and, from his point of view,

En Avant had two great advantages: she had a steel hull and she was cheap. He finally bought her for £750.

She had been involved in a serious marine accident which had left her temporarily sunk and with one crew dead; more cautious buyers might have pondered long and hard about this, and the possible structural damage to the ship's frames, let alone the superstition surrounding such a ship, which had been built by wartime slave labour – all ill-omens to old sea-dogs.

Richardson's determination overrode any such consideration and, having bought his ship, he set out for Holland to begin work on her. Dorothy Richardson's account of her son's conversion of *En Avant* emphasises the heroic efforts he made to change the tug to a sailing yacht. There is no question that he put an enormous effort into it, along with his youthful companions, once the hull had been brought back to Southampton.

It has to be said, however, that everything was done on the cheap; the photographs of *En Avant* leaving Southampton on her voyage south show her in a sorry state, her name crudely painted on her stern. Even Bill was appalled that she had not been fitted with guard rails above her low deck coaming for the trip across the Atlantic. Letters written by him from Rio express a pleasant surprise that they made the trans-Atlantic crossing with no major mishap.

In the aftermath, the details of how *En Avant* was converted and what might have happened have to be investigated. Four theories have surfaced about the loss of the ship. The first and most comforting to those who believe the expedition was not ill-conceived, is that the yacht was simply 'overwhelmed'. This theory, of course, does not answer the awkward question as to why a well-found appropriately converted and equipped yacht should be overwhelmed in anything other than a huge storm. There is no concrete evidence to suggest that *En Avant* was far enough south to have encountered the worst of Southern Ocean weather. There are, however, williwaws, fierce squalls, to be found anywhere off the coast of South America and, more significant, *En Avant* was anything but 'well-found'.

One theory, in part propounded by some of those who worked at the Berthon yard in Lymington, where Bill's Bristol pilot cutters were laid up and repaired, was that either the huge electric battery system *En Avant* was carrying had broken loose in bad weather and had burst the hull, or that those same batteries were leaking and eventually the hull failed catastrophically underneath them from the corrosion this could have caused.

A third theory is that the yacht was rolled by a large sea and that, given her build and high centre of gravity, she did not roll back, having been turned over. Such a roll could have been initiated by a breaking sea, combined with high winds. What lends weight to this theory is that

Simon had himself welded a hollow steel keel to the mainly flat bottom, and that he had welded this on himself. That is to say, the keel, which counter-balanced the sails and the steel mast, was not bolted through the hull (an important safety consideration). Further, Simon had installed a very heavy and large marine diesel engine, whose upper works intruded above deck level, raising the yacht's centre of gravity.

The fourth theory, compounded possibly by parts of the third is this: did the new keel fail, causing the yacht to invert at high speed, or did a breaking sea begin a heavy roll which, given the high centre of gravity and the stresses involved, cause the keel to fracture where it was welded to the old hull? Underlying these speculations is the question of the conversion. *En Avant* was changed from one kind of vessel to another of a completely different kind, using a different means of propulsion with all that implies, being sailed in conditions for which she certainly was not designed.

As far as the issue of keel failure goes, I am indebted to Sandy Lee, who took a close interest in this last voyage and who, indeed, did his best to help Simon Richardson in his refitting. He says of the keel that

a frustrating feature of *En Avant* was that from the time she was moved from the Belsize yard to her berth (27) in Southampton docks below Northam Bridge, virtually no one, apart from the crew, ever saw the keel. Mary and I saw about four feet of its forward end when she was beached at an obscure public hard at Northam for anti-fouling on July 21st. By the time we found this little hard the tide had risen to the extent that she was almost afloat again.

It was a box-section of welded steel plates (15mm thick) which it was intended to fill with iron pigs to create a substantial ballast keel, but this was never done. Simon had mentioned to the Belsize yard proprietor when *En Avant* was there, that he might have to cut openings in the hull plates to insert the pigs, and then weld up again. As regards the effective weight of the keel, it was reduced to the displacement weight of the plates which went into its construction. This would be about three tons.

It is clear that the idea of fitting the keel with pigs was too ambitious, even given unlimited time. What I can only visualise, with the greatest admiration, is Simon's ability to weld the overhead seams with the hull up on dunnage. It raises the question of whether he had to content himself with spot welds; and that brings us round to the question: did the keel tear away from the hull?

If her keel had been properly bolted, she might have survived. (But it is worth noting the accident to the Whitbread yacht, *Martela*, north of the Falkland Islands in 1990 when, with a bolted keel, it still detached: she turned over in less than ninety seconds.) For all the size of her scantlings, *En Avant* was a most unsuitable conversion. Bill Tilman, for all his experience of long-distance sailing, never seemed to bother or worry much about the actual condition of the yachts on which he dwelt. When *Mischief*, his first cutter, was found to be suffering almost terminally from Teredo worm infestation after his epic circumnavigation of Africa, he remarked that perhaps he should have spent more money on the copper-plating protection he had ordered in Cape Town.

In any case, Bill Tilman is unlikely to have been bothered much by the state or conditions of *En Avant*'s hull because he would have taken on trust what he was told – as he always had. Watching Simon Richardson and his crew, Bill would have been more impressed by their enthusiasm and apparent knowledge, and not notice what we could justifiably call the 'bullshit' factor. Finally, and this is a surmise, Bill's innate trustworthiness would, in this case, have been coupled with his overwhelming desire to make this last voyage, suppressing any lingering doubts he may have had.

Richardson, though, acted like a man possessed from 1976 until the yacht left on her voyage south in October 1977. The accident he sustained had left him partly crippled, and in a good deal of pain. None of this prevented him, at some risk to his own health, pursuing his goal.

Immediately the sale was agreed Simon went out to Holland. It was fourteen weeks since his accident, he was still in cumbersome thigh-length plaster, walking with two sticks, and it was February . . . He put his rucksack on the roofrack of the Mini and packed it there with all his tools, including his big Bosch steel-cutter. By the time it was full the rucksack must have weighed about a hundredweight, and when we got to Winchester station we had difficulty in getting it onto his back [wrote Dorothy Richardson].

When Richardson arrived in Holland he was met by friends, who were appalled to see how ill he looked and how badly his injured leg had swollen. It was in these circumstances that he began work converting his ship. His plaster finally came off in June. There is, of course, nothing wrong in the determination shown by Richardson in getting *En Avant* into shape; the questions which arise derive from his judgment in apparently believing that circumstances do not alter cases. In many important – and with hindsight, highly significant ways – Richardson matched Bill Tilman, not for their mutual experiences of adventure, not even, as Dorothy Richardson would have it, in Simon's mystical affinity with Bill, but in a much more prosaic, and potentially deadly, way.

Simon Richardson had lost his father in the summer of 1974, an event which affected him deeply; Bill Tilman lost his sister later in the same year, writing to Simon that 'Death clouded the beginning and end of the voyage.' Simon's obsession with getting this project to run in 1977 must have in part been fuelled by a belief – a desire – that Bill should at all costs come with them and that, if they did not go then, it might be too late.

Bill Tilman's behaviour towards this trip, and his own wish to be somewhere exciting for his eightieth birthday, suggests a collusion, never spoken but understood between him and Simon. By her own account, Pam Davis, Bill's niece, says that the one and only time she cried when Bill left on one of his voyages was on this one, believing she would never see him again. Simon had already expressed the view that Bill might not survive the whole trip, suggesting that, when his time came, he would expect him simply to turn his face to the wall and die.

It is not too fanciful to suggest, then, that between the old and tired explorer and the young adventurer a plot had been hatched in both their minds. If Simon had read more he might have known that the old heroes of earlier times had taken young heroes with them on their avowed last voyage, as a sacrifice to the gods to ensure a welcome in Valhalla.

It is worth noting that Pam Davis expressed forceful and, for her, unique, opposition to Bill going. When he arrived back from Iceland in the summer of 1977, and went to see her and her husband, Derek, at their house near Basingstoke, almost her first words to Bill were to ask if he really had committed himself to going with Richardson. Horrified at his reply, she was unable to get past his muttered excuse that he had given his word.

When he had decided is unclear. In a letter to Bill written in March 1977 Richardson says, 'Can I repeat on paper that your place is secured on the boat if you decide or want to come.'

This is to move ahead of events. Richardson's major task, in the work he put into *En Avant* in Holland, was to install the large marine diesel he had been given, a Deutz. Once this had been accomplished, he set out for England with a single crew member, an English doctor he had consulted for an eye problem. A flavour of that voyage is given in a comment from that same doctor to Dorothy Richardson. *En Avant* was still basically just a hull with an engine – no superstructure – and she was being sailed in the busiest waters in the world.

It got dark as we turned into the fairway off Calais an hour later, and we had no lights, none at all, which appealed to me. The problem was the lights worked off the generator and we'd come to enjoy the peace and quiet by then, so we didn't want the generator . . . shortly after we just missed a yacht, so after that we kept the generator running and the navigation lights on.

In Southampton, even Dorothy Richardson was moved to write: 'The first time I saw her again she looked exactly like all the other hulks waiting to be cut up for scrap,' adding that 'Simon redesigned her as a gaff-rigged cutter.' (That is to say, she would look superficially not dissimilar to a Bristol pilot cutter.)

In December 1976, the Richardsons had Bill to stay. He went and looked at *En Avant*, but still apparently did not commit himself. It was after this visit that Simon told his mother that he believed that Tilman wanted to die at sea and that he (Simon) would be quite prepared for that. Shortly after this visit by Bill, still in December, and due to carelessness in the way *En Avant* had been moored, she caught her coaming under that of an adjoining ship as the tide rose. As a result, she sank. This speaks volumes about the freeboard this 'yacht' conversion was to have, as well as about the seamanship involved on the part of her youthful skipper.

To Bill, Richardson wrote on January 23rd:

It seems that fate is trying to exact her ounce of flesh from me. The low tide after we launched the boat rolled over onto her beam ends and filled with water through a small hole some two feet above the water line. Instead of the keel breaking through the mud, which is what the yard expected she didn't. Amazingly I had just returned the bung from that hole to use somewhere else assuming that one's boat was safe from the vagaries of the sea in a such a sheltered spot.

Bill seems to have decided some time between this date and March. Was pressure put on him to come as the one person who might keep Richardson from the kind of mistakes he was making – elementary as many were – over the care and maintenance of *En Avant*? A little later he wrote again to Bill: 'I can see one problem in your coming to Smith Island and that is the notion that you are always, or at least have, been called "skipper" for the last 20 years. If we could change this to "Tilman" or "you" or some such term, the problem will disappear.'

But, significantly, he continues:

With regard to your use on the boat I do not wish to flatter you, but can I point out a few facts. 1) You know more about handling sailing boats in ice and unfrequented parts of the globe, than anyone alive today; 2) You have more experience in the way of expedition running of this kind than anyone else I know; 3) You should be able tactfully to temper my impetuousness and any other faults of my leadership; 4) and most important – you would be the last person to quit, should the going be difficult. There are a host of other reasons why you will be of use to me and the expedition.

In short, this letter says, 'help'.

Dorothy Richardson writes of her son: 'I could understand anyone who found him tiresome . . . slapdash . . . undisciplined . . . loutish,' tempering these comments by suggesting that only precise, pedantic and conventional people would have judged him this way, but she also quotes Rainer Marie Rilke: 'even between the closest human beings infinite distances continue to exist,' a sad comment from a woman who has had to come to terms with her son's death.

More broadly, the Smith Island expedition, despite gathering to itself some recognition and some sponsorship, was ill-conceived – and would have been even if it had been successful in its goal. Much has been made of the fact that Bill Tilman 'endorsed' it by going. But it is quite clear that he did not have any other offers; where would he have looked? He knew, too, that from the summer of that year he would no longer have a yacht of his own, after twenty-five years. He also knew that Richardson was obsessed enough to go to Smith Island. This would be the last voyage – he must have realised that as well.

Determined to keep to his schedule, come what may, Richardson allowed nothing to come between him and his avowed goal. At the same time, expedition planning the Richardson way was heavily based on Bill's 'envelope' principle. Unlike Bill, though, Richardson seems to have taken Bill's throwaway comment as a serious means of organising a major undertaking such as the one in hand.

Advertisements for crew came late, at the end of April, although by then Bill had committed himself along with one or two of Richardson's friends. In this Richardson was emulating Bill, although, as it turned out, he had better luck, not least because he did take one close friend and, with Bill excepted, they were all much of an age. Richardson refused to contemplate taking any women, espousing Bill's philosophy about no women on expeditions. And again, perhaps, he was mindful that if a woman was to come along, Bill almost certainly would not. In another letter to Bill, dated March 10th, he says: 'One good woman has applied – a glaciologist, done some climbing in the Alps and sounds keen, but I reckon must be an unreasonable bet, though women could be all right if there was only one of them? I don't know.' His hesitation was due in part to knowing that he had been unable to acquire any climbers for the ascent of Mount Foster on Smith Island. In part, of course, it was for Bill's benefit.

Eventually, Richardson picked three crew out of the response to his advertisement: Rod Coatman, Robert Toombs and Charles Williams, supplemented by two others, an old school friend Mark Johnson, who was a merchant seaman, and an American climber, Joe Dittamore. Bill Tilman was the seventh and the plan was to pick up a New Zealand climber (eventually two) on their way south through the Falkland Islands.

Bill had come to stay in the Richardson house – Longstock Mill in Stockbridge – in June, and had henceforth travelled with the rest down to Southampton to work on *En Avant*. Dorothy Richardson remembers him as charming, if somewhat aloof. She never called him anything other than Major Tilman. He had by then invited Simon and the rest of the crew to call him Tilly, the name his First World War troopers had used. He still appeared strong, surprising everyone with his agility; 'wiry' was a word much in use by his youthful friends.

He was old, though. One account of him – Dorothy's via Simon – has him scrambling easily up a rope from the deck of *En Avant* to the quayside. Another, by his long-time friend, Sandy Lee, who witnessed this, was that Bill could hardly manage it; Richardson stood by below, making no effort to help. Lee also recalls how badly *En Avant* rolled when a ship passed by in the river, and how Bill, in turn, rolled his eyes heavenward at Sandy after this had occurred. In yachtsman's terms *En Avant* was dangerously 'tender'.

The crew, apart from Simon, appeared to have been intrigued by Bill, rather than overawed, a situation that Bill no doubt enjoyed immensely, relieved as he also was by the burden of leadership. One of the photographs taken at this time of him, though, shows him on the deck of *En Avant*, doubt expressed in every line of his body; one of the very last, taken on board the yacht in the Atlantic, shows him sitting while Richardson's birthday party is in progress. He looks merely puzzled, as if uncertain as to why he is there.

En Avant left Southampton on August 9th, 1977. There was some last-minute trouble with Board of Trade officials, still never satisfactorily explained by anyone who was there. Part of their interest may have been occasioned by the siting of the main compass. As *En Avant* was steel, and maybe also because of the size and siting of the main engine, she created a huge magnetic field, so bad that the compass was positioned, not by the helm but in the bows. To steer a course the helmsman had to have shouted instructions from a man placed forward, fifty feet away.

Sandy Lee says of this:

I do not recall seeing the Board of Trade inspectors on the morning *En Avant* left; they certainly did not step on the deck that morning. In fact, I was the only non-crew Simon allowed aboard that morning, and that was to let me replace some temporary steel screws with brass in the makeshift binnacle housing the compass and to cover the correcting magnets with brass plates.

It never came to my knowledge that the BoT inspectors concerned themselves with the modifications from tug to gaff cutter, or with the compass arrangements. They insisted on a seven-man life-raft and on fire precautions in the galley and elsewhere. What happened to the compass was Simon's affair and, for the record, it was this.

On Saturday, July 30th, Simon had to move *En Avant* away from Berth 27 to let a frigate into the adjacent dry-dock. Being thus disturbed, he took the chance to motor down to the compass swinging grounds in Southampton Water. Tilman was aboard and I went with them. On our return about noon Simon motored up to the Southampton container terminal with the intention of feeling his boat under sail for the first time. It was a flawless day for many activities but for an exercise under sail it was a complete failure.

From the container terminal the current of the River Test brought us back at about one knot, during which time vague movement the two jibs and mainsail were set and then handed. They hung limply in the still air and the only purpose it served was to discover that the boom end would not clear the backstay. The backstay was thereupon dispensed with, permanently, although the steel mast looked as if it would cope. So ended the one mile of sailing trials which *En Avant* was afforded.

The result of the compass swinging that day was to set more questions than it answered when Simon and Mark Johnson came to interpret them that evening. Simon decided to take *En Avant* down again early next morning for another try. This second result, too, was perplexing, so Simon sought the services of a compass adjuster from Hamble. He first established that the instrument was showing a deviation of 30–40° due to the proximity of the steel boom above it and the steel deck and cockpit. He advised the resiting of the compass forward of the mast and as far above the deck as practicable.

To achieve this, I made a wooden binnacle which was mounted on a stainless-steel tripod which Simon made at short notice. Considering its vulnerable position on the foredeck, the whole thing looked frail, but the tripod was welded to the deck only a day before they sailed, and the compass mounting completed just ten minutes before their departure on the morning of August 9th.

The main compass now had a deviation of the order of 3° on the main points, but its reading had to be relayed back to the helmsman in the cockpit at the stern . . . No doubt they established the relationship between the main and hand compasses in due course, but a wave on the foredeck could have altered things dramatically.

But the yacht sailed – first for Las Palmas in the Canaries, arriving there at the end of August. Two points need to be made about that maiden voyage. First, that when they raised the sails on her, as she moved down Southampton Water, it was the second time they had ever done so; there had been no serious trials of her sailing capabilities at all; second, they enjoyed a large high-pressure system down to the Canaries – no real test of how *En Avant* would – or could – sail on the wind. Bill wrote to Sandy Lee from the Canaries: 'All the way down Channel and across the Bay we had calm seas and light winds.' On the one occasion they were obliged to heave to, he wrote that the crew were a nimble and active lot: 'they need to be to handle the cumbersome gear and to remain on deck and not in the sea . . . With nothing to hang on to I find it hard enough to get about on deck.'

No doubt, he thought, they would rig lifelines when they got to the other side of the Tropics. Gybing, he noted, had no effect on the boom or gear of 'this steel monster'. But he added, poignantly, 'I don't know why I'm here, but in spite of the damnable difficulties in getting about the boat, both below and on deck, it is an enjoyable experience (so far) and better than languishing at Bodowen.'

From the Canaries, the trade winds blow from behind; again, relatively easy down-wind sailing. They arrived in Rio on October 25th. Richardson reported in a letter that *En Avant* was able to 'carry full sail in 30 knots with no problem' (this being the trade winds, blowing astern). He added, oddly, 'so my dream is over. It would have been worth the terrible struggle just to get this far. I have started planning my next dream.'

Bill, in a letter to Sandy Lee, wrote from Rio:

I am having a very easy time doing little or nothing beyond watch-keeping . . . In fact I begin to doubt whether I am really worth the run of my teeth. The gear is too heavy for me and I find it difficult getting about the wide deck with nothing to hang on to. After leaving here I imagine we shall rig some lifelines. Still it would have been a mistake to refuse Simon's pressing invitation.

In another letter home, Richardson was estimating they might take two weeks to the Falklands (Bill thought six to seven), where he was now expecting the New Zealand climbers to be waiting. There was no more communication. Dorothy Richardson, at home, took the view, when the yacht had not turned up on schedule, that this could be interpreted as quite normal. In fact, a search of a kind was finally begun on January 9th, 1978, although 'search' suggests something active; ships in the vicinity were merely asked to keep a good lookout.

Dorothy Richardson, for the most obvious of reasons, insisted to anyone who asked – and by now these included journalists – that Simon had changed his plans and had taken a direct route from Rio to Smith Island; no news would be likely for a long time. A glance at any map would have told her the direct route to Smith Island from Rio is through the Falkland Islands where the climbers waited.

Nevertheless, a helicopter search of Smith Island, directed from HMS *Endurance* in March 1978, found no trace of men or of a landing. Former expeditionary colleagues of Bill's, including Colin Putt from the Heard Island expedition, suggested that perhaps *En Avant* had been disabled – through the loss of her rudder – and might be drifting towards Africa. People, in general, were grasping at straws.

A report from Colin Putt and David Lewis giving possible explanations does contain one interesting point, already made:

> *En Avant* is a small tug hull, built of steel, converted to cutter rig and redesigned with an old simple low-powered compression ignition engine. Tug hulls are both deep and beamy as power vessels go, with considerable stability, even to the point of carrying sail effectively, although this ability may be limited by the usually low freeboard which limits the amount of ballast which can be carried. A strongly constructed hull of this type, like *En Avant*, should be very resistant to the worst effects of a knockdown or broach-to in a big sea . . .
>
> On the other hand power hulls, and even tug hulls, are notoriously unhandy when converted to sail; they lack the stiffness [i.e., they are 'tender'], freeboard, and lateral resistance which are required especially when sailing to windward, and at the best they tend to be slow and unweatherly.

The Royal Institute of Navigation also made a report on what might have happened. Pointing out that Richardson was an experienced yachtsman, along with Tilman, and that they carried on board an ex-merchant sailor, who was an experienced navigator, the authors also mention the 'delay' in completing registration formalities. The report concludes the yacht most likely foundered; it was dated August 1978, a year after they had left.

We must assume the yacht foundered, in some way or another. In this case, especially had it happened at night, the crew would have had little chance of even getting clear of the hull, let alone inflating their life-raft. As no wreckage of any kind has ever been found, catastrophic failure of the hull – like the keel detaching – seems quite likely.

Years before, in 1965, on the Heard Island expedition, one of Bill's most successful sailing trips, he and his Australian compatriots had been lying ahull in a gale in *Patenela* when conversation had turned to what to do if the ship then had foundered. One of the crew confessed he could not swim.

Then, said Bill, you are lucky, your struggle will be the less. In the South Atlantic, when *En Avant* sank, we may at least hope he remembered those words and, although a swimmer, having been granted his last wish not to die in his bed, he parted this life in a true peace, surrendering gently to death, the ultimate healer.

EPILOGUE

H. W. Tilman:
An Assessment – Beyond the Myth

Bill Tilman's life was so full, so expressive of adventure, in all its forms, that it is nearly impossible to take it all in, to summarise it. To a more cynical age much of what he did can be dismissed as the whim of a gentleman adventurer, a man without a purpose. Certainly, it is hard to understand some of what Bill did – his endless quests to Greenland, for example. Perhaps, after all, he was just filling in time. Or perhaps he was seeking a silent solace from the sound of gunfire which twice in his life had so influenced him.

It may be wrong to try to claw any meaning at all from his life, other than to celebrate its achievements, and to laugh with him at the absurdity of the world of men. Yet one lingers over what it all could mean to us, as we stand close to the edge of a new and possibly great adventure – the third millennium. That it has to mean something may be the kind of conceit Bill would have despised, or more likely laughed off. His attitude to adventure was as simple as his philosophy for having one: just put on your boots and go.

But the surface of Bill's life, as smooth as the early morning waters of the far northern seas before a breath of wind rippled them, hid a complex man. Bill's mind had fjord depths, and in those sunless abysses he kept his counsel, wisely maybe, but for us, struggling to understand what made him doggedly keep on going, adding to the general air of mystery.

Bill Tilman was not an imaginative man; he was a stoic and that, we may surmise, grew out of the simple fact of surviving the century's most terrible conflict. All the evidence about what he became, what he strived for, leads us back to the First World War. If some of his adventures were a literal attempt to escape, some part of that escape must have been about the guilt of the survivor. Some, as I have suggested, was about never fearing danger again, never believing – quite – in

269

the power of death. Bill was, from 1918 on, living on borrowed time and his indifference to hazards, in the sense of their life-threatening capacity, is well documented.

He was, too, a lucky man, surviving a number of minor, and one or two major, accidents. He was lucky, too, in his companions, most notably Eric Shipton, but also, later, Charles Marriott, who sailed with him on some of the very best of all the adventures, south and north.

If the First World War defined the parameters of Bill's character, then it was Africa which filled in the details. By the time Bill returned from Africa and began on the course that was to take him into the halls of fame as a legendary climber, sailor and explorer, certain aspects of his character were already clearly defined. He was a solitary man, a man who could sit for hours with a companion and say nothing at all. He has also gained a considerable reputation for liking hazard, if not actually courting danger. None of this is particularly unusual. What became a much more firmly established part of the Bill 'legend' was that he actively disliked the company of women, a legend he in part encouraged because it saved him embarrassment on many occasions.

In fact, like many good stories told about Bill, this has to be so modified to fit the facts as to become a parody of the truth. There are no discernible reasons for Bill's growing detachment from women; during the First World War he wrote home about enjoying the company of women nurses; he was known for his love of dancing and, as I have quoted from his own letters, he asked girls out. But by the 1930s when Bill went to a dance he took Adeline, his sister, not a girlfriend.

As Bill's life story is one of a larger-than-life character, we need to explore the reasons for a change in Bill which seems to be dated to his time in Africa. We can dismiss out of hand any suggestion that he was either a latent or active homosexual. The hundreds of men who shared a tent with him, or were in close proximity to him in his yachts, over many months, are testimony to his lack of physical interest in them. No one I have interviewed has ever mentioned or suggested that Bill made any kind of advance, or that they noted any tendency by him to homosexual ideas, let alone practices. It would seem to stretch the bounds of human reason to beyond breaking point to suggest under these circumstances that his homosexual proclivities were so latent that even he did not realise he had them.

Was he a mysogynist? The answer to this question would again seem to be an emphatic no. Over the years he met, corresponded, dined and conversed with many women outside his family. Two kinds of response can be found in their accounts. There was the Bill who cut them dead, ignored them or made it plain that he wished himself to be somewhere else; and there was the Bill who was the soul of courtesy and kindness, who smiled and laughed and happily kissed the ladies.

Bill was a very self-effacing man in many respects; he was certainly a very shy man. What he actively disliked was the coquettish, eyelid-fluttering woman who believed she could win his attention by acting in a 'girly' fashion. All the evidence suggests that Bill either ran from this kind of woman or made it very plain he did not want her company.

To women who expressed themselves as they were he is remembered as a gentleman – an old-fashioned word but a completely accurate one in this case. Bill was old-fashioned, a Victorian in many ways, and no worse for that. He did not believe women should come on expeditions, for example, yet he could be won over – as he was by Betsy Cowles. He none the less applauded women who made their own adventures; a number contacted him in his later life to ask for advice and they got it, straight from the heart.

So what prevented Bill from – apparently – forming a long-term attachment, marrying someone? The answer is complex and there are inevitable gaps in our knowledge. One part is that there was a simple lack of opportunity. From just before his eighteenth birthday until nearly his twenty-first, he was at war. From the age of twenty-one to thirty-five he lived in the African bush where the chances of finding – or keeping – a woman were remote. At that point he took up climbing in the Himalayas and that continued until 1939 when he went away to war again. In 1945, when he might have taken stock, he was forty-seven years old and clearly very set in his ways. By then, more or less, he had a family in Adeline, and her daughters and their families.

We have examined his emotional experiences in the First World War. It is clear that he never fully recovered from that conflict and that he could never bring himself to let his emotions out – to feel in any public kind of way. Watching his fellows die, day by day, in front of his eyes may well have destroyed any further chance he had of ever allowing any kind of deeply felt emotion out. In this sense he was, from 1918, emotionally on ice. That he chose to spend his time in the great mountains amongst ice, and, later, in the icefields off Greenland and other northern waters, is probably no accident.

It is also more than probable that he saw a twin unhappiness in the death of his brother and the widowing of Kenneth's wife and in the break-up of his sister's marriage. He may well have thought a close personal relationship not worth the pain and suffering; we do seem to return to that as an underlying emotional reason for his not having formed a close relationship with a woman outside his family.

There has been a suggestion that he found his near neighbours in Africa, Ron Buchanan and his wife, who had committed suicide, but this is circumstantial evidence again that an experience like this would have turned him away from women as close companions. Probably, it was a mixture of all the above which led Bill to eschew marriage, along with his terrible shyness which would have created a first barrier to intimacy.

At the other end of the twentieth century to these events, there is no way of finding out for certain.

We have become sex-obsessed in western society. Sex is everywhere in our lives; it pervades almost every element of both adult and childhood thinking and, in many cases, acts. We are endlessly fascinated by the sex lives of others – especially the famous – and we cannot believe that if a man or woman does not have an overt partner, then they have none. If a man is not with, or pursuing, a woman then he must, perforce, be a homosexual. The concept of asexuality, of celibacy, seems a nonsense: such people are hiding from, or denying, their true desires, it is said.

This is a conceit (and an indictment of us and our attitudes). Celibacy, or indifference to sex, pervades history. In many respects Freud may have been right on this one issue to do with sex (and he has a lot to answer for, in bringing sex to the forefront of our thinking). He said that part of becoming an adult (in his meaning), or becoming civilised, was in sublimating sex into other, cultural, activities. He would have entirely approved of Bill: mountains and oceans have their own Freudian meanings.

Enough has been said, perhaps too much. Bill was a very great man, a man of immense physical toughness who could endure more hardship than most of his fellows – and for longer in his life. But he was not just an explorer, a mountaineer and a sailor. He was a family man, too. His letters home are full of homely comments and discussions; he always ends his letters to Adeline by asking her to pass on his love to Joan and Pam, before adding 'best love, or 'yours ever'. These little endearments express a great deal.

But there is much more. Once again, I am indebted to Pam Davis for these memories of 'Uncle' Bill. This is him at home in his very set routine:

> After my mother bought Bodowen, in 1947, they moved in together. Every day he was home he had a set routine. Breakfast was at 8.45, a boiled egg, coffee, toast and honey – which he got himself. He collected and read his mail. He answered letters the day they came, a rather irritating habit as one was always behind and owed him a letter. But he was punctilious to the extent of thanking people for birthday cards and even Christmas cards.
>
> He would glance at *The Times* crossword puzzle over elevenses coffee and a digestive biscuit; then there would be more writing – a new book, lecture notes, a letter. The typewriter would be constantly tapping from his study.
>
> Lunch was dead on one o'clock, a light cheese or egg dish, or soup; then he would have another go at the crossword and dead on two o'clock he would rise, put on his boots, and with the dogs

at his heels he would disappear around the Panorama [a local walk above the house].

Exactly at 4.28 he would reappear, dogs panting, Bill imperturbed, and he would go into the drawing room for toast, honey, fruit cake and three cups of China tea. He would fill in the crossword clues he had thought about on his walk. If he had no writing, he would work away in the garden or in clearing away the rocks outside the front door, planting things perilously close to the edge.

He always appeared at 7.15 tidy and ready for a whisky before dinner which was at 7.30. He had a thing about meals being punctual and he could not understand if they weren't. I am a very bad time-keeper and on one occasion when I was cooking supper he appeared at the kitchen door at 7.35 to enquire what the hold-up was. In the midst of my gravy-making I hurled a spoon at him, to my mother's horror but which amused him greatly.

He never sat over his meals. He would leap to his feet as the last plate was cleared which used to irritate my mother: 'You'd think he had a train to catch,' she'd mutter as plates and cutlery were sloshed about in the sink. He would always do the washing-up and never the drying or putting things away. It was a point scored when one found something not quite clean and could shout 'reject' and toss it back at him. Scrambled egg pans were usually his undoing.

Reading occupied him greatly. He was not a television fan although he watched the news, test match highlights and some documentaries. The programmes he never missed were Harry Worth and Leonard Sachs. He would wait expectantly for Harry Worth to begin his programme by putting out his arm and leg in front of a corner shop window which then reflected the image as if both his arms and legs were going up at the same time. He thought that was hilarious.

With Leonard Sachs he would chuckle as the string of adjectives were read out introducing each act. He would sing along with the old music hall songs, especially the 'Old Bull and Bush'.

Bill was a great beer- and bread-maker. The former was potent and usually muddy looking. I christened it estuary water, but his bread-making was quite something. He usually started to knead it with hands fresh from painting a shackle or binding baggy wrinkle [used to keep ship's running gear from chafing], or knotting ropes round knives or handles on a bucket. He had his pipe eternally in his mouth and flakes of tobacco would drop down into the dough, and the odd whiff of linseed oil would mingle with the yeast. It all helped the flavour, the cook would mumble, and I must admit all who ate it proclaimed it. I remember the many occasions when I would wink at him as the paeans of praise from some visitor rang out at his skill; a delighted chuckle would bubble up.

His sense of humour was enormous. In my opinion the tragedy of his life was that so few people appreciated it. He loved having his leg pulled, and if one could cap one of his quotations, which was seldom as he was a past master at that, he would chuckle until the tears ran down his face. So many people hung on his every word and lionised him which he really didn't like, but he was too courteous ever to rebuff them.

He could be grumpy and unsociable but it was usually bad back pain which all the family came to recognise. A grey look would come over his face. This back pain was a legacy from the climbing accident in the Lake District.

Of course, he was most awfully shy. He could not make small talk about the weather and stuff like that; he really found it quite impossible. He was infinitely better in male company, but his sense of propriety overcame him with women. There was nothing he liked better than his hot pot suppers with the local lifeboat crew. They were all pals together, and when the singing became a little more rugger song based, at the end of the evening, he would be joining in with the rest.

He was not a man given to expressing emotions. He felt things deeply – of that I am sure. But he expected family and close friends to keep their troubles to themselves. He kept his and was no moaner or whiner; he could not understand anyone who was. That is not to say that he would not have listened or helped if he could but I, for one, would have had to be desperate before I asked him for help.

He was slow to praise but his 'That was a good effort' was worth more than anyone else's fulsome expressions. He could be intolerant but he set himself exceptionally high standards which he kept, and woe betide those who didn't measure up. Pain he accepted as an inevitability . . .

After my mother died I was sent for as Bill was in a bad way with flu. When I got to Bodowen I immediately said that I was sending for the doctor. 'No, you're not,' he croaked. But I did and he was told to take antibiotics and stay in bed. The next day he was up and hacking away at the rocks in the garden. I left cursing him and saying, 'Well, I hope you fall off and lie there till the dogs eat you,' which got a laugh. He really was impossible in that way.

He was remarkably good with children, treating them as small adults. My boys loved him dearly. He was always interested in their progress and achievements and this interest was carried through to the next generation of his great-great-nephews and nieces. I well remember seeing him having a long conversation with my son John who was aged eighteen months and in his playpen. It was a charming sight but I kept well hidden as I knew if I'd showed myself Bill would have been covered with confusion and embarrassment.

Another time my other son, Simon, then aged about ten, casually mentioned that hot water freezes quicker than cold. Bill would not believe it. My mother, ever anxious, said, 'Now, don't argue with your Great-Uncle Bill,' but he and Bill went ahead and boiled some water and placed it in a saucer alongside another of cold water. Simon was right and Bill was the first to admit it.

People have called Bill an eccentric. If the old-fashioned virtues of fearing God, honouring your King and serving your country are now considered eccentric then he was. I do not think so. He had an enormous influence on my life and on many others'. He had humility, modesty and great humour which showed up mostly in the endless self-mockery of his own writings.

The examples of his quiet courage in the face of adversity were a legend. The way of his going was so very right for him. It was so merciful that it was not his boat nor his expedition. He was just, in the end, a crew member. I shall always be sad for the youngsters who did not return but for my uncle I feel the gods were kind. He sailed into a legend and is for ever climbing the high peaks of eternity.

Pam Davis is a true Tilman; Bill was always proud of her and, late in life, when he began to think he could not go on sailing, he asked her if she would teach him gliding (she was a champion glider pilot). She readily agreed and Bill repaid her by putting his hand through the wing fabric as they moved her glider. He enjoyed his flight but realised it would all prove too much.

Others who knew him less well, or even hardly at all, have their own memories. Bill was not a man about whom people had no opinion, having once met him. There is no enigma here – despite Bill's own best efforts to create one. Bill Tilman, though, through his extraordinary efforts in the Great War, as it once was called, and then in the Second, was by those events alone a heroic figure. In his chosen course, between and after those wars, he reinforced that heroism: the application of will and tenacity to the overcoming of peril, the mastery of the elements.

Pam Davis says Bill Tilman embodied Rudyard Kipling's great, but now sadly often derided poem, 'If . . .' Reading it over, and comparing it with Bill's life, I think, in the final analysis, she is right. But there is no parody in this juxtaposition. By these tenets Bill appeared to live. If that makes him unfashionably straight, politically incorrect in his iron judgments, so be it. I, for one, am with him, to the end. He was, after all, the last hero.

Bibliography

Anderson, John:	*High Mountains and Cold Seas*, Gollancz, 1980
Bonington, Chris:	*The Climbers*, Hodder and Stoughton and BBC Books, 1992
	Quest for Adventure, Hodder and Stoughton, 1981
Keegan, John:	*The Face of Battle*, Jonathan Cape, 1976
Madge, Tim:	*Long Voyage Home*, Simon and Schuster, 1993
Purves, Libby:	*H. W. Tilman, Adventures Under Sail*, Gollancz, 1984
Richardson, Dorothy:	*The Quest of Simon Richardson*, Gollancz, 1986
Shipton, Eric:	*Nanda Devi*, Hodder and Stoughton, 1936
	Upon That Mountain, Hodder and Stoughton, 1943
	Mountains of Tartary, Hodder and Stoughton, 1950
	That Untravelled World, Hodder and Stoughton, 1969
	The Six Mountain Travel Books, Diadem/Mountaineers, 1985
Tilman, H. W.:	*Snow on the Equator*, G. Bell, 1937
	The Ascent of Nanda Devi, Cambridge University Press, 1937
	When Men and Mountains Meet, Cambridge University Press, 1946
	Everest 1938, Cambridge University Press, 1948
	Two Mountains and a River, Cambridge University Press, 1949
	China to Chitral, Cambridge University Press, 1951

Nepal Himalaya, Cambridge University Press, 1952

Mischief in Patagonia, Cambridge University Press, 1957

Mischief Among the Penguins, Rupert Hart-Davis, 1961

Mischief in Greenland, Hollis and Carter, 1964

Mostly Mischief, Hollis and Carter, 1966

Mischief Goes South, Hollis and Carter, 1968

In Mischief's Wake, Hollis and Carter, 1971

Ice With Everything, George Harrap, 1974

Triumph and Tribulation, Nautical Publishing Company, 1977

The Seven Mountain-Travel Books, Diadem/Mountaineers, 1983

The Eight Sailing/Mountain-Exploration Books, Diadem/Mountaineers, 1987

Unsworth, Walt: *Everest*, Oxford Illustrated Press, 1989

INDEX